PRAISE FOR *Hoosiers: The Fabulous Basketball*

"Will appeal not only to basketball fanatics but ... mainstream readers as well. It is a knowing, respectful and caring look at heartland America."
—*New York Times*

"The finest book ever written on Indiana Basketball."
—Bob Collins, Sports Editor, *Indianapolis Star*

"Hoose develops a narrative that transcends sports and operates as cultural history . . . Warm, graceful, full of the happy savor of letter jackets and cheerleaders' sweaters . . . includes the great personalities of the game —Larry Bird, Rick Mount and the maniacal Bobby Knight— yet keeps the locus local, social and intimate."—*Boston Globe*

"To say this little gem is a sports book is to say *The Sun Also Rises* is about bullfighting."—Scripps Howard News Service

"Terrific reading."—*Sporting News*

"The best book ever written on Indiana high school basketball. Hoose not only writes well, but his vignettes and anecdotes are fascinating. His chapter on Larry Bird is probably the best short piece ever written about him."— Author Lee Daniel Levine, in *Bird: The Making of An American Sports Legend*
"One of ten recommended sports books for kids."
—*The Kids' World Almanac of Records and Facts*

"A thoughtful, elegantly crafted and shrewdly entertaining examination of a fascinating American subculture . . . An amusing, vital and intelligent book about a slice of America too easily ignored."—*Kirkus Reviews*

"This superbly written piece of sports journalism will alternately tickle the funnybone and pluck at the heartstrings of basketball fans everywhere."
—*Booklist*

"Phillip Hoose examines the phenomenon of Indiana basketball with wit and whimsy."—*U.S. News and World Report*

"Of all the books written about high school basketball in Indiana, this is the one that has lasted and will last, for good reason: None better explains the whys and wherefores, the context, culture, and fascinating history behind the hysteria. Read it to better understand Indiana as you would read Friday Night Lights to better understand Texas, or The City Game to better understand Harlem."—Alexander Wolff, *Sports Illustrated*, Senior Writer

OTHER BOOKS BY PHILLIP HOOSE

The Boys Who Challenged Hitler: Knud Pedersen and the Churchill Club
Moonbird: A Year on the Wind with the Great Survivor B95
Claudette Colvin: Twice Toward Justice
Perfect, Once Removed: When Baseball Was All the World to Me
The Race to Save the Lord God Bird
We Were There Too!: Young People in U.S. History
Hey, Little Ant (With Hannah Hoose)
*It's Our World, Too! Young People Who are Making a Difference
    (and How They're Doing it)*
Necessities: Racial Barriers in American Sports
Hoosiers: The Fabulous Basketball Life of Indiana (first and second editions)
*Building an Ark: Tools for the Preservation of Natural Diversity
    through Land Protection*

HOOSIERS

HOOSIERS

THE FABULOUS BASKETBALL LIFE OF INDIANA

Third Edition

PHILLIP M. HOOSE

FOREWORD BY **BOB PLUMP**

INDIANA UNIVERSITY PRESS   *Bloomington & Indianapolis*

This book is a publication of

Indiana University Press
Office of Scholarly Publishing
Herman B Wells Library 350
1320 East 10th Street
Bloomington, Indiana 47405 USA

iupress.indiana.edu

The paper used in this publication meets
the minimum requirements of the American National Standard for Information
Sciences—Permanence of Paper for Printed
Library Materials, ANSI Z39.48–1992.

*Manufactured in the
United States of America*

*Library of Congress
Cataloging-in-Publication Data*

Names: Hoose, Phillip M., 1947-
Title: Hoosiers : the fabulous basketball
life of Indiana / Phillip M. Hoose ;
   foreword by Bobby Plump.
Description: Third edition. | Bloomington :
Indiana University Press, [2016]
   | Includes index.
Identifiers: LCCN 2016002163 | ISBN
9780253021625 (pbk. : alk. paper) | ISBN
   9780253021687 (ebook)
Subjects: LCSH: Basketball—Indiana—
History. | Basketball
   players—Indiana—Biography.
Classification: LCC GV885.72.I6 H66
2016 | DDC 796.32309772—dc23 LC
record available at http://lccn.loc.gov
/2016002163

1 2 3 4 5 21 20 19 18 17 16

CONTENTS

FOREWORD

Bob Plump

I first talked with Phil Hoose about thirty years ago. He had an assignment for *Sports Illustrated* that later became a book. It was a memorable conversation. Of course, we discussed the 1954 Milan High School Basketball State Tournament win. I was fortunate enough to be a part of that memorable game when my rural high school defeated a much bigger school whose gym could have seated seven times the population of our entire town.

Phil wanted to know what it was like to still have people be so interested in a guy who made a basketball shot in a high school game played over 60 years ago. I told him that it still baffles me, but it is humbling that people from all over are still fascinated by the shot, the game, and me!

To reach the state final game we played and defeated Indianapolis Crispus Attucks High, one of two racially segregated high schools in Indiana at that time. It was an all-black team versus an all-white team, played in the state's biggest city. Phil wanted to know what it was like for us as a team and if we had played against black players before. Yes, we had previously played against black players. As far as it being an issue for our team, it just wasn't. Our coach, Marvin Wood never even mentioned it. He DID mention that they were good though! As a result, it was just like any other important game for us. The team's focus was on winning the ballgame . . . not that the opponents were black.

Through painstaking research, skilled interviewing and fine writing, Phil Hoose has written the go-to book about Indiana basketball. *Hoosiers* is a great read for anyone but especially for those of us who love the sport of basketball. As *Sports Illustrated*'s Alex Wolff put it in 2003, "Of all the books written about high school basketball in Indiana, this is the one that has lasted and will last, for good reason: None better explains the whys and wherefores, the context, culture, and fascinating history behind the hysteria."

Through great stories and profiles of figures like Homer Stonebraker, Fuzzy Vandivier, John Wooden, Oscar Robertson, Jimmy Rayl, George McGinnis, Rick Mount, Larry Bird, Judi Warren, Stephanie White, and Glenn Robinson, this book gives us a unique insight into the heartbeat of Indiana high school basketball.

The first edition of Phil's book was published in 1986 and the second in 1996. This third edition collects the best chapters of the first two editions, but it also adds important and updated information. For instance, it details the trials and tribulations of going from a one-class state tournament to the current multiclass system.

Now we can all learn why, how, and when Indiana became America's capital of high school basketball. Phil details the bitter rivalries between schools and interviews officials from a few of those heated games. Read *Hoosiers*, and you'll understand why even today thirteen of America's fourteen biggest high school gyms are in Indiana.

I'm so glad Phil walked through my door all those years ago. I think I had an hour scheduled that day but we went way beyond that. In fact, we're still talking about the Hoosier obsession that fascinates us both. Now you too can pull up a chair and join the conversation. I hope you will.

ACKNOWLEDGMENTS

I would first like to thank the many players, coaches, fans, referees, entrepreneurs and administrators who allowed me to interview them as I researched this book and its two predecessor editions. They include:

Cindy Ross, Lisa Anderson, Jack Carnes, Gary Holland, Jerry Birge, Al Hardin, Everett Case, Oscar Robertson, Bob Collins, Jim Rosenstihl, Rick Mount, Steve Woolsey, Sam Alford, Judi Warren, Basil DeJernette, Gene Cato, Howard Sharpe, Skip Collins, John Wooden, John Wilson, Harold Engelhardt, Hallie Bryant, Ron Porter, Bobby Plump, Herb Schwomeyer, Bill Keller, Sue Parrish, Jim Jones, Pete Mount, Tony Hinkle, Cyril Birge, Steve Alford, Rodney Harden, the Simmerman family, Bo Mallard, Kevin White, Shandra White, Murray Sperber, Lin Dunn, Stephanie White, Rex Cronk, Larry Brown, Frank Kendrick, Rich Mount, Bailey Robertson Sr., Tom Sleet, Emma Lou Thornburne, Norm Held, Damon Bailey, Ron Heflin, Bob Summers, Stanley Warren, Ed Jones, Pluria Marshall, Alex Clark, Marcus Stewart Jr., Dave Krider, George McGinnis, Mark Bird, Beezer Carnes, Bob Knight, Jim Barnes, Linda Godby, Larry Humes, Brenda Weinzaphel, Phil Eskew, Don Bates, Graham Martin, Jeannie Woolsey, Tom Jones, Jim Jones, Gene Keady, John Barratto, Tom Higgins, Jim Nelson, Jim Duncan, Bill Matt Winter, John Griggley, Tom Brown, Ann Brown, Cinda Brown, Harold Stolken, Bob King, Bob Jewell, Bill Scott, Willie Merriweather, Willie Gardner, Ray Crowe, Hallie Bryant, Tyson Jones, and Ron Hecklinski.

Dr. Herb Schwomeyer, Wilma Gibbs, Wendell Trogdon, Ralph Gray, James Lane, Steve McShane, Gilbert Taylor, Scott Williams, and Stanley Warren are foremost among the historians and archivists who generously shared their work and/or steered me toward other important references in the first two editions.

I thank Linda Oblack and Sarah Jacobi at Indiana University Press for restoring this book to life, and for working tirelessly to make it the best it can be.

Kelley Eskew, Graham Honaker, Ralph Gray, Garry Donna, Chris May, Judi Warren, Allison Nash, Julie Nash, Tom Smith, Rick Mount, Brad Stevens, Kyle Neddenriep, and Mack Mercer contributed generously to this edition.

I wish to thank Patti Williams, and Darwin and Tim Hoose, for support and encouragement through the years. I am happy to say that Grace Hine, my high school English teacher, expressed pride in this book and its author.

I thank my wife, Sandi Ste. George, for critiquing chapters, listening to me as I read them aloud, and for sharing the excitement of this project. My daughters Hannah and Ruby Hoose—West Coasters as I write—remain honorary Hoosiers to me.

INTRODUCTION

Like many expatriates, I didn't really understand how special basketball was to Indiana until I left. A few months after graduating from IU, I moved to the Chelsea neighborhood of New York City. In December of 1971, I got the itch to see a high school game. A story in the *New York Times* previewed a showdown between two nationally ranked city powers scheduled for the following Wednesday at an uptown high school. Tip-off was set for 3 PM. It seemed a bizarre time to play a game, but I took the subway up, carefully arriving an hour early to beat the crowd.

There couldn't have been a hundred people in that gym. Probably half of them were college scouts, lined against the wall, taking notes throughout the game. There were only a few pull-out seats on one side of the room. The place was so quiet you could hear shoes squeaking and picks being called out and coaches whining to refs. There were no cheerleaders, for they were not needed. Just a few students straggled in. It was unreal: these were successful teams bursting with talent in America's largest city; if that game had been played in Muncie or Anderson or East Chicago or Newcastle, there would have been thousands of fans there, raising a din. For the first time, it began to dawn on me that what people back home had always said about Indiana—and what I had assumed to be just talk—might really be true, that maybe I had grown up in some sort of basketball republic. I wanted to find out.

In 1984, *Sports Illustrated* magazine, responding to my written proposal, offered me the dream chance to research a feature story about Indiana basketball. They set up an expense account for me and gave me free rein to interview the legends and ordinary Hoosiers who made the game. I jumped at the chance and drove back home. It was an amazing opportunity. In the following months I put nearly 5,000 miles on my Rambler. I was able to talk with John Wooden, Larry Bird, Oscar Robertson, Judi Warren (the first girl star), Bob Knight, and Bobby Plump, the star of the team after whom the movie *Hoosiers* was modeled, as well as more than one hundred players, coaches, administrators, cheerleaders, fans, reporters, historians, religious leaders, and other cells that compose the warm-blooded organism called Hoosier Hysteria.

I learned that for most of the twentieth century, Indiana was an isolated kingdom of rivalries and grudges, of eagle-eyed sharp-shooters and sheriff-like coaches, a landscape of outsized gyms connected by excellent two-lane roads. Public funds appropriated for bridge building and road repair had been hijacked by community leaders to build monstrous gyms for the sole purpose of seizing the home court advantage in the state tourney. Even now most of the biggest high school gyms in the United States are in Indiana. Not so long ago almost every Hoosier town had a high school gym that could seat the entire student body several times over. A few could hold the entire town.

And back then, every school, no matter how big or little, played in the same high school postseason tourney. Boys and, beginning in 1976, girls representing their communities faced off against their neighbors to settle scores and provoke grudges. Family members screamed through cupped hands and the whole town was hoarse and exhausted on Saturday morning from the effort of rooting on Friday night. Pumped for battle, little schools regularly sent teams from urban institutions sprawling in the sawdust, especially in the tourney's early rounds.

* * *

The first edition of this book was published in 1986 and the second—with new chapters on the Calumet Region, Stephanie White, Larry Bird, and Damon Bailey—in 1996. Now, nearly twenty years later, Indiana University Press has offered me the opportunity to republish most of the stories and to update the volume. The IU Press saw the work as an important part of Indiana's history, something not to be lost. We are also taking steps to transcribe and catalog the recorded interviews constituting what Indiana historian Ralph Gray once called "Indiana history through the bottom of a net."

My research taught me much about Indiana history. I remember especially one comment Oscar Robertson—the LeBron James of his day—made during an interview in his lawyer's Cincinnati office. "You know," Big O remarked, "the Klan started my high school." He said it almost offhandedly, and it caught me by surprise. I knew his school, Indianapolis Crispus Attucks High, very well. In fact I had briefly taught English there during the school's final year as a racially segregated school. But I had never gone to the trouble of learning how Attucks—as we all called it—became a school for African-American students and teachers. As I was growing up near Indianapolis, it had had always seemed weird that the city had an all-black school. We were in the North, not Mississippi. My ancestors had fought for the Union. And what did Oscar Robertson mean about the Klan?

The comment led me to research the chapter about Attucks that appears in these pages. Among other things, I discovered that members of my own family, people I love and who had always been kind to me, had been among the multitudes of Hoosiers who wriggled inside hoods and robes in the early 1920s and went out to make life hellish for people of color, Catholics, and Jews. They caught a virus of intolerance and nativism that gave rise to segregated schools in Gary, Evansville, and Indianapolis. My aunt told me that her very first memory was climbing onto her father's back to watch a cross burn in a field near their home in Clay County. Many of my friends have similar stories in their families.

The interview project confirmed that scale and passion of community basketball and the investment in facilities was far greater in Indiana than anyplace else. And even after I moved away, I came to see that I would always be part of a worldwide diaspora of Hoosiers who remain infected by Indiana basketball in strange ways. We can be watching the world news on television and when the word "Lebanon" crops up, a synapse takes us briefly to Rick Mount. We can read the word "Milan" in a novel and be transported not to northern Italy but rather to a quiet hamlet in southeastern Indiana whose residents pronounce the name correctly: MI-lan.

★ ★ ★

So I re-upped for a chance to revisit the stories and legends that compose Hoosier Hysteria, and to see what was left of Indiana's national reputation as basketball's address. I was well aware that there had been at least one massive change since I last checked in. In 1997, just after *Hoosiers'* second edition was published, the Indiana High School Athletic Association abruptly divided Indiana's 382 high schools into four enrollment classes and staged separate season-end tournament for each class, boys and girls. Indiana—whose legendary tourney gave everyone a chance and no one a handout—had suddenly become ordinary. Every school belonged to a class now. The basketball teams of my old high school—the Speedway Sparkplugs—were now in class 2-A. Our boys' team actually won the class 2-A state title in 2002. Did it mean as much as winning the sectional had in 1965? Did it mean more? How were people taking this? Was there still outrage? Did young players rankle at the insinuation that they weren't good enough to lick the bigger schools around them? Did players burn for a chance to compete against the best, as had their parents and grandparents, no matter how big? Or did the 4-class tourney now seem fair after the weight of twenty years' experience. Maybe more to the point, did anyone even remember how it was in the old days?

This book will give them a chance. Eighteen years later, I went back home to see what was left of Hoosier Hysteria.

Phillip Hoose, Portland, Maine, 2015

Welcome to Lagootee. *Courtesy of Phillip Hoose.*

· ·

"Round my Indiana Homestead" (as they sang in years gone by)
Now the basketballs are flying and they almost hide the sky;
For each gym is full of players and each town is full of gyms
As a hundred thousand snipers shoot their goals with deadly glims
Old New York may have its subway with its famous Rum Row trust
And old Finland with its Nurm runs our runners into dust
But where candlelights are gleaming through the sycamore afar
Every son of Indiana shoots his basket like a star.

GRANTLAND RICE, "Back in 1925"

1

FARM BOYS

How Indiana Became the Basketball State

. . . .

THE COLD FACT IS THAT BASKETBALL DIDN'T START IN INDIANA. IT should have, but it didn't. It took Indiana University coach Bob Knight to come up with this face-saving explanation: "Basketball may have been invented in Massachusetts," Knight explained in 1984, "but it was made *for* Indiana."

The vector of "Hoosier Hysteria" has been identified as the Reverend Nicholas McKay, a Presbyterian minister born in England. In 1893 McKay was assigned to a YMCA in Crawfordsville, Indiana. En route, he visited Dr. James Naismith's YMCA camp in Springfield, Massachusetts, where a new winter game called basketball had been invented two years before.

McKay gave it mixed reviews. It was active enough but there were still bugs to shake out. After all, it was only by sheerest happenstance that they weren't playing "boxball." Naismith had told the janitor to bring out two boxes, but all he had been able to find were peach baskets. They had nailed the baskets to a balcony railing that went around the gym and placed a stepladder under each basket. After every goal someone had to climb up and toss down the ball.

Reverend McKay knew he could do better. After he found space above a tavern in Crawfordsville for his YMCA, he hired a blacksmith to forge two metal hoops, sewed coffee sacks around them and nailed them to the walls. It did not occur to him to slit the sacks so the ball could fall through, but at least they no longer needed a stepladder as long as they had one tall player. "It became my job, right off, to jump up each time a goal was made and knock the ball out of the sack," Dr. James Griffith, the tallest player in McKay's first organized game, later wrote. "The thing I remember most vividly is having a pair of bruised knuckles next morning."

Basketball was indeed made for Indiana. It was a game to play in the winter, something between harvest and planting, something to do besides euchre and the lodge and church and repairing equipment. At the turn of the century, when Indiana was a landscape mainly of small towns and crossroads hamlets—settlements of a few houses, a church, a schoolhouse and maybe a lodge—basketball was a godsend.

Most towns were too small to find enough players for a football team and too poor to buy all the pads and helmets anyway. But it was easy enough to nail a hoop to a pole or a barn, and you could just shoot around by yourself if there wasn't anybody else, just to see how many in a row you could make.

Basketball was epidemic in Indiana within a year after McKay carried it in. In Madison, they played in the skating rink; in Carmel, they played in the driveway of a lumber yard, with spectators hooting from atop skids of walnut. Other towns shoved the pews back against the church walls or dragged the desks from the schoolhouses out into the snow.

Rules, such as they were, were highly customized. The town of Amboy surrounded its court with chicken wire, so that the ball would always be in play. In Clinton, shooters were allowed to bank the ball in off the ceiling. Brawls were common, and in the Dodge City days, an athletic supporter was someone who came to watch you play.

Each March since 1911, Hoosier schoolboys have played in the state high school basketball tournament. The first "tourney," as it has always been called, was sponsored by the Indiana University Booster's Club, who viewed the occasion mainly as a chance to recruit players away from Purdue and Notre Dame.

The club invited each of Indiana's thirteen congressional districts to send its best team to Bloomington, no questions asked. Usually, local play made it clear who was best, but sometimes there were mitigating circumstances. For example, South Bend High School once informed the boosters that Rochester High had compiled the best record in season play only because one of their forwards was really a Notre Dame student who came home on weekends. The boosters held themselves above this ugliness, perhaps because they knew that the boy, Hugh Barnhart, was also the son of the local congressman.

When news reached Crawfordsville that their very own Athenians had won the first tourney, citizens ran shouting through the streets, men with their coats turned inside out. Church bells tolled throughout the town. Everyone danced around a mighty bonfire until a train whistle was heard above the clamor. Then they all sprinted to meet the Monon, steaming in from Bloomington. It took several minutes at the platform for them to realize that the players weren't on the train. Exhausted, they had spent the night in Bloomington.

Indiana's first superstar was a farm boy named Homer Stonebreaker. He played in 1913 and 1914 for Wingate High School, a crossroads schoolhouse whose enrollment included only twelve boys. Like many Hoosier schools at the time, Wingate High was a single room with a stove, a place in out of the cold where a few kids might learn something useful until the ground could take a plow. Having no gym, they practiced outside, except for the one evening a week when Coach Jesse Wood hitched up a team and cantered six miles to a gym at New Richmond.

"Stoney," as the boy was called, was a square-shouldered, 6'4" center who scored most of his points from far outside, by squatting suddenly and spinning up long, looping underhand shots. It is said that opposing coaches ordered their players to pick up Stoney at midcourt, but often even that was too late.

The Wingate players were ridiculed in Bloomington. While everyone else wore monogrammed tank tops and short pants, the Wingate boys took the court in sweatshirts, baseball pants and long socks.

The laughter stopped once they stepped onto the court. Wingate won four games—three by lopsided scores—and then faced South Bend High School for the state championship. The game was a classic; Wingate won, 15–14, on a shot by forward Forest Crane late in the fifth overtime period.

Stoney and the "Gymless Wonders," as they were called, became instant folk heroes. Challenges came from all over the state the next season. Great convoys of Model T's formed in the town square, and out over the fields they rumbled. Five hundred fans chartered a train for the Kokomo game alone.

Wingate repeated as tourney champions in 1914, with Stoney scoring all of Wingate's seventeen points in the closest game, against Clinton. Not many are left who saw him—coach Wood outlived all his players—but Stoney's memory shines bright. "I used to ask the oldtimers if there were any players from the early days who could still play today," said Bob Collins, former sports editor of the *Indianapolis Star*. "Three names usually came out: Johnny Wooden, Fuzzy Vandervier [who led Franklin High School to three consecutive championships] and Homer Stonebreaker."

To cope with the tourney's explosive growth—entries increased twentyfold in the first ten years—officials in 1915 divided the tourney into local, single-elimination tournaments called "sectionals." Winners met for the state championship.

With local bragging rights at stake sectional games became even more intense than the games at Bloomington. These were mythic events, played on hallowed battlegrounds with maple floors, where martyrs fell and true heroes emerged. Losses were seeping wounds that festered in coffee shops all summer long.

The sectionals were organized basically at the county level, and in Indiana counties typically amounted to several hamlets connected by pure rancor to the local Kremlin, the county seat. The litany of complaints against the county seat became a part of Indiana's special script, as even and soothing as a chorus of locusts on a summer night. It was common knowledge in the provinces that the school in the county seat typically had the following advantages:

1. The home court in the sectional.
2. An amoral coach.
3. A county all-star team, full of players who should have been going to other schools.
4. A pair of forwards who had voted in the last election.
5. A center in his third year as a junior.
6. A network of grade school teams, controlled by the varsity coach, that would shame the Yankees' farm system.

Winning was everything; amateurism was a cynical joke. Merchants rewarded winning coaches with bonuses—once a Pontiac sedan—and players with gold watches. Coaches went after the parents of any tall boy who could shoot a lick, promising the father a better job in their town.

"It was just dog eat dog," recalled the late Phil Eskew, former commissioner of the Indiana High School Athletic Association (IHSAA). "The basketball players were important kids in anybody's town, and they could go anywhere they wanted. There were married and overaged kids playin' kids that hadn't passed a subject."

The minutes of the early years of the IHSAA, formed in 1903 to regulate high school sports, read like a police docket: damage claims for broken windows, referees assaulted, brawls, illegal rewards, and more brawls. One letter from Anderson High accuses rival Cicero High of "re-oiling" its players in a 1916 contest. Regrettably, the author did not provide a description of the crime, nor did he explain why the original oiling went unpunished.

In 1916, the IHSAA hired a lawman. Arthur L. Trester, 38, a veteran school principal and superintendent, was the stern, uncompromising son of Quaker parents. He had grown up on an Indiana farm and worked his way through a master's degree in education at Columbia University, where he formed a close friendship with the famed educator John Dewey. Trester was a huge, lantern-jawed man, almost always formally dressed, puritanical, shrewd, and intimidating. He was given a free hand to clean house.

At once, Trester set about straightening out the Association's financial records, codifying its existing rules and making new eligibility standards for players and teams. Then he turned to the matter of enforcement.

Overnight, Trester's office became the state's woodshed. Anyone accused of violating an ISHAA rule received a letter from Commissioner Trester stating the charge. Defendants had the entire trip to Indianapolis to reflect on the matter, confidence ebbing by the mile. Hearts hammered against their ribs as the groaning elevator lifted them to the eighth floor of the Circle Tower Building. There they faced The Commissioner and stammered explanations through dry lips. They were usually found guilty and often suspended from competition. "The rules are clear, the penalties severe," he would say curtly to those who sought a discussion.

Strong personalities tested him. Charles O. Finley, who, as the owner of the Oakland Athletics baseball teams of the 1970s, made a reputation for bedeviling Baseball Commissioner Bowie Kuhn, cut his teeth on Arthur Trester. As a high school student, Finley was accused of enrolling in a Gary high school to play a sport without changing residence from a nearby town. He was summoned to Circle Tower. Trester heard him out and banned Finley from competition for a year. The rule was clear, the penalty severe.

As the tourney grew the Indiana legislature repeatedly tried to take over the IHSAA and its huge booty of basketball revenue. It galled the lawmakers that they could not deliver tourney tickets to their constituents. When the challenges came, Trester would stay up all night, phoning and telegraphing coaches and principals to come to Indianapolis for "their" association. Trester

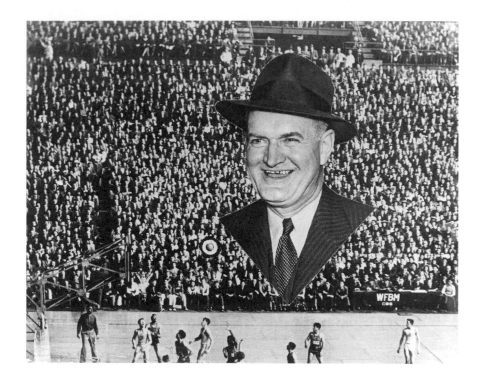

Arthur Trester and his showplace, 15,000-seat Butler Fieldhouse.
James Naismith, inventor of basketball, watched the 1925 tourney
at Butler and wrote, "The possibilities of basketball as seen
there were a revelation to me." *Courtesy of Dale Glenn.*

sat silently through hearings, letting others defend him against charges of
greed and gross megalomania. Then, when the bell rang, he rose to leave and
the lawmakers scrambled out after him, begging for tickets.

Trester was even the chief referee. In the 1932 Muncie regional tournament,
with Muncie Central leading New Castle by one point, a New Castle guard
named Vernon Huffman heaved the ball toward the basket from midcourt at
the buzzer.

Unbelievably, the ball swished through the net, but one official was signal-
ing that the goal had counted and the other was gesturing no basket. As fans
poured onto the floor, the referees made it into the dressing room and managed
to push the door shut.

Soon they were able to agree, but there was no way they were going to announce their decision before talking to Trester; he signed the cards that *made* them referees. They called him again and again. No answer. So they drove off to Yorktown for a bite, leaving thousands in anguish. At six that evening Trester returned the call, listened to the story and told the officials he would back their decision against the storm that would surely come. Not until then did the two feel at ease to announce New Castle's victory.

In 1925 Dr. James Naismith, the inventor of the game, visited the Indiana state finals as Trester's guest. The two men sat among 15,000 screaming fans and watched a superbly-played game. Naismith was stunned. He could not believe what had happened to the winter diversion he had started three decades before with two peach baskets. Thousands of fans had been turned away for lack of space. And this for a high school tournament. "The possibilities of basketball as seen there," Naismith wrote in Spaulding's Basketball Guide when he returned home from Indiana, "were a revelation to me."

Until Henry Ford began to mass-produce affordable cars, Hoosier engineers dominated the American auto industry. At least 375 models have been made in Indiana, most of them in the first third of the century. Spring would come, and the tinkerers would push back their shop doors and roll out elegant custom touring cars like the National, with its pushbutton electric gearshift, the Cole, with its revolutionary V-8 engine, and the Waverly, advertised as the darling of the ladies with veils and linen dusters.

High school basketball was important to the small-town life of several Midwestern states in the early part of the century, but the game exploded with greatest force in Indiana in part because Indiana was such an easy state to get around. Hoosierland is small and mainly flat, and an early, statewide network of roads was built to carry and test the great roadsters. Soon a statewide newspaper, the *Indianapolis News*, emerged, and one barnstorming reporter named William Fox Jr. made it his mission to bring the tourney personally to every Hoosier. His scheme was to give fans a dateline and a story from each of the sixteen regional tournament sites before the state finals. He had four days to do it.

Each year between 1928 and 1936, Fox and Butler University coach Tony Hinkle vaulted into a donated Stutz Bearcat at the final buzzer of the Indianapolis regional afternoon game, raced to Muncie for the evening final and tried to make it all the way to Fort Wayne for their tourney celebration.

Barnstorming *Indianapolis News* reporter William Fox and Butler University
coach Tony Hinkle prepare to board a Stutz Bearcat for their annual tour
of the sixteen final schools in the tourney. During the final years of their
circuit they raced an airplane. *Courtesy of Herb Schwomeyer,* Hoosier
Hersteria: A History of Indiana High School Girls Basketball

After that they had three days to criss-cross the state from Lake Michigan
to the Ohio River in order to make Fox's deadline. Hinkle drove by day and
Fox wrote by night; they rarely saw each other awake. But it worked. "Shootin'
'Em and Stoppin' 'Em" became every Hoosier's column. Fox's turgid dispatches
from the sixteen fronts gave those whose world view ended at the county line
a surpassing knowledge of statewide geography.

Unlike its neighbors, Hoosierland had no major-league franchises to distract
fans from its obsession. Illinois was the Chicago Cubs and Bears and White Sox,
Ohio the Cleveland Browns and Indians and Cincinnati Reds, Michigan the
Detroit Lions and Tigers. Indiana was the Frankfort Hot Dogs, the Vincennes
Alices, the Delphi Oracles, and the Martinsville Artesians.

Fox magnified local heroics into mythical events. Players and coaches
achieved almost scriptural stature. Johnny Wooden, who three times played
in the state championship game, probably came to mean more to a kid in Indi-

ana than Ty Cobb to a kid in Michigan. "Wooden, to the kids of my generation, was what Bill Russell, Wilt Chamberlain and Lew Alcindor were years later," broadcaster Tommy Harmon has said. "He was king, the idol of every kid who had a basketball. In Indiana, that was *every* kid."

Fox's gravel-filled accounts and predictions became so popular that the *News*' chief rival, the *Indianapolis Times*, hired an airplane to race Hinkle and Fox around Indiana.

"Don't take basketball season or life too seriously," advised Fox in one column, perhaps thinking about the increased weight of Hinkle's foot on the pedal as he glanced nervously toward the heavens. "Both are too short."

While New York City tried to scrape the skies with office buildings of Hoosier limestone, back home they piled it up against the schoolhouse. Even small towns built gyms that could hold everyone around, for everyone went to the games.

"I've been in places where I was having dinner on Friday night," says Bob Collins, "and the owner would shout 'Fifteen minutes and we're closin' up!' and everybody cleaned their plates, settled up and went to the basketball game."

Friday night was the perfect time to rob a small-town Indiana bank. "The game was the only activity in town," says Collins. "They had the bake sale at the gym, and the mothers conducted their raffle. I remember one time I went to a game in a place called Grass Creek and watched a kid play tuba in the band. Then he showed up in the reserve game a few minutes later, still dripping wet from his shower after the band quit playing."

"These gyms are our nightclubs," explained Fox to the nation in the *Saturday Evening Post*, "and we don't have to import any Billy Roses to put on our shows. At any ordinary high school game you will see bedizened and bedimpled drum majorettes leading bands through intricate formations before they toss their batons over the baskets in big league football game fashion. Our floor shows are second to none."

Along with the standard two- to three-thousand seat gymnasiums in little towns—structures built only for basketball and capable of seating far more fans than the population of the town—genuine monsters began to shadow the snowscape as well, facilities bigger than all but a few college gyms. The incentive was simple: the team with the biggest gym got to host the sectional round of the tourney. As more and more high schools entered and new sectionals were added, Hoosierland erupted into gym wars, with communities emptying their building funds and floating bonds to finance bigger and bigger gyms.

"No distinctions divide the crowds which pack the school gymnasium for home games and which in every kind of machine crowd the roads for out-of-town games," wrote sociologists Warren and Helen Lynd of Muncie in 1929. "North Side and South Side, Catholic and Kluxer, banker and machinist—their one shout is 'Eat 'em, beat 'em Bearcats!'"

During a 1929 meeting in which a motion to put up an extra $300 to hire a librarian was voted down, the Muncie City Council decided to reward Muncie Central's 1928 champs by spending $100,000 for what was to be the "biggest gym in America." School administrators pressured teachers to buy construction bonds costing fifty dollars, or two weeks' salary. Today, with its 6,576 seats, the seating capacity of the Muncie Central gym is surpassed in the United States only by fourteen high school gyms in Indiana and one in Texas.

Other Indiana communities turned the Great Depression to their advantage. President Franklin D. Roosevelt created the Works Project Administration—or, as many Hoosiers called it, "We Piddle Around"—as a way to get America's laborers back on their feet by giving them things to build. "I attended grade school in Spurgeon, that's eight miles south of Winslow," says Eugene Cato, a former IHSAA commissioner. "I can remember we'd go outside on the playground to play basketball and these gentlemen would be working on the gym. A lot of them were black, and I doubt if we had a black living in Pike County."

F.D.R. may have had roads and sidewalks and bridges in mind, but Hoosier politicians knew what was essential. Hell, went the reasoning, you could always build a road.

In 1930 the first black player appeared on a tourney championship team. His name was Dave Dejernette. It would have been Dave Miller, except that at the age of 16 his grandfather had been sold from one slavemaster named Miller to another named Dejernette.

Dave's father, John, was a railroad worker who had grown up in rural Kentucky. One day in 1913 a white man came through offering twelve cents an hour for 'good colored workers' who would travel to Indiana and help dig the B&O railroad out from a flood. John went and the next spring came back for his wife Mary and their two young children. They moved to Washington, Indiana.

David Dejernette, the third of John and Mary's six children, grew up in the early twenties, at a time when nearly half the white males in rural portions of Indiana were members of the Ku Klux Klan. A few black families, the Ballous, the Cotts, the Johnsons, and the Dejernettes, most of them headed by railroad workers, lived together on the west side of town. There they had their own small

Methodist church, with Mary Dejernette as pastor. They lived in an atmosphere of tension. John made a point to talk clearly to the children about how to handle themselves in town and at school. "He told us always to be respectful," says Basil Dejernette, Dave's younger brother. "He said, keep to your books and learn everything you can. And don't go making wisecracks. But he said, don't let anyone hurt you, either. If someone tries to hurt you, stand your ground."

One on one, Dave Dejernette would have stood his ground well. He grew to be 6′4 ½″ in high school and weighed 225 pounds. He was an intimidating basketball player, usually the fastest runner and almost always the most powerful rebounder on the court. He was widely regarded as the best player in Indiana.

The week before the 1930 tourney, Washington was to play Vincennes High School, whose team Washington had already beaten twice that season. A few days before the game a letter arrived at the school, addressed to Dave. It was a death threat warning him not to play against Vincennes and signed "the KKK." Dave took the letter home to his parents.

That evening his coach, Burl Friddle, walked out to the Dejernette home. John appeared at the door and Friddle got right to the point. "You going to let Dave go to Vincennes?" Friddle asked. "No, I don't think he'd be safe," John Dejernette replied. "You let him go and I'll protect him," said Friddle. "How?" "I'll see that he's protected." According to Basil, it took Friddle most of the night to convince John, and John until dawn to convince Mary. The next morning John told Friddle that Dave could go, but he was going too.

John took a pistol to Vincennes and watched closely from the bleachers. There was no attempt on Dave, although during the game there was a commotion in the bleachers when an overwrought fan died suddenly of a heart attack. When John and Dave got home, Mary was waiting up. Shocked, she saw John remove the gun from his coat. "What happened?" she asked, eyes wide. "Well," said John, unable to resist, "a man died in Vincennes tonight."

The tourney grew and divided again and again through the Great War and the Great Depression. So many new schools entered that two more weekend rounds—called regionals and semistates—were added to the tourney. By 1936, with almost 800 schools entered, the tourney took a month to play.

For the country schoolhouses, the regionals and semistates expanded the universe. To play a game before a multitude in a great house in Fort Wayne or Evansville, with the press corps taking up one entire end of the court, was like a field trip to a foreign capital. The new rounds gave the big schools a chance to dress up and look their intimidating best.

Dave Dejernette, the first prominent black player in Indiana Basketball History, soaring above all others. *Courtesy of Indiana Basketball Hall of Fame.*

ISHAA officials struggled constantly to find a fair way to satisfy the demand for tickets. Fans would do almost anything to get in. Tickets for the 1940 Kokomo regional were to go on sale at the school on March 12 at 7:00 AM. The first customer appeared at 5:30 the afternoon before. By midnight there were 600 in line. They made blanket tents and tried to deal euchre and canasta with frozen fingers around kerosene heaters. Enterprising kids shuttled coffee and short order meals to those in line. At 4:00 AM, police, fearing a riot, forced school officials to open the ticket windows. All the tickets were gone within a half-hour.

Despite the odds against the little schools, Hoosiers chose not to divide the tourney into classes by enrollment, like most other states, when the tournament became unwieldy. Though more than half the teams entered represented small-town schoolhouses, everyone deserved a chance for the big prize. The tourney had become a perfect metaphor for the Hoosier outlook: it gave everyone a chance but no one a handout.

In 1928 Butler University, a small college known for its pharmaceutical program, built America's largest basketball field house, seating 15,000, to give Arthur Trester a home for the state finals. Trester gave Butler $100,000 for ten years' rent. "We sure never had any trouble building a great schedule," laughed the late Tony Hinkle, Butler's coach at the time. "Teams would come through from the west, headed for Madison Square Garden, but they always wanted to stop here, just to play in this building."

The finals were held in Butler Field House, now renamed for Hinkle, until 1971. Perhaps no building has meant more to Indiana, and perhaps none has provided a better place to watch a basketball game. In the afternoon, the sun pours down through mammoth windows onto a mirror-like hardwood floor. The seats are painted in bright pastels. There are no columns to obstruct the view of play. "When other schools started building field houses, architects used to come in here all the time," says Hinkle. "They said they liked the way the space flowed out."

A ticket to vintage "Hoosier Hysteria"—as Fox called the tourney—was a pass to the "Sweet Sixteen." Between 1921 and 1936, before the tourney's semi-state round was created, the winners of sixteen regional tournaments met in a dawn-till-midnight two-day elimination to decide the state champion. It was like a marathon dance. Teams that made the Sweet Sixteen were said by Fox to pass through the "Pearly Gates of Butler Field House"; those that survived probably felt ready to meet their Maker.

Almost all the tickets went to the high schools of Indiana, who honored their best senior athletes with a trip to Indianapolis. When the sunlight struck their brilliant letter sweaters, the bleachers blazed with color, like autumn in Vermont. "Ah, it was just a *beautiful* sight," recalled Hinkle.

Herb Schwomeyer, 78, known throughout Indiana as the "Hoosier Hysteria Historian" saw the first of his sixty-two consecutive state finals—a Sweet Sixteen—as a high school junior in 1932. "That Friday was the only day in my whole school career that my parents ever let me miss school without being sick," Schwomeyer says, smiling at the memory. "My dad bought that ticket for me for three dollars—that's three dollars for fifteen games, Friday and Saturday. He gave me three more dollars and told me to buy a ticket for him for Saturday if I could.

"So my mother packed a big twenty-pound grocery sack full of lunch for me and I went out. At eight-thirty in the morning Vincennes, which was highly favored, got upset by Cicero. Soon as the game ended I went down to Gate three to try to buy a ticket for my dad. The Vincennes fans were already going back home. I was able to buy twelve tickets for a quarter apiece, and another two people *gave* me their tickets.

"I saved the best ticket for my dad and at noon I went outside and sold thirteen tickets for three dollars apiece. That's thirty-nine bucks." Schwomeyer, in the telling, still seems to be marveling at such a fortune. "That's more money than I had ever had in my life. I remember I went back in and watched the rest of the games with my hand in my pocket so the money wouldn't get stolen. I haven't missed a tourney since."

"People would hide in here the day before," Tony Hinkle said a few years before his death, gesturing toward the upper reaches of the great room. "We'd have to have the police come in and sweep the field house. Once I caught a guy climbing up a drainpipe toward a window. I said, 'What are you doing up there?' and he said, 'Oh, just trying to see if I could make it.'

"I remember once telling Arthur Trester, 'If you want, I'll put in another five thousand seats for you at two dollars per seat,'" says Hinkle. "He just laughed. He said, 'No, Tony, five thousand would just make things worse. If you can figure out how to squeeze in another hundred thousand, let me know.'"

By the 1940s Indiana smoldered with basketball "hotbeds," clusters of settlements where three generations of rivalry had made basketball the strongest thread in the community fabric. The thump of cowhide against maple had become the drumbeat of the Hoosier tribe.

Dubois County, an unlikely pocket of German and Dutch settlements, was as hot as a hotbed got. The towns have names like Holland, Jasper, Huntingburg,

Schnellville, Bretzville, and St. Marks. Many residents are connected by a common Bavarian heritage, but they recognize distinctions, especially at sectional time: the good burghers of Jasper were said to speak "Low Dutch," while folks from Ferdinand, eight miles away, spoke "High Dutch."

Likewise, Jasper was Catholic, Huntingburg Protestant. After a contest between the two, the winners grew to expect a call from the losers in the middle of the night. A voice would scream "Catlicker!" or "Potlicker!"—whichever the occasion demanded—into the phone, and then it would go dead.

It could get nasty. When Holland upset Huntingburg in the 1952 sectional, the citizens of Huntingburg nearly starved Holland out by canceling deliveries of milk from the Holland dairy. In the '60s, when the Holland and Huntingburg schools consolidated—a move violently opposed by Holland, which lost its high school—the lone Holland school board member who voted in favor of the merger found his barn in flames one evening.

In 1951 Huntingburg went for the groin. In a successful attempt to become the host—and gain the home court advantage—of what had always been the Jasper sectional, they built a gym big enough to hold everyone in Dubois County. Even then it wasn't big enough. Each year at sectional time they had to build temporary seats to hold the overflow crowds. This led to perhaps uniquely Hoosier liability problems.

One year, an elderly man reached down behind him to find his seat in the temporary bleachers. His finger became caught between a board and a cross-brace. After the National Anthem, his entire row sat down and the man's fingertip was severed. "He came into school the next day looking for his fingertip," says Dale Glenn, the Huntingburg coach at the time. "His wife told him to go find it, but he didn't want to miss the game. He was hoping we'd kept it for him."

The ticketless would try almost anything to get inside. Glenn remembers two men who walked past the ticket window, each with a fifty pound block of ice slung over his back between wooden tongs. "Concessions," they mumbled, heads down, ballcaps pulled down low over their brows. Once past, they ditched the ice—and the tongs—in the restroom and headed upstairs. The halftime mob had to wade to the urinals.

The seat of Dubois County is Jasper, a town from the Rhine that somehow turned up in Hoosierland. Nearly all the restaurants feature sausage and *Bier*. The streets are lined with prim red-brick houses which stand in contrast to the white frame dwellings in surrounding towns. The Jasper phone book is a marvel of vowel postponement, especially at the S's.

"While I was growin' up, Jasper was 95 percent German, Catholic and Democratic, and 100 percent white," says sportswriter Jerry Birge, 64. "I remember the Greyhound'd stop at Wilson's Drug Store, and now and then my buddies'd come runnin' back to me sayin', 'Hurry, there's one in there eatin'.' All us kids'd climb up to the window to watch a black guy eat. That'd be a big event."

Birge was in fifth grade in the year of the Miracle. It started the night before he was to return from Christmas vacation to St. Joseph's grade school, run by the Providence nuns. A few hours before dawn, the town's Wildcat whistle woke his family. Sirens sounded everywhere. In nightclothes, the Birges scrambled to the crest of a hill and watched the grade school burn to the ground. Three days later, the nuns had arranged for the children to share Jasper High School, the teenagers attending in the morning and the children in the afternoon.

"Come February, when the sectional started, it was really exciting for us little kids to see all the halls decorated, and all the signs sayin' '"Good luck, Wildcats,'" says Birge. "But we were almost laughing about Jasper's chances to win the sectional. Winslow was undefeated. Huntingburg was ranked. Holland had a great team.

"Well, this one nun, Sister Joan, stood up in class and said, 'Kids, don't worry, I've got it all figured out.' She was a real sports nut, had all sorts of Notre Dame stuff on her desk. She said, 'Jasper's going to win the state championship this year.' We thought she'd finally lost it. She said, 'Look on the calendar. The state finals are going to be on St. Joseph's feast day.' She was right, March 19. We said, 'So what?' 'Well,' she said, 'we're from St. Joseph's school, and God's going to reward Jasper High for lettin' us use their school.'"

No one could have blamed Birge and his pals for laughing. Jasper High School had finished the 1949 regular season 11-9, fourth in their local conference. They had lost four of their last five games. It would dignify their status to say they were unranked.

The Wildcats were coached by Leo C. ("Cabby") O'Neill, a former baseball and basketball star at the University of Alabama. Cabby had the courtside manner of a drill sergeant. He believed that basketball boiled down to fundamentals: If you learn it right in practice, you'll do it right in the games, he often said.

The Jasper squad had its share of rough kids. Some of them had a hard time taking O'Neill's regimen. One who could take anything Cabby could dish out and seemed to want even more was named Bobby White. White was a good shooter with a nice head for the game, but he'd stopped growing at 5'6" and 135 pounds. Cabby cut him from the team as a freshman and sophomore, but

White kept hanging around the gym after school, pestering O'Neill for at least a chance to scrimmage with the teams.

Cabby gave in and kept him but rarely used him as a junior and had no special plans for him as a senior until after the first game of the season. It was then that someone reported to Cabby that one of his regulars had been seen smoking a cigarette. Cabby summoned the player, extracted a confession and stripped him of his uniform.

The next game, when Bobby White's name was announced in the starting lineup, the gym thundered with boos, a great rolling wave of disapproval that functioned as a pointed finger. Many townspeople felt certain White had ratted on the dismissed player to gain a spot in the lineup. They couldn't prove it, and he denied it again and again, but that didn't matter. Evidence was not a factor. To them, it was *like* Bobby White. White was, in the vernacular of the day, a "clean Gene," one who didn't hang out, an outsider who had moved into Japser too late to have grown up on the grade school teams with the other kids. He kept his nose in his schoolbooks, and, worst of all, the nuns seemed to love him.

They knew he went to Mass every day, but until later they didn't know what he was discussing with God. Every morning for years Bobby White had asked God for a chance to improve himself that day so he could help Jasper High School win the state championship when he was a senior.

His life was focused like a laser. "I'd go to Mass, go to school and go to practice," White recalls. "Then I'd get off from practice about 4:00, get a sandwich and go back and play until about 9:00." For ten years the prayer was the same. "The concept was to *win* the state championship," he says. "I prayed to improve myself so I could contribute more."

"I was in a play with his mother, Louise, once," recalls Jerry Birge, "and we got to talking about Bobby. She said she told him, 'Son, if it doesn't happen, please don't lose faith. She said he told her, 'Don't worry, Mom. We'll win.'"

Two headlines juxtaposed in a mid-February Jasper *Daily Herald* convey Jasper's priorities as the 1949 tourney approached:
"Winslow Draws Tournament Bye"
and
"Munich Spy Trials Partially Opened"
The Wildcats somehow beat Dubois, Holland and Huntingburg in the first three games of the sectional. When they fell behind the Winslow Eskimos 24-14 at halftime of the final game, Jasper fans were thinking that at least they'd have bragging rights all summer long. Again, there were things they didn't know.

"I remember Cabby O'Neill walking up the ramp to start the second half and saying to me, 'I want you to take it over and make it happen,'" recalls Bobby White. As the next morning's *Daily Herald* put it, Jasper roared from behind to beat Winslow 48-39 "on the sensational, hard driving of little Bobby White." Quietly, after the sectional win, the other Catholic boys on the squad began to go to Mass with Bobby.

Tourney fever had consumed Jasper. The next Saturday's headlines tell the story:

"Battle Today for Regional Title"

and

"Employee of Justice Dept., Russ. Diplomat, Seized"

They nipped Monroe City 57-55 for the regional title, again coming from behind. The Jasper *Daily Herald* reported that "the first three rows [of Jasper fans] went repeatedly onto the floor to protest calls." The following morning, Bobby White noticed a throng at Mass, including, to his surprise, a few Protestant teammates.

The next week, forward Bill Litchfield, a poor shooter, banged a shot home at the buzzer to beat Bloomington for the semistate title. Most of the town dragged themselves out of bed and went to Mass that morning. Something unusual was definitely happening.

Jasper's local radio station, WITZ, had broadcast the Wildcat games all year long, but a huge forty-eight-station network out of Indianapolis had the license to broadcast the tourney. It was infuriating for Jasperites to hear the big-city announcers make repeated fun of the German names. *Schutz schoots!* was only so funny after the hundredth time.

The WITZ engineers decided to do something about it. License or no license, the Wildcats were in the finals, and God knew when they'd get there again. Very illegally, they pirated a frequency assigned to a Canadian clear-channel station that had already signed off, summoned the local announcers, and put WITZ back on the air over a four-mile radius.

The Friday before the state finals, the *Daily Herald* featured ads like the following:

NOTICE:
Our office will be closed Saturday, March 19,
to give our employees a chance
to boost the Wildcats to victory.
—*Link Twins Loan Co. (over Flick's Drug Store)*

On March 19 Jasper roared from behind twice to win the Indiana state championship, the final game a 62-61 thriller against Madison. The Jasper-Madison final is still remembered as one of the best games ever played in Indiana. The lead changed constantly; the pressure was crushing. In the final minute, Cabby O'Neill glanced over at his rival coach, Ray Eddy, and found Eddy looking back at him. In the heat of it all, each had seemed to realize how special that moment was, that maybe there would never be another like it, and had turned to catch sight of the only other person who could know in the same way. Cabby winked, and Eddy winked back.

Jasper won the tourney by rallying from behind in eight consecutive tourney games. A few smaller schools had won the tourney, but no champion had ever entered the tourney with a poorer record and less momentum.

How did they do it? It seemed like everyone in Jasper had a hand in it. Maybe it was because Mrs. Dr. St. John Lukemeyer had kept her vow never to stop pacing during the tourney until Jasper had won. Maybe it was because Bill Litchfield's dad never took off his hat until the final buzzer against Madison. Maybe the numerologists who found a clue in the three consecutive nine-point sectional victory margins had it right. Sister Joan had no doubts about what had happened; the tourney was indeed won on St. Joseph's feast day. And it seemed no accident that Bobby White, who seemed to contribute more with each game, scored twenty points in the final contest. His prayers had been answered. He was right: there had never been any reason for his mother to worry. A few days later, the nuns of the local order gave Bobby a plaque bearing Rudyard Kipling's poem "If" in recognition of his influence on the religious life of the community.

Cabby O'Neill was asked not long before he died if he thought God had a hand in the 1949 tourney. He professed little expertise in the area of miracles. "I know more people came to church when we started winnin'," he said, "but I wasn't at the door countin' heads. That wasn't my line of work."

"Let Joy Be Unconfined," blared the *Daily Herald*, "for we have crashed the circle of the basketball elite. This morning, the former Jasperites who are living in almost any part of the United States can point proudly to the sports pages or the front pages and say to anybody within earshot, 'Brother, that's my hometown, good old Jasper.'"

Hoosier basketball chauvinism reached a peak of sorts during World War II, which gave soldiers from Indiana a grand occasion to spread the gospel to other

GIs. To hear some of them tell it, they spent much of their noncombat time teaching non-Hoosiers how to play.

"In 1944, when I was in the Navy," says Bob Collins, former sports editor of the *Indianapolis Star*, "we had a barracks basketball team. Most of the guys were from Ohio and Minnesota. They were big, rawboned kids, and they played that same highpost game, a couple of fakes and the center shot." Collins illustrates this style expertly with leaden gestures.

"We played about three games and just got larruped. I went back to the barracks and said, 'I want to talk to everyone here from Indiana.' Some guys came up, and I said, 'Did you play? Did you play? Did you play?' Some had played in high school, some just in the schoolyard.

"I said, 'All right, we're going to be a team and we're going to play a game. We got one rule. The ball does *not* touch the floor.' We went out and beat those guys something like 75-30. We gave 'em Indiana basketball. When it was over, I said to those other guys, 'Now you know what basketball's about.'"

There was good reason for pride. To America's colleges, Indiana was "the basketball state," which produced annually a bumper, cash crop of playmakers, sharpshooters and rebounders. Scouts came in from everywhere at harvest time.

One year in the early '40s, all of Michigan State's starters were Hoosiers. In 1938, seven of the ten University of Southern California Trojans came from Indiana. When USC invaded the University of California that season, the Berkeley band struck up "Back Home Again in Indiana." Bobby White, who after Jasper played for Vanderbilt College, remembers a game against Ol' Miss in which twelve of the twenty players came from within a fifty-mile radius in southern Indiana. 'It was like a homecoming,' says White.

For a while it didn't hurt so badly because the emigrants cast glory back on the Homeland. Besides, some of their own were doing the harvesting. Nine coaches of Indiana high school champions had moved straight into head coaching jobs for major colleges. Everett Case, an Indiana high school coach who spent much of the '20s and '30s in Arthur Trester's doghouse for recruiting high school kids away from their hometowns, later established and popularized college basketball in Dixie by filling his North Carolina State lineups with players from Indiana.

But in 1948 it went a little too far. That year, while Indiana University finished in the Big Ten cellar, Kansas University stole away 6'9" Clyde Lovellette, the state's best college prospect. Everett Case took several others. After the University of Kentucky won the 1948 NCAA championship, their head coach, the despised Adolph Rupp, rubbed it in. "Indiana has not only lost its leadership as

BEST BASKETBALLER

JANUARY 15, 1940 **10** CENTS

In 1938, seven of the ten USC Trojans came from Indiana, nationally known as "The Basketball State." One was ex-Frankfort Hot Dog star Ralph Vaughn, proclaimed by *Life* magazine as the best player in the United States. *Courtesy of Indiana Basketball Hall of Fame.*

the top basketball state," Rupp gloated, "but the South has replaced the Midwest as the home of basketball."

Indiana University coach Branch McCracken promptly declared war. He announced that henceforth he would recruit only five boys a year, those being the five best Indiana high school seniors. Furthermore, he asked the state's high school coaches—his lieutenants in this crusade—to identify and bring forth those very special young men. To speed up the transition, he organized clinics and taught high school coaches the "McCracken system," a pell-mell fast break style ridiculed in the East as "firehouse basketball." Wherever they went, the best seniors heard people tell them, "You're too good to play anywhere but Indiana." And in 1953 it all bore fruit: Indiana won the NCAA championship with ten small-town boys from Indiana.

It seemed like a wonderful dance, one that had gone on for three generations and would go on forever. Until eternity, little towns would mill out thick-waisted sharpshooters who would walk out of fields and from under hoods and into college lineups. No matter how many wars and depressions, at least Indiana would always produce the most and best basketball players: Indiana would always be a small town, and it would always be Friday night.

But seeds of change were already in the wind. In 1940, Hammond Tech won the tourney. It was a big-city school from the Calumet region, a place that always seemed to belong to Chicago. Hammond's players had strange-sounding surnames: Bicanic, Shimala, Kielbowicz and Abatie. Like Lebanon or Martinsville, Hammond had a victory parade, but its parade drew a crowd of 50,000 on a Sunday morning.

In 1951 the world shrank again. WFBM in Indianapolis began to televise the tournament. The next year WTTV began its immortal telecasts of the Indiana University games, which began with announcer Paul Lennon holding up a bag of Chesty Potato Chips and stating, "I've got my ticket; have you got yours?" Suddenly kids in Bloomington and Indianapolis could see the images of players from Wisconsin and Ohio without leaving their homes.

By the early '50s, black players were no longer lone figures in small-town team photos but instead appeared in groups of four and five—and were often the best—players on city teams. Indianapolis Crispus Attucks High, one of three all-black schools which had been banned from the tourney until 1942, made the state finals in 1951. Their players seemed to play a different game, faster, less patterned, somewhere up in the air.

In the early '50s Jim Dean, a nice little guard from Fairmont High who in 1949 had beaten Gas City with a last-ditch shot in the Marion sectional, turned into

Fairmount High's clutch-shooting guard James Dean, later the "rebel without a cause." Dean's mother was also a fine Indiana high school player. *Courtesy of Fairmount Historical Museum.*

James Dean, a bigtime movie star who, to many Hoosiers, seemed to become famous by sneering back at everything that had made him. *Rebel Without a Cause* summed it up pretty nicely.

In the late 1940s, Indiana townships began to consolidate their rural school-houses into larger schools, in an effort to provide a better education for Indiana's rural children. Few movements have caused such turmoil in Indiana. When one community in a two-community township had more power than the other, it simply annexed the other's school, name, team and tradition and kept its own. There was genuine panic in the hamlets; lose your high school, lose your basketball team, and you stood to lose your very identity. For a small town, to consolidate was to be erased.

Some communities defended their schoolhouse as if it were the Alamo. In the summer of 1950, Township Trustee Virgil Turner announced that the high schools of the towns of Onward, population 171 and Walton, population 835, were to be consolidated beginning in September. Walton would be the high school, Onward the grade school. Onward residents refused to surrender their school and their basketball team. They set up a round-clock-defense brigade, surrounding the schoolhouse with trucks, chaining the school doors shut and stationing children inside the building against any attempt to remove the desks and chairs. State troopers stormed the building and were repelled until Governor Henry Schricker called them off to avoid bloodshed. The state switched to a strategy of attrition, refusing to pay teachers and discontinuing state aid. Residents kept their school alive for nearly two years, financing operations through chicken dinners which drew supporters from surrounding counties.

Before long it was happening everywhere. In 1954 Wingate High School— Stoney's school without a gym—simply disappeared, inhaled with five other little country schools to form something called "North Montgomery."

It was all changing, and too fast. For a half-century's winters the excitement had crackled on Friday night. Going to the games had been little different than going to church. You came together in a room built wide and high enough for the spirit to swoop and soar. Each space its iconography, the saints or apostles in one room and the team photos in another. Winter after winter, the prospect of glory or vengeance had brought the community together on Friday night and the hope of redemption had reconvened it at daybreak on Sunday.

In March, 1954 the curtain came down on the farm-boy era that had begun when Reverend Nicholas McKay had crossed the Indiana-Ohio line with a new game. After the 1954 tourney, fourteen of the next seventeen champions were to come from big-city schools. And after 1976, the girls who had also been playing since the turn of the century, but usually without funds or the support of their school's athletic department, had a tourney of their own.

The final act of classic Hoosier Hysteria took place on March 20, 1954, in Butler Fieldhouse. It was seen or heard by nearly everyone of age in Indiana, and was to be the most remembered sporting event in Indiana history. It was high drama worthy of everything that had gone on before.

. . . .

And David put his hand in his bag and
took out a stone and slung it.

·1 Samuel 17:1–58 ESV / 22

2

MILAN HIGH SCHOOL

The Hoosier Dream

• •

THE TELEPHONE SHATTERS BOBBY PLUMP'S DEEP SLEEP. HIS FUMBLING fingers encounter the receiver on the third ring. Plump drags it across the pillow to his ear. There is country music. Laughter. He glances at the clock: 2:15 A.M. "Hello, man . . . is this Bobby Plump?" The caller's voice is thick. This is not an insurance call. It's the other call, about the game.

"Yes, it is."

"Are you the one that hit the shot?"

"Yeah."

"Well, we was bettin' here whether the score was 31–30 or 32–30 when you did it. Can you help us out?"

Each year bus-loads of schoolkids visit the Indiana Basketball Hall of Fame Museum, in Newcastle, Indiana, about 40 miles east of Indianapolis. Boys and girls from Muncie and Anderson, Plymouth, Gary, Fort Wayne, and South Bend race around the rooms full of trophy cases, automated exhibits, and yellowed headlines. They laugh at basketballs stretched and laced like corsets over inflated bladders, inspect the primitive shoes in which only a god could have dunked, and then settle down to watch a video of an Indiana state championship game.

Among the most popular choices is a half-hour of scratchy film labeled "Milan v. Muncie Central, 1954." They know it as is the game on which the Hollywood film *Hoosiers* was based. There are few young people in Indiana, especially those who play on organized sports teams, who have not seen the movie about the farm kids who beat the big city team in the Indiana state finals.

Well, say their adult guides, popping in the videocassette, here's what it really looked like. The lights go out, and what flickers before them isn't like *Hoosiers* at all. The film is silent and the images are in black-and-white. The players seem to play in slow motion, pushing chest passes at each other and lifting prehistoric-looking set shots and one-handed jump shots toward the basket. Kids giggle. No one dunks. For a long while at the end no one does anything at all; everyone just stands around.

Then, right at the end, a slender, crew-cut white player wearing the number 25 on his dark jersey bounces a basketball very steadily, while being guarded intently by a taller black player wearing the number twelve. All teammates on both teams seem to have disappeared. Suddenly the offensive player fakes to the right, dribbles the ball hard, cuts to his left, leaps, and releases a soft, one-handed jump shot over his defender's outstretched hand. The ball falls through the net and the film expires.

★   ★   ★

Captured on that video is the Hoosier Dream. The images surely would find a place in any time capsule intended to show survivors what Indiana was like in the mid-twentieth century, and before. The event they capture reminds all Hoosiers that old fashioned values—hard work, boldness, and imagination—will still prevail in a fair fight. And if the world no longer seems a fair fight, the State Tournament still comes around each March to remind everyone what it once was like before the deck was stacked.

In 1954, when Milan High played Muncie Central for the championship, all other states but Delaware and Kentucky had divided their state basketball tourney into classes by enrollment. Typically, big city schools played in one tourney, medium sized and rural schools in events of their own. But in Indiana, little country schoolhouses confronted great city institutions named Washington and Central and Lincoln in a single tournament. Not as many players got trophies in Indiana, but, those who won woke up the next morning not as the champ of division 2A but as the ruler of all Hoosierland.

But only once did Hoosiers had a chance to savor the upset the event was designed to produce. That was in 1954, when Milan High School, with an enrollment of 161 students—seventy three boys—brought down Muncie Central High School, a school ten times as big, to win a tournament in which 751 schools were entered. The game was won on a shot with three seconds left by a boy named Bobby Plump.

It has been estimated that on that March evening, 90 percent of all Indiana families were watching or listening to the Milan-Muncie Central game. The contest is one of the most remembered events in the lives of many Hoosiers, along with the events of World War II and the births, deaths, and passages of loved ones. Milan struck a blow for the small, the rural, the stubborn; Milan stopped the highway, saved the farm, and allowed many to believe that change was still merely an option.

By hitting a fifteen-foot jump shot, Bobby Plump delivered the dream to which many grateful Hoosiers still cling. That is why his sleep is interrupted by strangers, why many of his personal belongings from the early fifties are preserved in various museums, and why a few moments in his late adolescence are enshrined in Newcastle for everyone to see.

★ ★ ★

Bobby Plump grew up in Pierceville, Indiana, population 45, about thirty miles northwest of Cincinnati. He is the youngest of six children, raised by his father and eldest sister after his mother died when he was 5.

It was not an easy life, but the Plumps were not the kind to complain about what they didn't have. Bobby's father taught school for a while, but when the Depression hit he took on a chicken route to Cincinnati, selling eggs until he found factory work in Lawrenceburg. There was a good roof over their heads, but nothing unnecessary under it. There was never running water, and no electricity until Bobby was 12. Four years later they were finally able to bring home a refrigerator, but phones and television sets were always to be for others. It was a warm and supportive family, and Plump today recalls his as a wonderful childhood.

"I may have run the world's smallest paper route," he says, "but I always had some money. I think I delivered eighteen or twenty papers. We had it for twenty-four years. When you got six kids, after the two brothers came back from the war, you could always get a card game up. We used to play pinochle with an aladdin lamp. Dad did the trading—that's what he called it—in town every Saturday. He'd go to the Oddfellows Hall, and if we had a dime we'd go to the movies, five cents to get in and five cents for popcorn. Then we'd meet him back over at one of the stores and ride back to Pierceville. It was a wonderful time."

"Town" was Milan, a center for Ripley County's hog, tobacco, poultry, and cattle markets, whose population was about 1,100. Though it was named after the Italian city, it is pronounced *My*-lan. One can also find Athens, Cairo, Paris, Rome, Shanghai, and Vienna without leaving Indiana.

A town of 1,100 could seem a jungle to a Piercevillian. "I remember getting lost in Milan in fifth or sixth grade," recalls Plump. "I went to a movie and couldn't find anybody. I was standing there crying and a man working in a furniture factory saw me and picked me up and brought me home. I just didn't know my way around."

When Bobby was in fourth grade, his father nailed a backboard to a shed for him on Christmas Day. Bobby spent most of the day shooting at it, entranced. He soon could hit the basket regularly. Better still, before long he found that he could freeze whoever was guarding him with a fake and a quick stride to the basket.

In 1949 the boy heard his first Indiana high school basketball tournament on the radio. He and Glenn Butte, who lived across the tracks, made it a grand occasion. They strung up some lights out back and together they choreographed the play by play, imagining how the players looked and moved.

In the final game, Bobby was Madison's Dee Monroe and Glenn played Jasper's Bobby White. Thirty years later, when Plump was introduced to Bobby White at a Hall of Fame banquet, he was astonished to discover that White was only 5'6". Only then did he realize that, assuming White was much taller, they had choreographed the shots all wrong.

Even in a community of 45, it was easy to get ten or twelve players up after dinner, when everyone came home. You played with the older kids, your brothers, fathers, and in-laws. The games were rough, especially on a gravel surface; "No blood, no foul" was the Pierceville code.

Bobby and Glenn and two other pals named Gene White and Roger Schroeder played together constantly. After a while, they developed a common experience of each other, each one understanding what the others were going to do on the court, the way voices in family quartets seem to reach for each other and blend.

Milan's cheering section—most prominently Bobby Plump's sister and brother-in law—fourth quarter 1954 state finals. *Courtesy of Bob Plump.*

Roger's family, the Schroeders, were the town merchants—they owned the one store in town—and day or night their place was the hub. At first everyone played in the barn behind the store, but the roof slanted down so you had to angle a shot from the corner too much. Besides, a nearby manure pile seemed to exert a magnetic pull upon the ball. So they moved the goal outside, trapped two shovels under a sheet of tin and strung electric lights between them; that way they could keep playing until midnight.

In the winters everyone went into Milan to see the Milan high school team play basketball. Milan's was not a glorious tradition. Over the decades the school had won two or three sectional tourneys but had never won a game in the regionals. Batesville, one of the other big schools in Ripley County along with Osgood and Versailles, beat Milan so regularly in the county tourney that it became a sort of custom, something you expected.

The Pierceville kids were especially attracted to a Milan player named Bill Gorman. Rather than lifting his leg mechanically and hoisting up one handed push shots like everyone else, or stopping to twirl the ball like a squirrel sizing up a nut and then lofting a two-hand set shot, Gorman leaped in the air on the run or off the dribble and fired up the first jump shots anyone around had seen. Gorman died in Korea in 1952, but he left his legacy in his jump shot.

★ ★ ★

From first grade on, they all went to school in Milan. That meant a three-mile walk or bike ride home, unless somebody's parents could find the time to go in and pick them up. They felt clumsy and ill-dressed around the Milan kids, who seemed to have a zest for ridiculing them.

Plump was acutely shy and easily embarrassed. He tells a story about two Milan kids tearing off his new green coat and throwing it in the snow. The memory still brings color to his cheeks and causes his voice to break. He became a legend at Milan, but he remains a Piercevillian at heart, and to him there remains a huge, living difference between the two.

The four Piercevillians—Plump, Schroeder, Butte, and White—made the eighth-grade team at Milan. Here at last was a way to shine. Milan, too, had skilled players who had grown up together. The team lost only one game all year and began to attract the attention of the town. In Milan's coffee shops it was said that these kids were "comers." The stigma of being from the country meant nothing in such quarters; you could be from Mars and it wouldn't matter as long as you could shoot or rebound.

Milan's varsity coach was Herman ("Snort") Grinsted, a veteran high school coach whose nickname derived from his explosive temper. Grinsted quickly recognized Plump's shooting ability and began to plan for the future. Though one-handed shots or even overhanded free throws had been forbidden in grade school, Grinsted told Plump as a freshman to perfect one move: start with the ball on one side of the court or the other, dribble across to the free throw line, and then stop and shoot the one-handed jumper.

By the time Plump was a sophomore, he and two other classmates were dressing for the varsity games but not really expecting to play much on a team with seven seniors. Then, early in the season, county rival Osgood humiliated Milan 85–38, and after the game Snort banished all seven seniors from the team and moved three sophomores, including Plump, into the starting lineup.

lenn Butte, Roger Schroeder, Bobby Plump (with ball), and Gene White in downtown Pierceville. This photo has become a postcard. *Courtesy of Bob Plump.*

No Ripley County team beat Milan again for the rest of the season, and twice they avenged their loss to Osgood. The team was the toast of Milan. Plump remembers being late for class one Monday after he had played especially well. He approached the classroom door, embarrassed as usual about his clothing, in mortal terror of standing out. He hesitated for a few moments outside the door, then gathered himself and opened it. When he appeared, his classmates stood up and applauded. "It was then I really knew I had something going for me," he says.

Grinsted rewarded his young charges by buying everyone new uniforms at the end of the year, without permission from school officials. When the word got out, Milan's principal was furious. He summoned Grinsted and pointed out that the athletic fund was now bankrupt and this time Snort had gone way too far. Shaken, Snort offered to pay for the uniforms himself, but it was too late. Like his seven exiled seniors, he was a man without a team.

★   ★   ★

There was good reason for all the grumbling you could hear around Milan in the summer of 1953. Snort was gone—some thanks after the year he'd had. To make matters worse, the guy they hired to replace him was only twenty-four years old, two years out of college and, rumor was, he was a set-offense man.

Indiana at that time had achieved a national reputation as the heart of "race-horse" basketball. Most high school coaches took their cues from Branch Mc-Cracken's Indiana University squads—the "Hurryin' Hoosiers"—whose grey-hounds usually won games by scores like 102–99. To slow the game down on purpose was worse than soft; in Ripley County it was near treasonous.

After Snort Grinsted, Marvin Wood was indeed going to take some getting used to. The new coach was a soft spoken, highly disciplined, and devoutly religious young man. In all the years Bobby Plump was to know Wood, he heard Wood raise his voice in anger only once, and on that occasion—after the team turned in a sloppy performance in a tournament game—Wood kicked a medicine chest and injured his foot.

Wood was convinced that these smart, sharpshooting kids could win by using the offensive system he'd learned from Tony Hinkle, his coach at Butler University. He knew firsthand that its inherent order could neutralize faster and taller players. Hinkle's system amounted to fourteen variations of a single pattern involving two players. The trick was to execute the plays perfectly. On your first day at Butler you were shown the fourteen patterns. On your last day you were teaching them to the freshmen.

Wood had been all set to sign a contract to coach at Bloomfield High when his high school coach told him of the sudden opening at Milan and advised Wood to go check it out. Word was, there was some real talent down there.

So one summer morning Wood drove to Ripley County, sat down on a basketball, and watched two groups of youngsters, one in Milan and one in Pierceville, play game after game. They were small but quick, smart, and good shooters. Above all, they were obviously close friends, kids who acted like they had been playing together a long time. Though the money—$4,000 to teach and coach—wasn't as good as the Bloomfield job, Wood applied for and won the job at Milan.

Wood's first challenge of the 1953 season was a personnel matter: fifty-eight of Milan's seventy-three boys tried out for the team. And, as much as Wood disliked zone defenses, that was the only way any of them had ever played. At first Wood tried to force them to play man to man, but he soon gave up and asked the junior high coach to show him how they had learned to play defense.

Wood imposed few rules, but he enforced them relentlessly. He set a 10 PM curfew during the regular season, but on New Year's Eve he let the players stay out till 1 AM. On that evening Bobby Plump and a teammate were double dating. A flat tire stalled them, but the quartet managed to pull up to Plump's house at the stroke of 1, at least according to Plump's watch. Wood was waiting for them; his watch said they had just missed. There was no debate. As Plump recalls it, Wood said quietly, "I'm going to make an example of you." Plump did not dress for the next game.

The next to the last game of the regular season, Milan was drubbing Osgood again when play started getting rough. Wood called a time-out. Explaining that he didn't want anyone getting hurt before the sectional started, he told the team to try something totally new.

He stationed Plump in the middle of the court, put Ray Craft and Bob Engels deep in the corners near midcourt and told Gene White and Ron Truitt to stand in the corners down under the basket. He instructed Plump simply to hold the ball until someone tried to take it away from him. When that happens, he said, someone come out and meet the ball so Bobby can get rid of it and everybody else cut toward the basket and look for a pass. When the players asked him about it later, it turned out Wood had coined a name for the scheme; he called it the "Cat and Mouse." Hoosiers proudly claim it as the forerunner of all spread offenses today.

★   ★   ★

Entering the tourney, everyone in Ripley County knew Milan had a fine team. The team had had to move their final few home games to a bigger gym, and, for the first time in a long while, the school was forced to raffle sectional tickets to meet the demand. There were great displays of civic pride. Chris Volz, Milan's GM dealer, stood up at one rally and promised to provide the team a fleet of Chevys to drive to the sectional round of the tournament. After prolonged cheering, Volz held up his hands for silence. "That's not all," he said. "They'll be riding in Pontiacs for the regionals, Buicks for the semistate, and *Cadillacs* for the finals!" Though the statement produced bedlam, Volz must have felt pretty secure about the Caddys on the lot: in more than thirty years Milan had never won even a regional game.

Milan breezed through the sectionals and took the road in Voltz's Pontiacs to the Rushville regional tourney. There they got lucky. In a cliffhanger against Morton Memorial, Milan fell behind by two points with twenty-eight seconds left. The ball went out of bounds, and while it was being retrieved the time-keeper forgot to turn the clock off. When play resumed, Milan's Bill Jordan was quickly fouled, and when he looked at the clock, he was amazed to see that there was no time left. Calmly he hit both free throws and tied the game. Morton appealed without success. Plump won the game for Milan with two free throws in a second overtime.

Milan went all the way to Indianapolis before losing to South Bend Central in the afternoon semifinal game. Plump had a great tournament, scoring nineteen of Milan's thirty-seven points against Central. For the first time, he began to believe that basketball might carry him to college; that all the hours of in back of Shroeder's and in town might actually pay off.

It had been an unbelievable season, highlighted by one of the most remarkable coaching jobs in Indiana high school history: a rookie coach had taken a school with seventy-three boys to the state finals. Snort Grinsted was now all but forgotten, and Marvin Wood had every right to feel like a king.

Instead, he felt like a failure.

All summer he blamed himself for having let his team down. They deserved more, he told himself. Maybe a more experienced coach could have given them the chance for which they had worked so hard. He thought about quitting.

There was a biblical quality to his torment. One summer evening Wood was approached by a man who owned a tavern in Milan. He said he had a son who shot well and stood 6'4". At the moment the boy was living with his grandparents in Lawrenceburg, but one word from Wood and the boy could live with him in Milan. He reminded Wood that Milan's center was graduating and that entered the evening showcase against Muncie Central as prohibitive under-dogs, a familiar position for Wood and his players.

Muncie Central was—and still is—a big school with an intimidating tradition. The Bearcats had won the state championship four times, more than any other school but one. Muncie played its home games in a gym that could hold seven times the entire population of Milan. But the pressing problem was that Muncie's front line averaged 6'4"; by contrast, Milan's Gene White jumped center at 5'11".

Wood thought carefully about the job ahead. Nervousness would not be a problem. These kids had played together since they'd worn braces, and they weren't the kind to scare anyway. And nobody had taken them seriously enough for the fear of failure to enter in. But there was just no way a conventional approach could offset Muncie's height and muscle. Wood decided, for the first time, to try the spread offense—the Cat and Mouse—for an entire game.

The strategy worked perfectly during the first half, giving Milan 25–17 lead into the locker room. Now all they had to do was stay calm and hit the shots that surely would come once Muncie became anxious and started to press. But the third quarter was catastrophic: Milan failed to hit a single field goal and entered the final eight minutes of the game tied 26–26.

Most Hoosiers over 40 can tell you where they were during the final period of that game. Statewide television coverage of the finals had begun only three years before, but there had been a sophisticated radio network since 1921, and of course Butler Fieldhouse was jammed with over 15,000 Hoosiers. The state stood still that Saturday night, and the dream shimmered.

Muncie pulled ahead by two points in the opening seconds. Gambling that his veteran team would prevail in the frenzy that was sure to come, Wood stuck to his game plan. He told Plump, just as if they were playing Osgood for bragging rights to Ripley County, to stand there and hold the ball until someone came out to get it.

So for four minutes and thirteen seconds Plump stood with the ball cradled under one arm, the other hand on his hip, staring at Jimmy Barnes, the player assigned to guard him. Barnes stared back, knees flexed, arms extended in a defensive position.

Bobby Plump scores against Crispus Attucks High in the 1954 semi-state round of the tourney. Oscar Robertson watches, facing Plump. *Courtesy of Bob Plump.*

Most of Indiana thought Wood was insane, and many Hoosiers were furious. As the minutes melted away with no fouls to stop play, it sounded for all the world on the radio like Milan was quitting; Wood seemed to be mocking everything that every father told every son. They were *behind*, for Christ's sake, and they were *stalling* and the dream was ticking away.

Plump recalls those moments: "I kept looking over at the bench and Marvin Wood was sitting there as if he was out on the porch. He had his legs crossed, kicking his foot. If he would have told me to throw the ball up in the stands I would have done it, I had that much confidence in him. But when I'd look at him he'd just put his hands up, like 'Everything's okay.'"

Jimmy Barnes was likewise glancing over at Muncie coach Jay McCreary, who, ahead, was quite content to let time expire. "We wanted to go out and guard 'em, but coach said to lay back," recalls Barnes. "I wanted him to put the ball on the floor, 'cause I figured I could steal it from anyone.

With about two minutes left, the frenzy began: Wood let Plump shoot for the tie. He missed, and Muncie got the rebound, but then Milan's zone press forced a turnover and a field goal by Ray Craft tied it at 28 all. Muncie coughed the ball up again, and Plump put Milan ahead with two free throws. Muncie's Gene Flowers retied the score at 30. With all of Hoosierland on its feet, ear against the radio, eyes on the tube or in the berserk field house itself, Plump and Craft brought the ball downcourt very slowly for the last time.

With eighteen seconds left, Wood called time out. In the huddle, Gene White suggested that everyone move to one side of the court and let Plump go one-on-one against Barnes. Plump was a little surprised since he was having a terrible game, having made only two of ten attempts so far. Wood agreed. Plump was the shooter and it was time for a shot.

Ray Craft was supposed to inbound the ball to Plump, and then the entire Milan team was to shift to the left side of the court, out of Plump's way. But Plump, who had felt jittery in the huddle, nearly blew the play right away. He took the ball out of bounds himself and threw it in to Craft, who somehow found the presence of mind to catch it and toss it back.

Then the nervousness disappeared. After all, it was the play Snort Grinsted had told him to perfect years before, and he had done it a million times out back and at Schroeder's and against Osgood and Cross Plains and Aurora.

Alone and with nothing to do but what he knew how to do better than anything in the world, Plump worked the clock down to five seconds. Then he suddenly cut across the lane, stopped quickly at the top of the key, leaped in the air, and flung the ball over Barnes's fingers and toward the hoop. As the

Today Bobby Plump has his own insurance agency, one which provides nicely for his family. His first clients were college athletes, kids who were thrilled to meet him. He had impressive careers at Butler University—which he chose largely because he knew Tony Hinkle's fourteen two man variations by heart, and he knew there would be lots of shots in it for him—and in amateur basketball, with the Phillips '66 Oilers. He very nearly made the 1960 Olympic team.

Hundreds of speeches and banquets and celebrity golf tournaments have forced Bobby Plump—it's Bob now—to conquer his fear of public speaking; he says if he can get an early laugh he actually enjoys these appearances.

The number of requests for engagements has skyrocketed since the movie *Hoosiers* was released in 1986. The film is based on the Milan story, though screenwriters augmented the basic David and Goliath theme by adding a coach with a haunted past (Gene Hackman), a love interest (Barbara Hersey), and a town drunk (Dennis Hopper).

Plump's character, whose name is Jimmy Chitwood, is a troubled, sullen boy who has quit the team apparently because he felt loved only for his pure jump shot. Plump sees few similarities. "I didn't identify with Jimmy at all," he says, "at least not until the last eighteen seconds of the final game. I would never have held out and not played on the team. To me it was an honor to have a uniform and even sit on the bench. And at the end, I would have never said in the huddle, 'give me the ball, I'm gonna hit it.'"

He says that celebrity has taught him that everyone, even corporation presidents, have basic insecurities. Though he still seems to have more fun talking about the pressure shots he missed than the one he made, he knows that he is forever consigned, like Don Larsen or Bobby Thompson, to recount his immortal jumper.

As the incarnation of the Dream, he is careful to tell an interviewer the whole story, with nothing left out, and as colorfully as possible. From time to time he'll say, "Wait, there's another story about that," or, "I forgot to tell you this," as if an omission would be irresponsible. Especially when you get to those final seconds, the stories peel away like layers from an onion. But the core is surprising: he says he really can't remember what he was thinking or what it felt like to hold the ball and look at Jimmy Barnes, except to recall, "He certainly was intense."

Jimmy Barnes is today a parole agent for the California State Prison System. He played college basketball for a year and was invited to an unsuccessful tryout with a professional team in 1961. Barnes says that although his relatives kid him a little about Milan when he goes back to Indiana, the people of Muncie did not hold Plump's shot against him. "They blamed everyone else but me, for some reason," he says.

Each year the Milan teammates get together at Thanksgiving to retell the old stories. Milan's victory did more than provide memories for these players; nine out of ten received college scholarships, and eight graduated. Before that game almost no one from Milan had ever been able to afford college. "I asked my father one time," says Plump, "if I had not gotten a scholarship, would he have sent me to college. He said, 'No, I couldn't afford to send the other five. It would not have been right to borrow money to send you.'"

Plump is amazed by his enduring celebrity. One of his high school championship jackets is in the Indiana State Museum, as is the outdoor basketball goal that his father made for him in Pierceville. There are questions about Milan High School on Indiana History tests, and a new biography is in the bookstores. Again and again, whenever an anniversary of the game arises or a new angle suggests itself to a reporter, Bobby Plump, now 57 and the grandfather of three, is invited back to Butler Fieldhouse to try the shot again. Sometimes he hits it on the first try and sits down. And some days, such as the day he missed eleven straight for ABC television, he couldn't throw a basketball in a lake. Some things, he laughs, don't change.

Hardly a day goes by when someone doesn't mention the shot or the movie. His wife Jenine has learned to live with the calls in the night and interrupted meals. The couple's three children, now grown, each have had their own experiences with their father's legend:

"I was waitressing at this restaurant in 1981," recalls Tari Plump, Bob and Jenine's eldest daughter. "We were at a bar having drinks after work one night, and I still had my name tag on my blouse. There were two gentlemen sitting next to me with very pronounced foreign accents. One of them looked at my name tag and said, 'Tari Plump? Are you any relation to Bobby Plump?' I said, 'Yes, he's my father.' He got very excited. He said, 'I come to United States, arrive in New York, fly to Indianapolis. We talk about sports. All I hear is Bobby Plump, Bobby Plump . . . did he do something special?'"

3

INDIANAPOLIS CRISPUS ATTUCKS HIGH SCHOOL

The Black and White of Hoosier Hysteria

• •

THIS IS HOW THE *INDIANAPOLIS RECORDER*, SERVING BLACK INDIANAPOLIS, began its editorial of March 19, 1955: "It is with a spirit of profound reverence and thanksgiving that we hail the new high school basketball champions of Indiana, the Crispus Attucks Tigers. Persons unfamiliar with our State may believe that we are overdoing it in going down on our knees and giving praise to almighty God that this glorious thing has come to pass."

What had come to pass was not the end of a war. It was not that a tornado had skipped over Indianapolis, or that a vaccine had been discovered, or that rain had finally come. What had happened was that a basketball team had won a basketball game.

But it wasn't an ordinary game or an ordinary team, and those weren't ordinary times. This victory sent black Indianapolis down to its knees in prayer and springing back up again in jubilation because, while nothing could erase the sting of thirty years' injustice and ridicule, at least it made sure that black players could no longer be disregarded. Every player and all coaches on both teams that night at Butler Fieldhouse had been African Americans. On that late winter evening the guard changed, and everyone knew it.

More than any other story, the rise of Crispus Attucks High School shows the power of basketball as a social force in Indiana. The school was established to socially quarantine blacks at an almost surreal time when the Ku Klux Klan controlled Indiana politics. Attucks's basketball teams were banned from the Indiana state tourney for fifteen years and were shunned by the other Indianapolis high schools for years afterwards. The new state champions had won far more than a basketball game on the night before the editorial: it had won a uniquely Hoosier form of redemption—through community basketball.

Attucks had also succeeded in removing a huge embarrassment from the City of Indianapolis. In forty-four years, no team from the state's capitol had ever won the tourney. Many residents of Indianapolis had to admit that for once it mattered more that an Indianapolis school had won the tourney than that every student who went to Crispus Attucks High was black. *Indianapolis* Crispus Attucks had won. And while celebrating "our" team, everyone's team, many whites and blacks mingled with each other, spoke to each other, slapped each other on the back for the first time.

And when the party was over, the sobering prospect that Crispus Attucks might forever dominate the Indianapolis sectional tourney probably did more to integrate the public schools of Indianapolis than all the policy changes and loophole-ridden plans had ever done. "The success of Attucks's basketball integrated the high schools of Indianapolis," says Bob Collins, sports editor of the *Indianapolis Star.* "They became so dominant that the other schools had to get black basketball players or forget about it."

The *Recorder* goes on to explain, as if there were someone in Indiana who didn't know: "Basketball—especially the high school variety—occupies a particularly lofty place in the Hoosier scheme of things. It is far more than a boys' sport—in fact, it is just about the most important thing there is."

Or, as Attucks's great star Oscar Robertson put it, "I don't want to take anything away from anyone else. But nobody did what we did."

*　＊　＊　＊*

Farming had never been an easy way to make a living in Indiana, not even in the rich glacial till of central Indiana. That is, not until World War 1. Then, for a few blessed seasons, everything changed: "Food Will Win the War" became America's mantra, and suddenly farmers couldn't yank corn and beans out of the ground fast enough to feed Europe. Money rolled in, money there had never been before, money to buy a Ford and a feathered hat and a piano for the front room.

But Hoosiers also became wary and suspicious of anyone from the outside who might want a piece of the prosperity, especially laborers who were pouring in from Europe and black workers from Southern states who were finding jobs in Indiana's cities. In 1926, Hoosier writer Samuel W. Tait Jr. described the Ku Klux Klan's appeal especially to rural Indiana: "Here at last," Tait wrote, "was a political weapon calculated to satisfy all the fears and hatreds the evangelical hell-hounds had been instilling in the faithful for so long: fear of the power of Rome; hatred of the wickedness of the cities; fear of the Darwinian heresy; and hatred of the evil individualist who persisted in having a private stock (of liquor)."

The Klan spread throughout many states in the '20s, but it roots sank deepest in Hoosier soil. "Nearly 500,000 Hoosiers, in white robes and hoods, burned their fiery crosses almost nightly to strike fear in the hearts of their neighbors," wrote journalist Irving Liebowitz. Roughly one in three white Hoosier males slipped under the sheet. The Klan took over Indiana's Republican Party—the party of Lincoln—which in turn controlled Hoosier politics. And for a while, the most powerful figure in Indiana was the Grand Dragon of Indiana, a pudgy, sharp-dressing demagogue named David C. Stephenson.

In 1921 Stephenson was in his late 20s, selling coal securities out of an Evansville hotel and looking around for what to do next, when the call came. The Klan's Imperial Wizard, a Dallas dentist named Hiram Wesley Evans, said he had heard good things about Stephenson, heard that he could organize, heard that he gave a good speech. Evans was willing to take a chance on Stephenson, to make him Grand Dragon of Indiana, to see what he could do. Stephenson had dabbled in Socialist politics and had even run for Congress as a Democrat, hoping the veterans who took in the stories he made up about his escapades as a war hero could put him over. All that had failed. With nothing to lose, he took the Klan job.

Stephenson didn't waste time. He hired professional salesmen to spearhead recruiting drives. A pamphlet entitled *Ideals of the Klan* described the Klan as follows:

- This is a white man's organization
- This is a gentile organization
- It is an American organization
- It is a Protestant organization.

"I am the law in Indiana," crowed
Ku Klux Klan Grand Dragon D. C.
Stephenson in the early 1920s, before
he was convicted of murdering and
mutilating an Indianapolis woman.
Courtesy of the Indianapolis News.

White Hoosiers—many rural and poorly educated—received membership applications in the mail, on stationery with sketches of Klansmen on horseback. Stephenson dreamed up solemn mumbo jumbo rituals and nearly wore out the letter K. Women were Kamilias. The house organ, called the *Kourier*, featured a Klan Kiddie Korner. Memberships, called "Klectokons," went for between $10 and $25, depending on your circumstances, of which Stephenson pocketed $4. White robes and peaked hats moved at $6 a set, of which Stephenson kept $4.25. D. C. Stephenson raked in more than $2 million dollars in eighteen months and moved into a mansion in the east side of Indianapolis.

On January 12, 1925 the Klan vote elected a new governor, Ed Jackson, who, campaigning on the Republican ticket in Stephenson's Cadillac, had captured ninety of Indiana's ninety-two counties. The tide also swept in dozens of Klan-influenced legislators, prosecutors, judges, and mayors.

Business executives found their way to Stephenson's house, cash in hand, shopping for help at the State House. Intolerance had become fashionable. Hoosiers threw sheets over their heads and formed vigilante squads, terrorizing blacks, Jews, and Catholics, tarring women accused of being prostitutes. There were public floggings. Crosses blazed on hillsides. Billboards reading "Nigger, don't let the sun set on you here" cast long shadows at town lines.

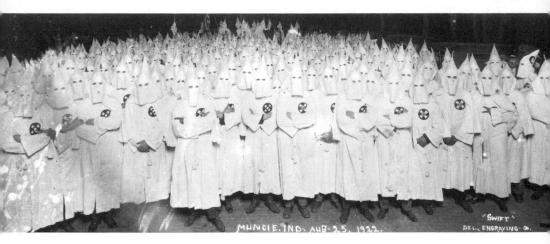

Citizens of Muncie pose for a nighttime photo in August 1922
—a time when nearly one of every three white males in
Indiana was a Klansman. *Courtesy of Ball State University,*
A. M. Bracken Library, and the W. A. Swift Photo Collection.

"I am the law in Indiana," crowed D. C. Stephenson, and for a short while he was. Months after the election he was convicted of kidnapping, molesting, and murdering an Indianapolis woman. "Ed Jackson'll pardon me," he said, grinning, as they led him away. Twenty-five years later another governor did, on the condition that the sun never set on him again in Indiana.

* * *

Indiana's black population doubled between 1910 and 1930, as a steady stream of workers abandoned the cotton and tobacco fields of the South and sought work in the factories of Indianapolis and the Calumet region cities of Gary, Hammond and East Chicago.

Alarmed, whites clamored for segregated schools. The Indianapolis Chamber of Commerce appealed for a "separate, modern, completely equipped and adequate high school building for colored students." The Indiana Federation of Community Civic Clubs added that segregated schools—grade schools and high schools—would shield whites from the menace of tuberculosis, a disease which was only slightly more prevalent among blacks, many of whom were crowded into drafty shacks in a river bottom on the City's near west side.

In December 1922 the Indianapolis school board formally recommended the construction of a high school for blacks. Citing the "laudable desire" of Negroes for a high school education, the board assured the city that the school would encourage their "self-reliance," "initiative," and "good citizenship."

The Klan-elected school board of 1925 appropriated funds for construction. As board members debated whether to name the school after Thomas Jefferson or Theodore Roosevelt, local black organizations aided by the NAACP, sued to stop construction of the school. They lost, and lost again on appeal. The school board agreed to allow the community to name the school themselves.

On September 12, 1927, the doors swung open to Crispus Attucks High School, named after the first black to die in the Revolutionary War. Thirteen hundred eighty-five students, kids uprooted from their neighborhood schools, filed into the classrooms, nearly double the number expected. The Ku Klux Klan organized several parades for the occasion. The *Indianapolis Star* reported that "One parade on Washington Street, consisting of row after row of masked Klansmen marching slowly to the beat of muffled drums, took an hour to pass." In this atmosphere, the black children of Indianapolis opened their books.

A few days after Attucks opened, three prominent black leaders, F. E. De-Franz, Reverend H. L. Herod, and F. B. Ransom—"The Big Three," as they were often called—met with Arthur L. Trester, permanent secretary of the Indiana High School Athletic Association to seek Attucks's membership in the organization that governed high school sports. Membership would let Attucks compete against other member schools and play in the Indiana state basketball tourney. There was no better way to show all Hoosiers that Attucks's athletes belonged among them.

Trester was 47, eleven years into his job, and at the height of a remarkable career. His organization, fat on revenues from the grandest basketball tourney in the United States, was the envy of the nation. He was a powerful figure in Indiana—reporters often referred to his puppet board of governors as the "Board of Controlled"—and editorial cartoonists caricatured him as a man on a throne. Whatever Arthur Trester's racial views might have been, there was little for him to gain by taking a pioneering stand in the Indianapolis of 1927.

The meeting was brief. Trester explained that since Attucks was not a public school—only blacks could attend—his organizations' hands were tied. It would be the same for Indiana's two other black high schools, all parochial schools, and even the Indiana School for the Deaf. Trester rose and the Big Three exited,

KING ARTHUR TRESTER

King Arthur Trester.
Courtesy of Dale Glenn.

furious and humiliated. It was the opening round in a struggle that was to last for fifteen years.

Until the late '40s most Indiana school officials showed little interest in playing athletic contests against Indianapolis's black school. In those years Attucks's typical schedule for football and basketball consisted of a handful of games with the other two all-black Indiana schools—Gary Roosevelt and Evansville Lincoln—maybe a game with Indianapolis Cathedral, the Catholic school, and a few games with schools in Chicago, St. Louis, Dayton, and Lexington.

The job of building a schedule fell to Alonzo Watford, Attucks's athletic director from 1932 to 1957, was above all a resourceful man. At 5'4", 160 pounds, he had led the nation in scoring as a college football player at Butler University. In his playing days, when your knee touched the ground you could bounce back up and keep running. No one had ever found a way to keep Alonzo Watford down.

When he could talk someone into playing Attucks, it usually meant the expense of chartering a bus for a long trip. Everyone wanted their cash up front. Watford developed a network of "angels," as he called them, local black businesses and Butler alums who would stake him to a game. If he fell short, he'd get the students to sponsor bake sales. He was able to talk Butler into giving Attucks hand-me-down uniforms and shoes, which he then turned over to Attucks's tailoring and shoe repair shops as class projects.

Once Watford found out about a national high school football tournament in Tulsa, Oklahoma. The sponsors were eager to have them. This, thought Watford, could put Attucks on the map. He shook down his angels, put $400 down for the bus, told the players to make sure they packed plenty of food—there wouldn't be many, if any, roadside restaurants that would feed a large group of black teenaged boys. To a great sendoff, the Flying Tigers took off for the Wild West.

It started to snow in Missouri. They kept going until the driver couldn't see anymore. He pulled over. There they were, two coaches and two dozen city kids stranded in a bus in the middle of Kansas. The wind rattled the vehicle and the kids bundled up in their pads. Remarkably, they made the game—which they lost—and turned around and came home.

The basketball team had an added burden of not being able to play in the tourney. That was how you mad your mark. Change was maddeningly gradual. In the mid-'30s, the Indiana High School Athletic Association (IHSAA) ruled that Attucks could play "contests [against member schools] in which not more than two schools should be involved at the same time," but the tournament was still taboo.

Watford booked games with tiny rural schools—Elletsville, Smithville, and Paragon were the first—whose athletic directors were either daring or sympathetic

The 1938–1939 Smithville High Schedule. Note the December 17 game against "Crispus Attuck." For two decades, Attucks could find games only against tiny rural schools like Smithville and against segregated schools throughout the Midwest. *Courtesy of Indiana Basketball Hall of Fame.*

and sticky summer days, black boys in Indianapolis waged war, teaching each other a form of basketball that bore little resemblance to the patterned game whites learned elsewhere in Indianapolis and in the surrounding towns. The Dust Bowl was the crucible for the best competition in the city, birthplace of the kind of city game that is celebrated in the playgrounds of all major cities today.

Many of the players went to junior high school right next door to Attucks, at Public School 17, where in 1945 a math teacher named Ray Crowe started an intramural basketball program. In contrast to his players, Crowe knew Hoosier Hysteria firsthand. The eldest of eight boys in a family of ten children, Crowe had grown up on a farm and attended school in a small town south of Indianapolis. He'd grown up like white kids, playing on grade school teams and shooting at baskets on backboards nailed to barns.

The tough kids who poured into his intramural program loved him. He was short, stocky, handsome, and tough. "He used to run up the wall, spring off it and slam-dunk," remembers Hallie Bryant, who now represents the Harlem Globetrotters. "That used to impress us little kids. He'd come into your neighborhood and take you to get a soda. He'd visit your home and get to know your parents. He became like one of the family.

"He demanded respect, and he respected us. If he came in and said, 'Be quiet,' and you weren't quiet, he would shake you up. He wouldn't hurt guys or anything, but if they were cuttin' up he'd jack 'em up against the wall. He spoke very softly, but we figured he carried a real big stick."

In 1950 Crowe was asked to become Attucks's assistant coach. The next year the head coach, Fitzhugh Lyons, resigned and Crowe was named to replace him. It was all very sudden. Having no high school coaching experience, Crowe hustled off to every summer camp and clinic he could find.

Crowe almost won the state tourney in his first year. When the 1951 season began, Crowe instantly placed Willie Gardner, a 6'8" forward who often came to school hungry, in the starting lineup and gave him free reign to run and handle the ball. Midway through one early game, Hallie Bryant's long jump shot bounded off the rim and went straight up. Gardner, crouched beneath the basket, leaped up, cupped the ball in one hand high above the basket, and smashed it down through the hoop. The crowd was at first stunned, then ecstatic. In the Indiana of 1951 that dunk was a revolutionary move, a stylistic breakthrough something like those that Julius Erving would bring later.

Emboldened, Gardner worked out a pre-game dunking routine. First he did a left-handed dunk, then a right-handed dunk, and then a two-handed over-the-head dunk. Often, opposing players, especially those from the little towns that still made up much of the Attucks schedule, would stop their own warmup drills to watch Willie Gardner dunk. Some coaches kept their players in the locker room until Attucks was finished warming up. It was a huge advantage.

After Attucks won the bitterly contested Indianapolis sectional in 1951 for the first time, defeating several schools that still refused to schedule games against them, Ray Crowe and the Attucks players became community heroes. Store windows along Indiana Avenue blossomed with good luck signs for the second, or regional round, to be played the following Saturday at gigantic Butler Fieldhouse in Indianapolis. The tourney was televised for the first time that year, and during the sectional games neighbors had clustered around big TV consoles in bars and hotels, squinting to make sense of the blurred images on the little screens.

Everything, even luck, seemed to be on Attucks's side. They won the semistate round of the tourney by beating Anderson High on a miraculous shot from the corner by Bailey ("Flap") Robertson, who was the third option on the play. Robertson's shot hit the rim, bounded straight up and fell cleanly through at the buzzer. Attucks finally lost to Evansville Reitz in the afternoon round of the finals. "The first mighty surge of Ray Crowe's Tigers, in 1951, aroused probably the greatest demonstration of genuine good feeling between whites and Negroes since the Civil War," wrote the *Indianapolis Recorder*.

It was indeed a monumental feat, achieved far too suddenly for many. There had been no time for anyone to get used to the notion of Crispus Attucks High—viewed by many as the City's outcast school—as a powerhouse. Crowe not only had to contend with whites who feared the Attucks team as a potential vehicle for social revolution, but also with Attucks's administrators, who feared the consequences of success.

"I would call the attitude 'defeatist,'" recalled Crowe of the mind set at Attucks when he arrived as coach. "It took some time for the principal to get adjusted to big-time athletics. He liked to come down and talk to the boys. He'd tell 'em not to be too rough, not to commit fouls, to be good sports. It was kind of a timid approach."

"They were total gentlemen," recalls Bob Collins, sports editor of the *Indianapolis Star*, who covered Indianapolis basketball for the paper at the time. "They played the loosest zone you ever saw in your life. Every time the whistle blew, the Attucks player put up his hand because he knew it was gonna be against him."

The 1951 Attucks team galvanized black Indianapolis. "When Attucks would win," recalls Marcus Stewart, now the editor of the Indianapolis *Recorder*, "all black people would celebrate. Indiana Avenue would go wild. It was like when Joe Louis would whip someone."

Best friends Willie Gardner and Hallie Bryant, with their beloved coach Ray Crowe. *Courtesy of Frank H. Fisse.*

One of Attucks's cheerleaders made up a song that rubbed the new order in everyone's faces. Called the "C-R-A-Z-Y" song, the Attucks fans, weaving back and forth en masse, would begin to sing it when the game was iced. "Oh, Tech is rough / And Tech is tough / They can beat everybody / But they can't beat us." The earlier the song was heard, the more delicious the goad.

In 1951 the tourney was televised for the first time, and the images of local heroes entered homes and bars and department-store showrooms. No longer did black kids have to wait for the Globetrotters, for right there on the screen were Hallie Bryant and Willie Gardner and Flap Robertson, guys from Lock-field, from the Dust Bowl, from Attucks.

And Attucks had a new style, high, fast, and flashy. They weren't interested in working the ball around for set shots. They ran hard all game long and made up shots to fit any occasion. They seemed to play the game above the rim. Attucks's center Willie Gardner—who the next year went straight from high school to the Harlem Globetrotters—was the first player many Hoosiers ever saw dunk the ball in a game.

After the tourney loss, Ray Crowe spent a grim summer blaming himself for not winning the championship, for not making the kids play tougher, for letting them back off. He vowed not to let it happen again. "It was the way they had been brought up," he says. "They felt they shouldn't knock heads the way you have to if you're going to be a winner. I came up playin' against white kids. I went to school with 'em. I finally got my point across, but it took me years."

While Crowe agonized, Alonzo Watford was having the time of his life. The phone was ringing off the hook. Attucks had become box office. "Do you think you could find an opening sometime in February?" the athletic directors would ask politely. On top of that, they were offering whopping sums, hundreds of dollars, bus fares included. Why? Because Attucks was the pride of black Indianapolis, and, for a growing number, white Indianapolis too. Thousands of people would flock to Butler field house for a chance to see them play.

In 1984 Alonzo Watford recounted these events from a bed in his home one evening a few weeks before he died. He spoke from an oxygen tent. Until he thought of those courteous phone calls, his face had been contorted with the punishment of struggling to build words syllable by syllable. But the memories made him chuckle, and soon laughter shook his frame. "Those people had never seen a Negro before," he said. "We were something unusual. One game with us could make the whole year for them. It got so I could play *Podunk* and make money." Tears of laughter rolled down Alonzo Watford's face. "Man, what a great feeling," he said.

★   ★   ★

Attucks could not escape the wicked Indianapolis sectional in 1952, but Ray Crowe saw something that year that looked like the ticket back to the state finals. Flap Robertson's younger brother Oscar, then an eighth grader at Public School 17, looked like he was going to be a special player.

The three Robertson brothers—Bailey, who hit the shot that beat Anderson in 1951, Oscar, and Henry—had, like nearly all Attucks's players, come to Indianapolis from the south. In the winter of 1944, Mazelle Robertson ushered her three sons aboard a Greyhound bus in Nashville and led them to the rear. She was leaving her home and family and the 300 acres of cornfields that her grandfather had begun to sharecrop after the Civil War. Her husband, Bailey Senior, had landed a job with the Indianapolis sanitation department. They should come on, now, he said. They could all stay with his sister. Of course it was a risk, but whatever Indianapolis was, it was North. It had to offer more for the three Robertson boys than a one-room schoolhouse unheated and without

Crispus Attucks High teams changed forever the way basketball was played in Indiana. Their opponents seemed to have square dances running through their heads, while Attucks played jazz—fast, soaring, and improvised over a sound structural knowledge of fast-break basketball. *Courtesy of the* Indianapolis Recorder *Collection, Indiana Historical Society.*

plumbing, in which a single saintly teacher named Lizzie Gleves taught every child between first and sixth grade in all of Dickson County.

Sometime after midnight—after an all-night ride with a dozen or more stops at shacks with whites only restrooms and fountains—the Robertsons finally pulled into the bus station in Indianapolis. Together they dragged their one stuffed suitcase down Illinois Street, pausing repeatedly to ask for directions to the address on the scrap of paper. Sixteen blocks later, they found the house and waited on the porch until morning, when Bailey Senior's sister came home from work and let them in.

Several months after their arrival from Tennessee, the Robertsons put a payment on a small house on Colter Street, across from Lockfield Gardens. The basketball court was a magnet for Bailey, who was soon hooked on the game. With all the farm work there had been no time to learn sports in Tennessee. Now he had found something he was good at, and a way to gain respect in a new neighborhood. He became obsessed with getting better. He cut out the bottom of a peach basket and nailed it to a telephone pole in the alley behind his house and played with Oscar and Hank, using a sock stuffed with newspaper as a ball. As the oldest and the biggest, Bailey had little trouble dominating the games.

But Bailey was shocked when one Christmas day Oscar opened a gift-wrapped box and pulled out a bright orange basketball. Oscar had begged his mother for a ball, but Bailey never thought she would take it seriously. How could she? Where would she get that kind of money? Mazelle explained that the lady she cleaned for had asked her what each of the boys wanted for Christmas. She had dutifully said that Oscar wanted a ball, and was as surprised as they were when the lady handed it to her, smiling, along with gifts for Bailey and Hank.

To Bailey, how it got there didn't matter. What mattered was that it was *Oscar's* ball. Oscar was now not only the only basketball owner in the family, but the only private ball owner in the *neighborhood*. Oscar made it clear to Bailey and Hank that it was not the Robertson Family Ball, but just his. In the mornings he took it out the door with him, and carried it with him wherever he went. At night, sometimes with Bailey looking on, Oscar soaped down the orange ball and placed it carefully beside his bed before closing his eyes.

Word got around about Bailey's little brother Oscar. Ray Crowe was in the bleachers as the tall, skinny kid scored half his team's points in leading P. S. 17 to the first Indianapolis grade school championship. Crowe was impressed. "He could shoot well and had all those moves and fakes," he later recalled. But at the end of each half, Oscar did something that impressed Crowe even more, just as it would impress fans around the world for the next two decades. Very deliberately, Oscar dribbled the ball while the seconds ticked away, and then gave a couple of fakes and scored just before the buzzer. "He just *ran* the game," Crowe recalls.

Hallie Bryant remembers him at the Dust Bowl: "There was this sense of combat about him. He was always challenging people. He was big for his age, but he had to gain the older guys' respect to get on the court. So he was always sayin', 'Get this, get this,' like, 'See if you can block this,' even to the guys with the big reputations."

Oscar started at forward his sophomore year, but Attucks's hopes were crushed in 1954 by Milan's team of destiny, a team from a rural school with 161 students enrolled, all white. Milan gave Attucks the soundest beating of any team Ray Crowe had ever coached. Two of Attucks's best players—Willie Merriweather and Winford O'Neal—were injured and could not play. Still, there was a sense that Attuck's wouldn't be denied forever.

★ ★ ★

Early in 1955 it became clear that Oscar Robertson and Crispus Attucks High School were a special team, maybe a once-in-a-lifetime team. In these early days of the Civil Rights Movement, Attucks represented hope in a City that stifled hope. Black fans throughout Indiana, and many whites as well wanted to see them play, but Attucks had no home gym. Seven of their first thirteen games had to be rescheduled, usually to a Tuesday or Wednesday night at mammoth Butler Fieldhouse. One frosty weeknight, Attucks played Indianapolis Shortridge before 11,561 fans at Butler Field House. Local papers called it "possibly a world's record crowd for a non-tournament game."

Attucks's share of the take for that game alone was $3,200. Before Oscar Robertson left Attucks, the athletic fund would swell to over $40,000, enough to finance printing presses and engineering equipment for the school. Watford could have chartered a bus to the moon.

Attucks no longer had to go out of Indiana to find games, but there were still no seats in their gym. Every game was an away game. Though they expected trouble on the road, it rarely came. Today, Attucks players and coaches remember the crowds as generous and the players as respectful. The officials were thought to be another matter.

Crowe and his players were convinced that referees would call any close call against Attucks. He told his players never to argue with the referees, but to assume they were playing against seven people—five players and two refs. He told them to get ahead early and play like the game was tied the whole way, because he didn't want a close game at the end.

Attucks entered the 1955 tournament 21–1, having lost by only one point to Connersville. Attucks had no trouble in the tournament until they met Muncie Central in the semistate final. Muncie and Attucks had been rated first and second in Indiana all year long, and the game lived up to all expectations. With Attucks ahead 71–70 in the closing seconds, Oscar intercepted a pass and flung the ball high in the air as the buzzer sounded.

* * *

As the state finals approached, the white citizens of Indianapolis were forced to consider Crispus Attucks seriously. For many whites, Attucks was above all a mysterious place. Few whites even knew where the school was; many, not knowing any better, called it "Christmas" Attucks.

"Black or white, these kids were in a position to do Indianapolis one immortal favor: win the tournament and end the nightmare. People who had never talked to each other were talking to each other," recalled sportswriter Bob Collins. "Attucks was a common denominator." Oscar Robertson remembers, "Before we got to the state finals we were just known as 'Crispus Attucks.' But when we got into the finals we were suddenly Indianapolis Crispus Attucks."

But even in a thaw, the years of estrangement between blacks and whites were formidable barriers. "The week before the finals, I got called into the Indianapolis school superintendent's office," Attucks Principal Dr. Russell A. Lane later recalled. "There were representatives from the mayor's office and from the police and fire departments. The mayor's man said, 'Well, looks like your boys are going to win next week.' I said, 'We think so.' He said, 'We're afraid if they do, your people will break up the city and tear down all the lampposts.' I said, 'There will not be one incident.'"

Dr. Lane spent much of the next week advising students to restrain themselves even in celebration. A car turned over in jubilation, he explained to them, might well be held against everyone as evidence of the Negro's violent nature.

It turned out to be an all-black final game, Attucks versus Gary Roosevelt, which made rooting for Attucks much easier for many Indianapolis whites. Roosevelt had a fine team, including Dick Barnett, who was later to star for the New York Knicks, but they were hopelessly undermatched. Attucks demolished them 97–64, scoring twenty-nine points more than any team had ever scored in a final tournament game.

4

ANDERSON, INDIANA

Basketball Town

. . . .

Author's note: The first section of this chapter, Part 1, was written in 1984 ʳ a time when Anderson's economy, neighborhood life and basic sense of hope were placed under siege by the collapsing auto industry. In a very real sense, high school basketball was the glue that was keeping the town together.

I've never visited a place where high school basketball meant so much as it did to Anderson, Indiana at that bleak hour.

Ron Porter's ear is mashed against a telephone receiver. "Turn it up, Earl!" he screams at the bartender 1,200 miles away. Between the bedlam at the Olympia Lounge back in Anderson and the noise at the Astrodome, where the Boston Celtics are playing the Houston Rockets, Porter can barely hear.

It is February 1982. Driven from Anderson by the collapsing auto industry, Porter and his roommate, Ron James, arrived in Houston six months ago looking for cars to sell. The summer and fall were all right, but now it is winter—although it doesn't feel like it—and back home the Indians are playing Highland in the Wigwam right now, right NOW for the sectional title. As Larry Bird and Moses Malone go at it, Porter is thinking, my God, this is the first Indiana high school basketball tourney I've missed since 1954, when I was ten: as the game goes on, the monkey bears down harder and harder on Ron Porter's back.

By halftime, he can't take it any longer. He leaps from his seat, sprints up the stairs two at a time to a phone booth, jams some coins in a slot, and dials Earl Alger at the Olympia Lounge. Alger knows exactly what to do, for he's known Ron Porter a long time, and he's had cases like this before. He places the receiver tight against a radio, turns up the broadcast, and goes back to mixing drinks. Porter never returns to his seat.

At that time Ron Porter was one of a diaspora of Anderson High School alumnae—"Old Indians," they are called—who depend on these long-distance radio hookups each March during the tourney. They pile up monstrous phone bills when the Indians survive into the tourney's advanced rounds, as they often do.

But Porter, now 50, knew he couldn't continue to live that way. Starting the next year, he set out to restructure his life so that his seasonal movements could match those of the Indians. Now, each year, usually around Christmas, Porter buys a low-milage used car that he thinks he can sell for a profit in Indiana—something like a Buick Park Avenue—flings his bags into the spacious trunk, punches cruise control, and settles back for a journey to Anderson. The distance is 1,025 miles, door to door. His best time is a radar detector–assisted 16 hours.

As he motors eastward, he is only vaguely aware of the changing landscape or fluctuating sunlight. His heart is filled with the romance of Wigwam, his mind dancing with images of last year's underclassmen. By the time he bypasses Naptown on I-465 and swings north onto 69, with Anderson less than an hour away, he is once again brimming with hope. If everyone plays up to his potential, if the center grew, if they study, if the freshmen jell and the new coach is as good as he's cracked up to be, this could be the year. In fact, it probably will be. As the Redbud City fills his windshield, Ron Porter is certain that this year, when he returns to Houston after the tourney, it will be later than ever before.

* * *

Anderson, Indiana, is the hottest grass-roots basketball town on earth. It is a tough, blue-collar city whose many auto workers live from contract to contract, a family town where drugs and weapons and crime have become increasingly worrisome, and a place where high school basketball is still celebrated on Fridays after sundown much as it was three-quarters of a century ago. Families have held season tickets to Anderson High School's games since the Great Depression. The townspeople have dressed up in red and green—Indian colors—to share popcorn and cheers and dances and songs that haven't changed for longer than anyone can remember. Many Andersonians can most easily mark the events of their lives by remembering what grade a star player was in at the time, or how the Indians did in the state tourney, year after year.

Travel around Indiana and ask coaches and players to name the hotbed of hotbeds, and you will hear a lot of replies like, "We have great fans, but those people in Anderson are crazy."

For much of its history Anderson, Indiana, thirty miles northeast of Indianapolis, has been a one-industry town whose residents have cranked out headlights and windows and doors for several General Motors parts factories. With a large and stable labor force and low taxes, Anderson was briefly promoted as "the next Detroit." But in the late '70s and early '80s, when high interest rates and foreign competition crippled the US auto industry, Anderson nearly collapsed.

Seemingly overnight, GM laid off 5,000 workers, Nicholson File and Anaconda Wire moved out, and small job shops dried up. By 1984 Anderson had the highest unemployment rate in the nation, over 22 percent. While welders and assembly workers stayed home, salespeople like Ron Porter took off for places like Houston, looking for showrooms with some action. Daybreak found the citizens of Anderson clinging to The Game.

In that desolate winter the bleachers became pews. Anderson High School sold 5,600 season tickets, nearly twice as many as the NBA's Indiana Pacers, and crosstown rivals Highland and Madison Heights each sold several thousand more. When all three schools had home games on the same night, one of every four Anderson residents was in a gym, sheltered in tradition. In the Wigwam, four generations huddled together in warmth and light and ritual. For a few hours the old problems—how to break Kokomo's press or contain Muncie Central's guards—left no room for brooding about the next paycheck.

Even jobless families could afford eighteen dollars for a season ticket, a pass to twelve winter evenings of blessed relief. "I mean, things were bad around here," said Jack McMahan, then mayor of Anderson. "I'm talking about real human needs. But basketball was the great stabilizing factor. I'm very serious about this. Even if they didn't have a job, people could look forward to the games. When snowstorms closed down the city government and the library, I've seen people walk down the railroad track in two feet of snow to get to the gym."

Elders of the tribe at the Wigwam. *Courtesy of Norm Johnston.*

* * *

Anderson High had already outgrown two gyms by 1925, when the doors were opened to the original Wigwam. Anderson's children hoarded pennies to buy bonds to pay for the Wigwam, the gym that would at last be big enough for everyone. The bonds were hawked with the fervor of the World War I bond drives of the previous decade. Seating over 5,000, the Wigwam was to be the Gym to end all Gyms.

It was too small from the first whistle. The town lived with it until the winter of 1958, when it burned to the ground. Many believe it was finally torched by a citizen who could not get in one Friday night too many. A new Wigwam began to rise from the ashes almost at once.

Today, from across Lincoln Street, Anderson High School itself, a practical, red brick institution built in 1910, looks something like a snail peeking out from beneath an oversized carapace. The shell is, of course, the Wigwam. Best examined from the parking lot behind the school, the Wigwam is a mammoth mint

Friday night fever: 9,000 fans attend a home game at the Wigwam.
Courtesy of John E. Simon.

green cube with an Indian's head emblazoned on the side. Judging from the size of the building alone, it is plain to see that this time the townspeople got it right.

It is more a temple than a gym. Seating 8,998 fans—nine times the enrollment of Anderson High—the Wigwam cost over $2 million, even in 1960. Ron Hecklinski, who became head coach of the boys' basketball team in 1993, takes a few moments before practice to guide a visitor briskly through the Wigwam's weight rooms and video rooms, past an Olympic-sized pool, and into the locker room for a glimpse of pantries full of new shoes and practice uniforms and bright orange balls.

Voices lower when one steps into the gym itself. This is the second largest high school gym in the United States, containing a mere 327 fewer seats than the Newcastle's Chrysler Fieldhouse, about thirty miles away (gym size is an raw nerve in this part of Indiana, one that Newcastle fans skillfully tweak by stretching a wall-to-wall banner across their gym proclaiming it, "the largest and finest high school fieldhouse in the world.")

The eye rises to meet endless sections of red-and-green painted seats. A four-sided, NBA style electric scoreboard is suspended high above a gleaming floor. A brave's head in full headdress has been painted into the center circle. It is a room much larger and better-appointed than those in which most NCAA Division I teams play their games.

★ ★ ★

Anderson High was the only school in town for three quarters of a century, until the mid-fifties, when Highland High was annexed into the city of Anderson and Madison Heights High was created to educate the sons and daughters of an expanding GM management. Although the Indians didn't welcome the prospect of competition, the threat at first seemed harmless enough, for Anderson High still had the most students.

A decade later, the civil rights movement transformed everything. School districts were redrawn, the most dramatic change splitting a large, predominantly black neighborhood, the source of many of Anderson's best players, almost in half. Students living south of 22nd Street were assigned to Madison Heights; north of 22nd Street, to Anderson. Still other residents were bused to Highland, and for the first time there was authentic competition in Anderson.

Most Hoosiers now rate the Anderson sectional as among the toughest of all the sixty four sectional tournaments. Sectional week is the most passionate time of the year, a few days in mid-February when three Anderson schools and three smaller local schools go hand to hand for the right of only one to survive to the regional round. Hostilities simmer within acceptable limits throughout most of the year, but at sectional time Anderson can feel like Ulster.

It was only a generation ago that everyone in town went to Anderson High, so there are many families with parents who bleed red and green and whose children and grandchildren go to Madison Heights or Highland. During sectional week there are a lot of unfinished meals.

"My daughter was a cheerleader at Anderson High, and so was her best friend," said Brenda Weinzaphel, a lifelong fan and former treasurer of the Indians Booster Club. "But her friend's mother was a secretary at Madison Heights and her dad taught at Highland. She'd get into it all the time with her parents. Finally it got so bad she had to come to stay at our house during sectional week."

The tension seems to grip adults harder than kids, who get to mix at parties and in back seats and on outdoor courts. But much of Anderson's service club life revolves around basketball in the winter, and it is harder for adults—especially Old Indians, who still regard the other two schools as bratty newcomers—to forgive and forget. There are those who will not shop in rival neighborhoods.

* * *

An hour before game time, the fragrance of fresh popcorn already fills the Wigwam. The Indian boosters are busy at their table, unboxing high school basketball's most complete product line. Tonight's assortment includes sweatshirts, tee shirts, posters, license plates, pennants, buttons, ballpoint pens, mugs, window stickers, and window shades. "Anything that's red and green," says a smiling booster.

After a while, fans start to trickle, then flow, then surge into the gym. Young families, guys in ballcaps, arrive first to begin their long trek upstairs to aeries that call for keen eyes. Then older, nicely dressed quartets, the boys steering the girls with a light touch on the back, dawdle momentarily at courtside to watch layup drills and then finally ascend into the top and middle seats of the floor level. Everyone seems to know everyone else.

Below them is a block of boosters, many of them elderly women decked out in red and green outfits. Some are wearing red and green lipstick. Finally, arriving fashionably late, are the town's gentry, including the ex-mayor (the current jobholder is a Highland graduate), members of the school board and the managerial elite. One of them turns out to be Carl Erskine, class of '45. The great Dodger curveballer is today president of the First National Bank of Madison County.

Erskine swears he is remembered locally more as a set shooter than as a major league pitcher. "Hardly a day goes by when somebody doesn't stop me on the street and say 'Carl, hey, uh, remember that game when you—' and I think they're gonna talk about the Yankees. Then they'll say, 'I was in the old Wigwam that day you made that one from the corner against Kokomo. Here, I'm not a Dodger, I am an Indian."

As tip-off time draws near, the opposing cheerleaders are squatting around the center circle, passing a peace pipe. Suddenly the lights go out. Everyone leaps to their feet, whooping in the dark as the Wigwam reels with the thunder of tom-toms. All at once a spotlight falls upon an Indian brave in full headdress, arms folded across his bare chest.

He dances in wide circles around the gym, then cuts abruptly into the center circle as the spotlight broadens. There, kneeling, is a maiden. The crowd noise would mute the Concorde. As the two hold a long, unblinking stare, she rises and they begin to dance slowly together, mingling rather sensually for high school fare in central Indiana. He bolts loose for a final circle, breaks in again, and leaps over her. They stride from the spotlight together and the crowd cuts loose with one last great whoop.

The Maiden and the Brave stare down the opponents during the pre-game ceremony. *Courtesy of John E. Simon.*

The Dance of the Brave and the Maiden is a sacred tradition in Anderson, perhaps fifty years old. Competition for the roles of the brave and the maiden is said to be as keen as that for starting forward on the team. The dance is believed to have an intimidating effect on the opponents, some of whom remain in the locker room until it is done.

Because the ceremony of the game means almost as much here as its playing, cheerleaders, majorettes, band members and dancers have long been respected at Anderson as they are in few other places. "I was a cheerleader at New Castle High," recalls Brenda Weinzaphel, "and to come to Anderson and see the maiden and the brave dance and pass the pipe, that was the high point of the year. At Anderson High a cheerleader really means something. When my daughter made cheerleader here, I was in ecstasy."

The lights come back on, and, when vision and hearing are again possible, a neighbor points out that all that the best seats in the house are occupied by very old people, mainly, it turns out, by members of seventeen families who have held season tickets for over fifty years, along with the interlopers who sat down thirty or forty years ago.

Season tickets for those seats are Anderson's crown jewels. You work your way down toward them row by row, year by year throughout the course of your life. At the Wigwam you begin at the top and descend when someone dies or moves away or forgets to renew. The players get closer as your ability to see them gets worse. From the young families up in the clouds down to the gerentocracy at courtside, Anderson's human geology is recorded in the strata of the Wigwam.

Word that one of these tickets has become available is whispered among family members and trusted friends, like word of a vacant rent controlled apartment in Manhattan. These tickets surface from time to time in wills, and Indian athletic director Jack Macy has three times been summoned to testify as to their proper custody in spiteful divorce hearings.

Dan Quickel, 90, has what seems to be the best seat in the house, front row center. He is happy to share the story of his marvelous descent. "I started out in the top of the old Wigwam in the student section," he recalls. "I bought my first season ticket in 1928, when I was a freshman. I had to sit with the students until I graduated in 1931." When he came home from Cornell and law school at the University of Michigan, opportunity knocked, hard. Waiting was the break of a lifetime.

"My father had become team physician. Because of that, he could get us into all the games, row three." From there it was all downhill, so to speak. "Then we were in the second row when the new gym opened. We had three seats together. Then Father died at the age of ninety nine. He was getting ready to go to the ball game when he fell down the stairs and couldn't come anymore. After that Charlie Cummins, the athletic director, put us in the first row, section D, down by the stage. Finally, two seats opened up front row center, and we were delighted to take them."

The Indians hold a drawing to distribute tournament tickets. To enter "Lottery Night" you hand in your regular season ticket stub one weekday before the sectional—during Red and Green Week, when everything in town looks like a Christmas package—and then return to the Wigwam at eight that night for the drawing.

Actually, you could show up at 8:00 for the drawing, because it is preceded by at least an hour of inspirational speeches and fight songs and syncopated cheers. Each team member gets to shuffle up to the mike amid riotous applause for a few defiant words, and the booster product line appears once more.

Finally, one blindfolded student cranks the drum and another yells out a number. There's a shriek and a woman in a red blouse and a green skirt bounds down the stairs to claim her tourney ticket. For more than an hour down they come, in every combination of red and green, until the drum is empty.

Although Jack Macy insists he's never been offered a bribe for a tourney ticket, that doesn't mean every rabid Indian fan is content to trust the tournament to blindfolded students. Ron Porter remembers scoring eight tickets for the state finals one year by stapling six season ticket stubs from the previous year to his two current tickets, and then getting lucky in the drawing: "And then I was walkin' out of the gym and a guy said, 'R. P., I'll give you a hundred dollars apiece for 'em.' I said, 'No way, no way.'"

* * *

Though Anderson High celebrates the game ritually and in multitudes, though the faithful have twice passed the hat to erect a truly flattering place of worship, though the prayers are earnest and the faith unbroken—the gods have not smiled on the Indians since 1946, when a 5'8" center named Jumpin' Johnny Wilson—a pioneer dunker—led the Indians to their only Indiana championship.

Since then, the Indians have escaped their cutthroat sectional—which surely can be likened to the Valley of the Shadow of Death—many times, captured regional and semistate crowns and have reached the final, final game for the championship of all 400 Hoosier schools, three times, only to lose by four points, and then two and finally one excruciating point.

"We're snakebit," explains Ron Porter glumly. "There's no other way to explain it. Year after year we have the statistics, the superstars, and something always happens." Porter can tell the story firsthand, for no matter where he has been or what has been going on in his life, he has been with the Indians in spirit or flesh every year since his graduation in 1962—and he has even made a little spending money on the side. A sampling of key events in Ron Porter's postgraduate years leaves no room for doubt about the intensity of his faith:

"In '68–'69 I was at the top of the gym when we got beat by Highland in the sectional. We were down by one point with about forty four seconds to go, and Artie Pepelea shot a shot from the ten second line that went over the backboard and into the stage. I just went wild. I was so mad I left my ex wife at the gym. I was screamin' and cussin' and stomped down those stairs and out of the gym and got in my car and drove to my buddy's house and got drunk. It was one of those days.

"In '73–'74 we were 27–0, ranked fifth in the nation by some magazine. We had to play in the Fort Wayne semistate. I went up to northern Indiana and bought 500 tickets from the different schools in the semistate. Me and four other guys, we left Anderson at midnight and drove to Elkhart and bought 150 tickets for four dollars apiece and I was sellin' 'em for twenty. That night we played Fort Wayne Northrup and we lost. Unbelievable.

"Let's see, '79 is when I thought I had the heart attack. We were in the state finals and this girl and I were drivin' to Indianapolis for the afternoon game. I was workin' for Stupes Buick and I made him give me a light green and dark green Regal to drive to the game. Then I started havin' chest pains. She had to drive me back to the hospital. I'm missin' the game, I'm pissed so I make 'em put it on the radio in the emergency room. Then the guy comes in and says, 'There's nothin' wrong with you, but tonight I want you to come in and get an upper GI.' We beat Argos in the afternoon and so I just got dressed and drove to Indianapolis. I went to Steak and Ale, had dinner, went to the finals and we got beat."

THE game, the one that sent Porter and nearly every other Indian fan combing back through the collective past for trace of some unpaid karmic debt—like, maybe somebody really did burn down the first Wigwam—was the one-point loss to Connersville for the 1983 state title. The game boiled down to one shot, a shot that high-scoring guard Troy Lewis took from eighteen feet.

The final seconds of the Connersville game remain hauntingly clear to all who were there: Behind by one point, the Indians took the ball downcourt and held it for about thirty five seconds. With three seconds left, Lewis dribbled it into the middle and shot a jumper. Norm Held remembers watching the flight of the ball convinced that all his trials were over. "The ball looked dead center, but it hit the front of the rim and bounced up and off . . . it just didn't go in."

Ron Porter was listening to the game by telephone from Houston with his roommate, Ron James. "I just went numb. My roommate was on the phone at the end, I couldn't take it. With about thirty seconds left, he says to me, 'Listen, I can't stand this, Norm's holdin' the ball for the last shot.' When Lewis missed, I just went numb. We were bigger than them, we could've gone inside and got fouled or got a last second shot . . . I couldn't believe it."

Brenda Weinzaphel was stricken. "I cried all the way home. My husband didn't know what to do with me. When that shot didn't go in, I went into the lobby at Market Square, and I don't even remember being out there. I cried all the next day. Even today, I can be in the car driving, I can think about it and I'll be there again. It hurts."

★ ★ ★

Part 2: November, 1995. Though Anderson's economic woes have continued, the Anderson Indians remain one of Indiana's elite basketball schools. When Anderson's coach Norm Held decides to step down, word of the coaching vacancy has the sizzle of a college opening. And for an Anderson High student, the chance to play in the Wigwam remains the dream of a lifetime.

Fifteen-year-old freshman Tyson Jones takes a pass from a teammate in a pre-season practice game and breaks for the middle of the court. Two players fan out to flank him as three defenders backpedal furiously. A step past the free-throw line, Jones fakes to his right with the ball and his hips, drawing a defender to him, then splits the defense with a burst of speed, maintaining his dribble. As hands flail to reject his shot, Jones smoothly passes the ball behind him to a trailing player who banks the ball in the hoop. The tension in Anderson High's head coach Ron Hecklinski's face dissolves. "I love to watch that kid," he says to no one. "He is just so skilled."

Tall, angular, a bank of straight brown hair halting in an even row above thick spectacles, Ron Hecklinski is already hoarse five minutes into practice on an autumn afternoon, just a week before the Indians' opener against Indianapolis Manual. There is too much to teach in too little time. Five of his players are freshmen, and their inexperience often shows as they scrimmage. Four assistant coaches, a team statistician, and a video coordinator patrol the margins of the court, tracking and recording every action. Again and again, Hecklinski stops play to lecture and instruct, his neck arching forward to reach for volume in the huge room. They listen carefully and repeat the mistakes. Exasperated, Hecklinski banishes one player to the custody of an assistant for not warning another that a pick had been set. Head down, the player begins to run laps as Hecklinski's lips move in a private prayer.

Hecklinski, 38, beat out 62 other applicants for the job of the Anderson Indians' head coach. Eleven of the applicants were assistant college coaches and another was a head coach. Hecklinski had been a key assistant at Ball State University during a six year period in which the men's basketball program became nationally prominent. He hated the frequent trips that kept him apart from his wife and young daughter. Having grown up in Indiana, Hecklinski saw the Anderson High job for what it was: a unique chance to live the life of college head coach, but without the family-crushing qualities of life on the road.

The job had suddenly become available when the previous coach, Norm Held, suffered a heart attack and resigned. Held had been an evangelical leader who had taken the Indians to three state championship games in his eighteen years. All were lost, and Held is remembered by many in Anderson not for the character-building journey but for the rank outcome of those games. Each of the three huge runner-up trophies was carried away quietly to a back corner of the coaches' room where no one could be reminded of the shame.

Shortly after arriving in Anderson, Hecklinski was invited to play golf with a trio of Indian fans. At the tee, one asked Hecklinski if he had heard they named a street after Norm Held. Hecklinksi shook his head. "Yeah," said the fan, "They named it 'Second Street.'" No one laughed. Hecklinski felt their eyes hard upon him.

Hecklinski inherited Held's complete business package: besides Norm Held's team, Hecklinski took over his radio show, his shoe contract with Adidas, his staff of paid assistants and his cable TV deal. He could take over Norm's basketball camp, or put in his own, his call. He could rely on the booster club to generate $10–15,000 per year for team equipment. "There's something a lot of people don't understand," Hecklinski says after practice. "This facility, for a thousand high school students, is probably better than three-fourths of the university facilities we played in when I was at Ball State. The community really takes care of this place. I've been all over and I don't think there's a better high school coaching job anywhere. Maybe not a coaching job of any kind. Basketball still matters here. Sure we have problems in Anderson, guns and gangs and drugs and whatever. But on Friday and Saturday night we come in here and we pretend none of it exists. On those nights, it's just ball."

★ ★ ★

Another of the gifts Hecklinski inherited is Tyson Jones, the fluid freshman guard whose name is on everyone's lips. Tyson Jones was born to be an Indian. His father was a star at Anderson High in the late '50s, and his mother has followed the Indians faithfully since her graduation from Anderson. Tyson has two stepbrothers who were also AHS stars and who played at major colleges. He lives with his mother in a large house in a racially mixed neighborhood which he describes as increasingly dangerous.

Like many young people throughout the United States, Tyson grew up dreaming of playing basketball before for high stakes in great arenas before massive television audiences. But unlike most young athletes, Tyson knew he can do this before he left high school. As a young boy his heroes were not Magic Johnson or Michael Jordan or Larry Bird, but Artie Pepelea, Tim Westerfield, Archie Fuller, Vince Tatum, and, first among all, Terry "Kojak" Fuller. Big dreams came true in the Wigwam.

Tyson grew up listening to the Norm Held show on Monday nights. Many times he heard coach Held explain to callers the reasoning behind Troy Lewis's last second shot, and once Tyson even met Troy Lewis. Like Dan Quickel and the other old-timers, Tyson Jones remembers the day that someone moved or died and he and his mom got tickets closer to the Wigwam floor.

Tyson Jones went to as many of Kojak's games as possible, even some on the road. Kojak Fuller was short, like Tyson, a smooth ballhandler and explosive scorer. Tyson was in Indianapolis's Hinkle Fieldhouse, for both of Kojak's semi-state losses to Indianapolis Ben Davis. After the first disaster, Tyson shut himself in his room and repeated the excuses he heard adults make: The refs stunk. Injuries killed us. The second time, when Kojak poured in 47 and the Indians still lost, Tyson just locked himself into a car where no one could see him and sobbed.

One day Tyson was shooting baskets at a recreation center and Kojak Fuller walked in. Before long, somehow they were playing one-on-one, just the two of them outdoors. Even when rain came, they kept playing. Finally, drenched and laughing, they walked inside together.

Coach Ron Hecklinski counsels the Braves: "There is no better coaching job in the U.S." *Courtesy of Brian Drumm.*

In the summer of 1994 Tyson began to hear rumors that he and perhaps four others from his undefeated eighth grade team might make the Anderson High varsity as freshmen. At the beginning of the school year, when Ron Hecklinski posted the names of those who had made the Indians varsity along with the date they were to gather for team photos, it came true.

The biggest moment of Tyson Jones's life was at hand. He was about to step onto the stage where his father, his stepbrothers and his heroes had performed, like their heroes before them. In those days just before Thanksgiving he and his mother talked a lot about what it would be like, and what it would mean to both of them. "The other night my mom said, 'Do you know, Tyson, ever since I was in high school, I get so excited when I hear that school song play and the players come out on the floor. I can't imagine what I'll feel like when I see *you* run out on the floor.' She said, 'You won't be able to imagine it either till it happens.' Well, she's right, I don't know how I'll feel. I know I'll be nervous, but I'll be ready.

"I can't wait."

Freshman Tyson Jones begins his career, hoping he can be as good as his heroes were. *Courtesy of Brian Drumm.*

· ·

I see a city rise as if by magic, in proportions vast and splendid, with a hundred busy marts of traffic and of trade, with palatial homes unnumbered and seats of learning multiplied

Governor Frank Hanley, in his speech at the first banquet of the Gary Commercial Club, 1907

People come to Gary expecting to be shot

Glenn Robinson, 1994

built a cushion in the third quarter and then began to fall apart as the game wound down. People throughout northwestern Indiana leaned closer to the radio as the play-by-play man stumbled over lines like "Kielbowizc to Bicanic . . . Shimala Scores!" Tech hung on to win by two points and, led by Thomas, defeated Mitchell easily in the final game.

When the championship buzzer sounded, everyone grabbed their coats and headed for Hammond. Parades jammed the downtown streets all night long, blocking all major Hammond intersections completely. Stacks of surplus railroad ties were jerked from the rail yard, piled up and set ablaze. The train bringing the team home from Indianapolis was delayed by fans who repeatedly attempted to board it before it could reach the station in Hammond. At ten o'clock on a Sunday morning 50,000 of Hammond's 70,000 residents, many of whom had not slept, gathered to greet their champions. Hammond Tech's principal made the most of his few moments at the microphone. "Basketball will bring to Hammond something it has needed for a long time," he proclaimed. "A new school building!" The multitude erupted at the good news. Hammond's city officials, probably still hung over, dutifully appropriated funds the following morning.

★   ★   ★

John Baratto gazed around the rickety 900-seat gym at East Chicago Washington High for the first time in September of 1943 and wondered why anyone would want to play in such a dump. No wonder their schedule was pathetic. They only played teams from around the Region. Who could blame a coach from Muncie or Kokomo for not busting his butt to come up here and play in this place? There was no money to be made, no excitement to be had, no glory in the offing.

Baratto had come to coach at Washington from downstate, where he had been plugged directly into the juice of Hoosier Hysteria. His baseball coach and mentor at Indiana State Teachers' College had been none other than the immortal Glenn Curtis, who had been Johnny Wooden's coach at Martinsville High. Curtis had helped Baratto get his first coaching job, at a schoolhouse near Terre Haute with a grand total of 64 students. Baratto had cheerfully led them to two straight sectional championships and then asked Curtis to see if

Fifty thousand of Hammond's 70,000 residents greeted the
Hammond Technical state championship team at 10 AM
on a Sunday. *Courtesy of the* Indianapolis News.

he could help him find something a little bigger. So Curtis drove Baratto up to East Chicago to look into an opening. When they crossed the viaduct over the Calumet River, Baratto caught his first sight of the gigantic smokestacks of Inland Steel belching fumes into the sky. He got cold feet. He wanted to turn around. "Look John," Curtis reassured him, "It takes a lot of big strong men to make that steel, and they have sons who'll play basketball for you."

So here he was. East Chicago was bigger all right, but it was a football town in a football Region. At least he had a gym. Some of the schools in Gary didn't even have that.

But John Baratto felt at home in the melting pot of the Calumet Region. He had been born in Texas and moved to Indiana as a young boy when his Italian father got a job in a coal mine near Terre Haute. He had grown up among Slovaks and Serbs in the little camp towns like New Goshen and Clinton. One of his early squads at Washington had five Serbs in the starting lineup. He enjoyed visiting the homes of his new players, sampling dishes from their home countries, and was happy to celebrate their feast days. He knew a few words in many languages.

And Curtis had been right: they were good players. He had no trouble with discipline: those strong, steel-making fathers were happy to tell his players that one wise-ass remark or slip-up at practice and there was a job waiting for them at the mill, starting Monday morning. Cocky, personable and full of laughter, Baratto cut the kind of figure that tough people responded to. Polio as an infant had left him with a limp on the left side and made him talk out of one side of his mouth. He looked like a permanent wise guy, a tough guy in a tough town. When a parent complained that his son wasn't getting enough playing time, Baratto found out where and when the father drank and simply took the stool next to him. "Sometimes we crawled out of those places," Baratto recalls, "But we crawled out together."

He set out at once to build a major program like the powers downstate. He filled up the little gym and beat the other teams around the Region, then went to the mayor and asked for a real gym. He didn't want a bond drive, he wanted an appropriation. He would build a winner, but there was no way the major powers, the money makers, would come up to play in that sorry excuse for a gym. And besides, what sense did it make for Washington to travel over to Gary to play the regional tourney there? How could you win that way? You needed a home court advantage. He would give East Chicago a winner, but they had to help him. And in 1952 they built him an 8,000-seat showcase, as splendid as any gym in Indiana.

East Chicago Washington's coach John Baratto in the huddle. "I just looked tough," he later said. *Courtesy of Indiana Basketball Hall of Fame.*

When it came to finding players, Inland Steel was always there to help the community achieve its goals. "Foss Mayberry was the general superintendent at Inland," Baratto says. "We had an area they called Sunnyside, with a lot of homes. Mayberry would say, 'John, if you have a player you think oughta move in, just get him in to see me and we'll have a job for his father Monday morning.'"

As Baratto's players improved and high statewide rankings became commonplace, as the great teams arrived at the new showcase and the City began to get some respect, the purse strings opened even wider. They gave him money for a defensive coach and placed paid coaches throughout East Chicago's grade schools from the fifth grade on, all of whom reported to Baratto. They paid him well, too, in some years nearly $50,000. He was simply mimicking the successful coaches he had seen downstate, although his private stable of harness horses, which he kept at the local track, added a certain unusual flair.

It was important to Baratto that wherever the East Chicago Washington Senators went, they went first-class. No burgers on the road for them. Again, when you needed help, you turned to the community. "In East Chicago we had 'the Big House,' which was the biggest gambling casino in Indiana," says Baratto. "They'd bus people in from the Palmer House in Chicago to play. It was right in the Harbor, there. Dr. Fletcher, our team physician, was a member of the syndicate that ran the Casino. He was always there for us. I'd say, 'Doc, will you feed the kids tonight?' and he'd say, 'Whatever you say,' and we'd go to Bill Smith's or whatever. He took care of everything. He dressed our boys up in blazers and slacks. Full outfits. 'I'll take care of it,' he'd say."

1960 was the breakthrough year. No team from the region had won the tourney since Hammond Tech twenty years before, though Baratto had taken Washington to the Final Four in 1947 and Gary Roosevelt had made it to the championship game in 1955. Baratto had a typically tough blend of Blacks, Serbs, Slovaks, and Hispanics.

His star center, Jim Bakos, was a classic Foss Mayberry special. Bakos was already well over six feet tall in eighth grade, and tough. But his parents were Catholic, which meant he might be headed to Bishop Noll, the Catholic school in Gary. This concerned Baratto. Enter Mayberry. "One night Foss and I were having a martini before dinner and I said, 'Foss, does Jim Bakos (the player's father) work for you? He said, 'Oh, yeah, I know old man Bakos.' Baratto told him about the tall son with a difficult choice ahead. "Foss said, 'I'll talk to Old Man Bakos.' Foss calls him over the loud speaker at Inland Steel: 'Mr. Bakos, please come to the superintendent's office.' Bakos came, wondering what was wrong. Foss said, 'I understand you've got a son that's a good basketball player. Well, Mr. Baratto's a good friend of mine and he's interested in him and he'd like to have him to go to Washington instead of Bishop Noll.'

"Two or three days later Bakos goes back to Foss and says, 'My boy's gonna play for Baratto.' That was fine, except pretty soon the word got around. One day I was leaving the Elks and I saw the priest over at Bishop Noll. I said, 'uh-oh. This guy's lookin' for me.' He was, too. When he saw me he started right out, saying, 'I never thought you'd stoop so low as to threaten a man's job just to get a basketball player.' It was the wrong thing to say. I hopped all over him. I said, 'Father, you make a living selling religion and I make a living selling basketball. But I never threaten anyone's job to get a basketball player.'"

From the start of the 1960 season Baratto knew he had a team that could go all the way. At the beginning of the season he tried to predict who they would be most likely to face in Indianapolis. He poured over lineups and records and schedules and kept getting the same answer: Muncie Central.

So eight times throughout the season Baratto drove to see Muncie play, often slipping off by himself when Washington had no game. "I went a couple of nights in below zero weather, travelling late at night, all the way to Muncie or wherever. And in the end, we knew them better than they knew us."

Muncie Central was favored by 19 points when they met East Chicago Washington at Butler Fieldhouse for the state championship. Muncie Central was undefeated and had won its games by an average margin of thirty points. Ron Bonham, their best player, was scoring nearly 30 points per game. Before the game, Baratto was extremely nervous and so hoarse from yelling at practice that he could barely whisper. He told his players to get physical, and to try to wear Muncie down with a pressing defense. "When you're playing in state tournament," he says, "in the finals it's a matter of who's the strongest. Who can last. They can all shoot by the time they get to Butler. And we were physically stronger than they were. I figured we would have beaten them in a street fight nine times out of ten."

Early in the game, Jim Bakos smashed a Muncie player to the floor while scrapping for a rebound and took him away from the middle for the rest of the game. By the end, Bakos, elbows flying, had hauled in 15 rebounds, and Washington had pulled off one of the biggest upsets in the tourney's history, winning by sixteen points.

It was the Region's first win since Hammond Tech's 1940 championship, and the team, its attitude, its class, the blazers, their dead-end toughness stirred the pride and spirit of the Region. It was a team that looked like the region, tough, unvarnished, a beer-and-a-shot team with a cocky coach. It was a cultural statement, an exclamation point of a win against a glamorous downstate team.

When they got back, John Baratto's angels took care of him as never before. After one dinner they gave him a ticket to the Rome Olympics and the keys to a new Cadillac. It was of course under the table, but who in the Region was going to hold it against him? Other coaches reported to the Indiana High School Athletic Association. Johnny Baratto worked for the Region.

It got easier after that. Before he retired in 1968, Baratto ended up taking six teams out of steel country to Indianapolis. Today, Baratto winters in Florida and summers in Indiana. And today, when East Chicago players suit up, they take the court in the gleaming, 8,100-seat John A. Baratto Auditorium and Civic Center, built in 1986. Now 77, he looks back fondly on the two-fisted steelworkers and their sons who gave him his best years. "Was I tough?" he repeats, chuckling. "No way. It just looked that way."

* * *

From the time Bo Mallard took over as head basketball coach at Gary Roosevelt in 1957 and long before as an assistant coach he and his wife Mary Elizabeth had been scavengers. His players were the sons of good, strong, struggling people, but poor people. There were few fathers in their homes. And it was a simple fact that no kid could play the running game Bo Mallard coached without food in his belly.

The Mallards organized a network of golfing buddies, faculty colleagues, merchants, coaching associates, and neighborhood women to help the players. Bo talked the cafeteria crew at Roosevelt into letting his players bus lunch; that gave them one extra meal. The Mallards hoarded clothes, surplus welfare tickets, anything that would give the players a few more calories and threads on their back. "Our basement looked like a secondhand store," laughs Mallard. "We had one electrician who stood 6'1" who brought in I don't know how many suits." Mary Elizabeth helped the gangly boys slip on suit coats and taught them to knot a tie. After a while some of the players had several outfits. "We had one kid who changed clothes all the time," Mallard says. "We had to teach him to pace himself."

Mallard nearly landed his center of the future through his basement store. One day Mallard saw an amazingly tall boy that everyone called "Big Bird" walking down a Gary street wearing galoshes on a blazing summer day. Realizing that the kid probably had no shoes, Mallard took him home, rummaged through the basement's shoe department and came up with a spare pair of black wing tips. The happy boy jammed his feet into them, and sure enough, came out for basketball the next fall. Mallard was certain he had anchored the middle of his defense with a pair of shoes. Wrong. "The kid had hands of iron," Mallard says ruefully. "Couldn't catch a cold."

Bo Mallard even scavenged time. From the '30s through the '60s, all Gary high schools practiced and played at Memorial Hall, a drafty old municipal civic center built in 1928. Each school was allotted an hour and a half to practice, but Mallard was always looking for ways to get more. When Roosevelt's practice was finished, Mallard would ask the next coach if they could just run up and down the stairs and around the bleachers while his team warmed up. "At first they'd laugh at us," Mallard recalls. "They'd say, 'You out for track? But that was fifteen minutes of conditioning, each day."

Sometimes Mallard took oranges to practice just in case another school didn't claim their practice time, as often happened on the coldest days. That way he could feed his kids right at Memorial and use the unclaimed time. "We'd have us a picnic right out there," he says." One custodian at Memorial, a diehard Panther fan could sometimes be convinced to shovel one extra load of coal into the furnace at the end of the evening so they could keep playing.

By the early sixties, Roosevelt was Gary's dominant team. Mallard was able to fend off competition for black players from the other Gary Schools mainly by developing a sense of pride and a winning tradition. Kids who had been in trouble got a second chance at Roosevelt if they could follow Bo Mallard's strict code of conduct and appearance and make their grades. "I told kids, 'forget your former troubles," says Mallard. 'You have a new day with me.'" Making the team meant a chance for glory, a chance to play in the footsteps of Dick Barnett and Jake Eison, who had led them all the way to Indianapolis in 1955. Gary boys could listen to a flamboyant broadcaster named Johnny O'Hare as he called the games on WWCA, imagining they were Reggie Lacefield or Loren Thompson or the great Manny Newsome. "I had kids, hungry kids, kids who went without breakfast and sometimes lunch, kid who would run for hours after school in our workouts," recalls Mallard. "They wanted to play for Roosevelt so much."

Each year two Indianas—The Region and downstate—collided like frontal systems in Lafayette. The weekend after the East Chicago Regional, winning players found themselves in a coach's car streaking south on highway 41, smokestacks vanishing behind them, flat fields coming into view south of Crown Point, blurring rows of beans or corn tapering to the horizon from either side of the car, then slowing down to pass through little towns with names like Enos and Morocco and Ade, where white people mingled and chatted on the sidewalks.

Bo Mallard usually took the starters in his car to talk some serious strategy. It was a mixed blessing. "Riding with coach Mallard could make you a nervous wreck," recalls Jim Rogers, who played as Jim Nelson in the late '60s. "He drove fast down 41, and a lot of the time he was turned completely around, talking to the players in the back seat. You had to have one eye on him, but you also couldn't help trying to look out the windshield."

The Saturday semistate games were played at the Purdue Fieldhouse. Coaches from the Region prepared their players for two foes: the opponent and the shock of a being in a different world. "In the early years I made the mistake of going down there the night before," says John Baratto. "Kids weren't used to it. Everything was so different, even staying in the hotel. The black kids would go down and stand in the lobby just watching people. I had to keep them in their room. After the first year, we waited till the morning, had a good breakfast and then drove down there. And we went straight to the gym, got dressed and played."

Usually the foe was Lafayette Jefferson High school, the largest high school in Tippecanoe County, or "Jeff," as they were called. Locally, they were all but invincible, winning 23 straight sectionals in one amazing stretch. Jeff's coach, Marion Crawley, was the most admired and resented coach in Indiana. He was a straight-laced, immensely disciplined man who was widely believed to recruit the fathers of good players from far and wide through an arrangement with a Lafayette-based manufacturer of pre-fabricated homes. But Crawley's greatest sin, as far as the other coaches were concerned, was that of being hard to beat. "Jeff was the gatekeeper," says Mallard. "Crawley was like a wolf down there, just lickin' his chops."

The Lafayette semistate was Crawley's court and Crawley's crowd. "Crawley knew all the tricks," recalls Mallard. "You'd have an outstanding player and he'd have one of his worst players taunt him to get him off his game. Get him mad. Get him to lose control. They'd say everything. 'Nigger.' Racial things. You try to prepare the kids for that but it's just too much for some guys."

Even in the years when they were eliminated in Gary or East Chicago, Mallard drove his underclassmen to Lafayette, just to prepare them for what it would be like the next year. They would sit together in navy blazers and dark grey slacks, a small island in an ocean of white people, often profoundly un-comfortable as they saw themselves through the eyes of others. It was hard not to feel different and unwelcome.

The games were hellish for referees. "Just by his presence on the bench, Crawley was one of the game's biggest intimidators," recalled a veteran official, Don McBride. "He didn't have to say anything or do anything to get your attention." Most officials were from downstate, and unused to refereeing the rougher, faster game played in the Region. "It was farmhorses versus racehorses," says Jim Rogers, "and since the refs were from downstate, it was farmhorse rules." Downstate coaches taught their players to stand in front of a flying player from the Region and take the charge. No one called that play an offensive foul in Gary. No one didn't in Lafayette or Logansport. Officials thought the Lafayette semistate was among the roughest of assignments. You couldn't win. Teams from the Region, having exhausted themselves in the Darwinian struggle to get out of their own regional, often found themselves headed back to Gary or Hammond or East Chicago empty-handed, trying not to blame the refs, or the crowd, or even Crawley, trying to think of some silver lining. Homecomings could be rough. In each of the two years before East Chicago Washington won the state championship, they were upset by Jeff and Crawley in Lafayette. The second year when they returned to the school parking lot they were greeted by effigies of themselves hanging from a light standard.

At 57, with 30 years in at Roosevelt, Bo Mallard had already made up his mind to retire at the end of the 1968 season. Gary, and coaching, and just about every-thing, for that matter, had begun to change. It was getting harder to maintain authority. The seniors were part of what was to be one of the largest graduating classes in Roosevelt's history, in a year of upheaval in the United States. Richard Hatcher, a Gary Democrat, just become the first black mayor in US history. Muhammad Ali was champ. Black Power was important in Gary. Some players seemed a little less willing to run through a wall for Roosevelt.

Some issues were easy to deal with; as for Afros, Mallard simply told his play-ers they could wear their hair as long as they wanted, providing it wasn't longer than the stubble atop his head. Other problems were more troubling. Early in practice, it became apparent that Roosevelt's best guard had developed a drug problem. Mallard tried to help as best he could, but had little experience. Finally he had no choice but to dismiss him from the team. Not only was he in agony for the player, but now his starting guards were 5'5" and 5'6". All season long he struggled to find ways to give them help against taller players.

His asset was a big, experienced front line, averaging about 6'5" in height. Forwards Cornelius McFerson and Aaron Smith could both shoot, though Smith, oddly, could hit consistently only from one corner. Jim Nelson, the center, was skilled but inconsistent, highly intelligent but not easy for Mallard to understand. He seemed to drift in and out of focus, and Mallard didn't always know how to bring him back. He loved basketball, having grown up tutored by neighborhood Roosevelt heroes, but he had other interests as well. He liked poetry. While most Roosevelt players were raised by their mothers and grandmothers, Nelson's father was very much in the picture. He had worked his way into a white-collar job at US Steel and wanted Jim to join US Steel's work-study program. When the coaching staff first spotted Jim Nelson as a stork-like adolescent, they had to convince the father that the Gary Roosevelt basketball program could teach his son life's important lessons—sticking to goals, finishing the things he started, having his work stand up to inspection—just as well as could United States Steel.

All year long the Roosevelt team walked a tightrope. They were never out-rebounded and rarely outshot, but any team with big, good guards had a chance against them, and it was a year of exceptional talent throughout the Region. Roosevelt lost six times during the pre-tourney season, including their last two games. But the team jelled for the sectional and struggled past East Chicago Washington in the Regional final. When they got to the Lafayette semistate, Jeff had already been eliminated, and only small town teams remained at the gate. Roosevelt crushed a school called North Miami 91–30 for the semistate title, and made ready to go to Indianapolis and the state finals the next weekend with a full head of steam.

The following Saturday they beat Vincennes in the afternoon game and prepared to face Indianapolis Shortridge for the State championship. Shortridge had won their game on a last-second shot by their star, Oscar Evans. In the few hours between games Mallard primed his defenses to shadow Evans and went over plays designed to get Aaron Smith the ball in his corner.

To Mallard, the championship game hinged on a single moment involving Jim Nelson, who was playing passively. Late in the first half, with Shortridge ahead and pulling away, Mallard called time out and put his finger in Nelson's chest as soon as Nelson reached the bench. Mallard glared straight into the eyes of his center. "I told him he was loafin'," Mallard recalls. "I said, 'You're in another world. Get in this one.'"

Nelson went back out and stuck two jumpers that seemed to turn the game around. Aaron Smith drilled shot after shot from the corner, ending with 28 points. Roosevelt won by eight. The team stayed in Indianapolis that evening, then drove back home through Lafayette and back up 41. The farther north they got, the more families came out to wave at them, and the more signs of congratulations they saw on the lawns of the rural families. For a while, at least, a team of black players and coaches from the south side of Gary now represented all of Northwest Indiana.

It was the sweetest of the hundreds of drives Mallard had made up and down 41, from the years when they couldn't play in the tourney to now, when he could retire a champion at the end of the school year. Some things had remained constant: in thirty years he had never made more than $3,000 as a coach, even when he had coached three sports. They had joined hands in prayer before each game. And through all the civil rights movement and the official integration of Gary's schools, he had never coached a single white player or taught a white student at Gary Roosevelt High. It was a wonderful way to go out: he had fed his players and clothed them and scavenged for them and his wife and daughter had even taught somehow to use silverware on the road, and now they were champions. The towns flew by and the people kept waving until the smokestacks of the mills came into view. He even found himself slowing down a little. "I had worked so hard," he remembers. "I had to pinch myself."

★ ★ ★

Glenn Robinson slides down against the wall of the Mallard gym at Gary Roosevelt and sits on the floor by himself. Fixing an impassive expression on his oval face, he tries his best to concentrate on the young players who are attending his summer basketball camp. Before him are several hundred boys, scattered in groups of 25 or so throughout the gym, going through ballhandling drills and one-on-one tournaments. Most sneak peeks at him whenever a counselor isn't looking.

The phone in Roosevelt coach Ron Heflin's office rings constantly for Robinson's agent, Charles Tucker, who is never far from it. Everything is still up in the air: which shoes will Glenn wear? Which sportswear company will he sign with? Which team will he play for? Will he even play? Earlier in the summer, Robinson was selected by the Milwaukee Bucks in the NBA draft. He was the first college player chosen. Tucker, who also represents Magic Johnson, promptly announced that it would take $100 million dollars to employ Glenn

Robinson. Herb Kohl, the Bucks' owner, half-jokingly proposed that he just sell Glen Robinson the team and let him run it. Later Robinson signed a multi-year contract with the Bucks for $68.8 million, one of the biggest sports contracts ever. It is an almost cartoonish sum of money where Glenn Robinson grew up. He is not yet 22.

Glenn's mother, Christine Bridgeman, was an unmarried teenager when Glenn was born. Though she was poor she was determined to give her son the best. As soon as he was of high school age, she moved them into a small frame house across Harrison Street from Gary Roosevelt High, which had been her school. She felt that Roosevelt, where strong teachers and counselors constantly remind their students that it is a good and proud thing to be an African American, was an important gift she could give her son.

He would need all the help he could get. Then as now Gary had one of the highest per capita murder rates in the nation and an unemployment rate twice the national average. Guns and drugs are everywhere, and much of the action centers around 25th Street, a main artery of Southside Gary, which everyone calls Two-five. Roosevelt is on Two-five. Trouble is all around. "Glenn's just like I was, and like every other kid who grows up around Two-five," says Ron Heflin. "He could have wound up on either side of that street, with a life of trouble or a life with possibilities. It all depended on who he listened to."

At first uncertain of this skill, Glenn did not go out for basketball until his eighth-grade year. He made the junior varsity as a freshman. While trying out for the varsity as a sophomore, Heflin noticed his toughness before his ability. "One day we were going through workout drills at practice. We call 'em 'suicides.' I ran them for about 40 minutes straight. The rest of the kids were grabbin' their stomachs and complaining but he didn't bend over and he didn't say nothin'. I got interested. I said to myself, 'I'm gonna see what it takes to break this guy. I couldn't do it. He always came right back to the starting line. That night I went home and told my wife, 'I got a special kid here.'

Robinson started on the Panther varsity as a sophomore, but didn't get the ball much. "We thought he should have been the first option but he was the last because he was the youngest on the starting five," says Rickie Wedlow, a teammate. "He didn't complain."

Gary Roosevelt coach Louis "Bo" Mallard cuts down the nets after Roosevelt won the 1968 state finals in Indianapolis. *Courtesy of Indiana Basketball Hall of Fame.*

When his grades slipped in the second semester, Christine marched him into Heflin's office. "She said, 'Coach Heflin, I wanna talk with you. If his grades drop any more—she put her finger up in his face—you won't be playin' basketball anymore.' 'DO YOU UNDERSTAND ME, GLENN ALLEN?' Here's this guy towering over his mom, and he just says 'yeah'. Total control. You don't want to cross Christine."

In his junior year Glenn took over leadership of the team. He was an explosive scorer and rebounder, a disciplined player with a versatile game. He loved to dunk. He loped down the court, arms down by his thighs, his face expressionless, in a way that seemed to lull opponents into complacency. Then he would strike. He did things nobody at Roosevelt had seen. "I remember this one time Daryl Woods, one of our guards, threw him an alley-oop when he was coming down the left side," recalls Rickie Wedlow. "We all thought Darryl had overthrown it and we were getting ready to go back on defense. Glenn leaped and caught the ball at the top of the square above the rim and jammed it down over Judah Parks of East Chicago Roosevelt. We were just shocked."

Gary Roosevelt lost only seven games in Glenn's three years. By his senior tourney, though all defenses were keyed on him, he was unstoppable. He hit the winning basket in both the regional and the semistate. "Everybody in the gym knew where the ball was going both times," Heflin says. "It didn't matter. Nobody had a chance. He can focus better than any athlete I've ever known." He led Roosevelt to the 1991 state championship, winning a heralded showdown with future IU star Alan Henderson in the final game. Glenn was named "Mr. Basketball."

After a brilliant three-year career at Purdue—during which a custodian gave him the name "Big Dog"—Glenn decided to postpone his senior year and enter the NBA draft. He announced his decision to the Nation's sporting press at Gary Roosevelt High, in the gym whose walls sported bigger-than life cutout figures of him and 1991 teammates. "One thing's sure," observed Ron Heflin. "His mom will make sure he gets that degree."

Gary has lost one-fourth of its population in the past fifteen years. The Steel industry has been crippled both by foreign competition and by its own inability to adapt to rapidly changing circumstances. The exodus from Gary to the suburbs has included thousands of whites and many black professionals. But

Glenn Robinson listens to a camper's question at his Big Dog Basketball Camp at Gary Roosevelt High, 1994. *Courtesy of Todd Panagoupoulos, the* Times, *Gary, IN.*

not Glenn Robinson. "Anyone who puts Gary down," he says defiantly, "doesn't know Gary. Gary is a good place. I want to give something back."

The first installment turned out to be Glenn's basketball camp, staged in August of 1994. Summer basketball camps are a major industry in Indiana. There are jumpshooting camps, big man camps, defensive camps, IU camps, Purdue camps, boys' camps, girls' camps, celebrity camps, and meatmarket camps where college prospects are trotted out in groups of ten to play before college coaches who inspect them like plantation owners at an auction. What most have in common is that they are expensive.

Robinson's camp is different. Three hundred campers, almost all of whom are black and from the Region, paid $95 for four days, but only if they could. About a quarter of them got in free.

On the first morning of camp they gathered near an entrance to Roosevelt High and then Robinson blew a whistle, leading them out of the shade and into the sticky heat for a mile run on the school's track. Some were looking at each other and muttering complaints. He paid them no mind. Then they practiced ballhandling drills outdoors on the new surface that Glenn had purchased for the school and shot on new rims he had given them. Finally they entered the Louis B. Mallard Gymnasium, the room in which Glenn Robinson learned to do the things that have made him a millionaire, for a talk about discipline. They listened.

At 21, Glenn Robinson had become the one player in a million that these boys wanted to be. His success had given him the means to see the world, to take up golf, to buy cars and condos and open businesses in his name. But that morning, as he divided the campers into teams, he was taking advantage of a bigger chance. It was the chance to instill among a group of boys a sense of pride in the part of Indiana, overlooked and scorned by so many, that is the real Hoosierland to him. And for a morning, at least, it seemed to be working. "I like Glenn better than Michael Jordan," said one camper. "I like him because he's here."

. . . .

No person in the United States shall, on the basis of sex,
be excluded from participation in, be denied the benefits of,
or be subjected to discrimination under any program
or activity receiving Federal financial assistance.

Title IX of the Education Amendments of 1972

6

JUDI WARREN AND THE WARSAW TIGERS

Into the Front Court

• •

PATRICIA ROY'S OFFICE WALLS ARE COVERED WITH GLOSSY PHOTOS OF a high school girl with her hair in a bowl cut, only with the ends turned neatly under. She is steering what seems to be a huge basketball around and through much bigger girls. Her body seems almost horizontal to the court, she is driving so hard.

Since 1972 Commissioner Roy has been in charge of all girls' sports programs for the Indiana High School Athletic Association. She pushed hard for a girls' basketball tournament, and its success, whose magnitude not even she could have imagined, is due in large part to the girl whose image fills her walls.

"I thank God for Judi Warren," Roy says of the girl. "She's our Billie Jean King. She's the spark that ignited girls' basketball in Indiana. It was scary to start out in what had been a boys' program, but she was a little kid with a lot of fire. She caught people's imaginations. We were lucky she started when she did."

Girls' basketball has become a major force in Indiana. The state championship game routinely draws over 15,000 fans, the largest tournament crowds in the United States. The TV ratings are impressive and growing. In several communities, girls' teams outdraw the boys' teams, and major stars have emerged. One Thursday night in January 1995, 7,100 fans wedged into a gym in East Chicago to see a girls' game between East Chicago Central and Lake Central high schools, both nationally ranked. The scores of reporters, the crush of the crowd and the noise left the players stunned at first. "When we came out for warm-ups I couldn't stop looking around," said Central guard Monica Maxwell. "This is something I'll tell my kids about," agreed her teammate, Kizzy Buggs.

Girls have forced their brothers to share the driveways and the boys' coaches to share the keys to the high school gym. Their knees are braced, their hair is pulled back from their eyes and their ankles are taped. Now they suffer torn anterior cruciate ligaments rather than skinned knees. Their mothers no longer wash their sweaty tee shirts—now their road grays or their home whites get tossed in the team's laundry bin. Many girls will not waste time or risk injury—and the loss of a scholarship—by playing other sports. It wasn't always this way.

★ ★ ★

Girls first played basketball in Indiana in 1898, wearing bloomers, middy blouses, and high cotton stockings. Sponsors cautioned the girls not to roll their stockings down—thus exposing the knees—when their legs got hot and itchy during a game.

For most of a century, girls played basketball a form of tranquil exercise staged in a largely social setting. Smiling girls faced off for the center jump standing erect, one hand raised above their heads, as if they were pairing off for a ball-room dance. "Better than winning honor in basketball is deserving credit for ladylike conduct," explained the Hobart, Indiana, *Gazette* in 1915, "not only in the game but before and after."

Since competition produced excitement and sweat, men were not allowed to watch girls play in many towns. Experts cautioned that the exertion required to play basketball could prove dangerous to young women. "It must always be remembered that the fascination of the game is so great . . . that there is temptation to play at the time of menstruation," wrote Dr. J. Anna Norris. "It is accepted by most authorities that there should be no basketball during at least three days at that time."

Little girls who enjoyed playing ball were called tomboys. Those whose enthusiasm persisted into high school entered rougher waters. They became "jocks," and it was assumed that boys who dated them did so because they couldn't get anyone else. Some women coaches who spent a lot of time with their players were called "dykes," and more than a few were driven from Indiana schools like witches in Salem.

When Judi Warren and her Warsaw High teammates first started, there were few competitive female role models, few resources available to them and little encouragement. But they didn't think about it, at least not at first. Like thousands of young people in Indiana, they were in love with basketball, swept up in the fun of a game involving a ball and a hoop.

"Enthusiasm without hysteria"—that was the goal of Miss Senda Berenson, who introduced Dr. Naismith's game to America's colleges in 1893. Applied to basketball in Indiana, that is an oxymoron. One dramatic winter night in 1976, Judi Warren and the Warsaw tigers proved to all of Indiana that Hoosier Hysteria—the heat and passion of basketball—is gender free.

⋆ ⋆ ⋆

Judi Warren had a problem: the Lions Club had chosen her "Miss Claypool," queen of the fair, and there was no way out of it. She didn't want to be "Miss Claypool," she didn't feel like "Miss Claypool," but there she was, and they had to do something with her hair.

This required a team meeting. Cindy Ross, the team's center and co-captain, went with her to a beautician, for this was not a job for a barber. Before, Judi had just gone to the barber with her dad on a Saturday morning and had her hair cut straight. She wanted it simple, for she had no time to bother with curlers.

Janet Warren had long ago given up on making a homemaker of her younger daughter. Judi wouldn't come in for piano lessons, dropped band, and seemed to drift away from housework. At least Janet had put her foot down on 4-H. A girl should be able to cook and sew, and besides, Janet Warren was the Claypool 4-H leader and her own daughter was going to be there.

Not that Janet hadn't liked sports herself. She had played a little basketball at Claypool High, six girls on a team. With only fourteen students in her class, she had done everything else, too: led cheers, blown horns in the band, hammed it up in the school plays. "The class just wouldn't have functioned if I hadn't have been there," she says.

But all Judi had ever seemed to want to do was play ball. As a little girl, when she got mad or moody, after dinner or before dinner, she'd take a ball out to the driveway and practice throwing it against the chimney and catching it. Then she started heaving it up and into the basket. Then, when her elder brother Jack's friends came over, she'd play with them. Even though she was six years younger and a girl, they all seemed to love her, partly because she'd chase the ball for them all day long. It worried Janet that Judi wasn't meeting any girls. It was good that she was dedicated to something, but this didn't seem, well . . . rounded.

Despite her misgivings, Janet Warren was above all a devoted and supportive mother. She made time to see Judi's games and arranged meals around her practices. As a Hoosier, and having herself married Layne Warren, a slick guard from Claypool, she had seen enough basketball to know that Judi was good. Judi was smaller than everyone else, but she seemed to get up and down the court twice as fast as the other girls. She had always been exceptionally well coordinated. There had been no training wheels on Judi's bike; one day she'd just pedaled off to kindergarten.

While Judi was in grade school, all the Kosciusko County schools, Claypool and Atwood and Leesburg and Silver Lake, were consolidated into Warsaw High School, absorbed like provinces into a central soviet. "Our towns disintegrated," Janet said. "The towns became shambles of communities. When you take the teenagers out of a community there's not much left." Though she had been condemned to go to high school in a faceless institution, Judi amazed her mother by remarking one night at dinner that she was happy to be going to a school that had a sports program for girls. It was hard to figure her out.

And when the time came, just as her mother had predicted, Judi found Warsaw High to be a lot different from Claypool. It was so big that Judi told her she couldn't find the john until the third day. To Janet's relief, she did find girlfriends, though, although there was a catch. These girls were as crazy about sports as Judi.

★ ★ ★

Lisa Vandermark, Cindy Ross, and Cathy Folk had known about Judi Warren for a long time, for Judi's Claypool grade school teams kept beating theirs. Actually, Judi had met Cindy by falling on her in a sixth grade basketball game. Judi swears Cindy tripped her.

Cindy was a head taller than Judi, with long blond hair. All through grade school, Cindy had worn short pants underneath her skirts, so she could whip off the skirt and play tag and dodge ball with the boys at recess.

The Rosses lived in town. Cindy's parents encouraged her desire to be an athlete. Bill Ross was a cheerful and muscular man who followed sports but who had himself started working too early in life to try out for the high school teams. He told his daughter that the main thing was to love something, learn to do it well, and not to quit when the going got tough.

The whole family played twenty-one and shot free throws in the driveway, mom spinning them up underhanded and dad overhanded and the three younger brothers heaving them up any way they could. On the day Cindy announced that she had entered the local AAU track meet as a javelin thrower, they were delighted. All six piled into the car and drove to the park for a Sunday afternoon of javelin throwing. It didn't matter at all that no one had a clue how to throw a javelin.

Judi, Cindy, Lisa, and Cathy ran track and played badminton in the fall, tennis in the spring, and basketball in the winter. They spent all their free time together. Their parents began to get to know one another, too, as the girls stayed at each others' homes on weekends.

They spent their winter Saturday afternoons like boys throughout Indiana, watching and listening to basketball games, munching chips, and tugging on sodas. If they didn't like the announcer on TV, they turned the sound down and listened to a second game on the radio.

At halftime they ran outside and practiced the plays they had just seen. UCLA was their favorite team, because the Bruins ran and pressed and played the whole court, just as their junior high coach, Vivian Eigemiller, had taught them to do. They worked on the timing of their own low altitude version of the alley-oop pass, with Judi as Greg Lee and Cindy as Bill Walton.

At night they went out and cruised around in Judi's older sister Jill's red and white '71 Olds Cutlass. They hit the Village Pizza Inn after the boys' games on Friday nights, and when there was no game they went downtown to the Lake Theater to catch a movie.

The night they went to see *Love Story*, there wasn't enough tissue for the whole squad. "Judi cried the whole time," says Cindy. "Everyone was sniffling but Judi had to bite her thumb to keep from getting loud. We were all sentimental girls. By the end Judi had about bitten her thumbnail off. The girl dies. We bawled. What else can you do?"

At school they were branded as "jocks." Girls snubbed them, and they felt the boys they knew best—mainly other athletes—were a little intimidated by their closeness to each other. They wore little makeup—maybe just a little blush, except for Margie Lozier, the manager, who was into mascara—and, as Cindy Ross put it, "It took at least a funeral to get us into a dress." They all had boyfriends off and on, but they weren't oriented toward dating, except around prom time. "I think right then we all got a little sweaty," remembers Cindy. "Everyone wanted to go to the prom.

"We weren't the ones the guys wanted to be with," Judi Warren recalls. "We weren't the cheerleaders and high society girls all the other girls looked up to. It wasn't cool to date a jock. At times it was discouraging, but we weren't trying to impress anyone or stand out as a group. We just went out and had a good time.

"At that time, my teammates were closer to me than my own family. We knew each other very well. We understood each other. We became a unique group. We would do anything in the world for each other. We would do anything in the world to keep one of the others from going down."

★ ★ ★

Even though the girls had a team, basketball at Warsaw High meant boys' basketball. Warsaw High was a county seat school with a long-standing tradition of winning big games. The boys' basketball team attracted sellout crowds every home game and made enough money to pay for all the girls' programs and the rest of the boys' sports as well. Any question about expanding girls' sports would have caught the men who ran Warsaw's athletic program by surprise; the girls should have been grateful they even had a team.

The girls saw things differently: Warsaw High was their school, too, and they didn't even have uniforms. They practiced in grade schools at inconvenient hours while the boys practiced in the Warsaw gym right after school. And besides, going into their senior year they had lost only four games in three years. That was far better than the boys had done.

The girls believed that their chief oppressor was Ike Tallman, the head boys' basketball coach. Tall, stocky, and given to dark suits, he was an imposing figure. A decade before he had coached a Muncie Central High team to the Indiana boys' championship, which only added to his intimidating stature. But they felt they had to confront him if anything was going to change. One evening after school Judi, Cindy, and Lisa entered Warsaw's athletic office, hearts hammering. Without speaking, Lisa handed Tallman the list of demands they had drawn up, including uniforms and laundry service, buses for the games, cheerleaders and, above all, equal access to the Warsaw High gym for practice.

Tallman studied the list for a moment, then looked up. He did not appear angry. Well, he told them, to succeed you'll have to promote yourself. First thing you'll need is tickets. He told them that he would have his secretary print up some orange tickets, the school's color, and the girls should see if they could sell enough of them to fill the gym. When they could fill the gym, like the boys did, why then they could share it. He returned his attention to his desk. Lisa, who had organized the event and written the list, grew livid. Cindy burst into tears.

When the secretary delivered the tickets, the girls didn't know what to do with them. They decided to try to sell them. Friends and relatives and people at church bought them faithfully, but few showed up at the games. This wasn't going to get them anywhere.

In their senior year the girls were granted permission to practice in the high school gym after the boys were finished. It was a bittersweet victory. Judi lived too far away to go home for dinner and then return to the school for practice. Instead, she would stay in Warsaw, study for an hour or so at school and then stroll with Lisa to Burger's Dairy Store for a couple of jars of baby food. Somehow "Fruit Delight," a mixed fruit, had become the official training food of the Warsaw Tigers.

Then they would walk back to watch the boys practice. Judi studied the drills carefully and tried them herself when the boys' practice was over. She found she could do anything they could except dribble between her legs on the run. At 5'1", her stride wasn't quite long enough for that.

It was usually 9:00 by the time practice was over. With luck, Jill would be waiting in the Cutlass. By the time she got home, Judi had just enough energy left to stumble into the shower and roll into bed.

"I can remember Judi coming home and telling me she had talked to the coach," says Janet Warren, "and I said, 'Judi, you shouldn't talk to your superiors like that.' Looking back, the girls knew what they were doing. I just wasn't in on it. What I knew was that she was never home because she was always at practice. That was kind of upsetting, because it's hard to work around a family when one member is gone so late. We are a family that likes to sit down and have our meals together. It was a sacrifice for everyone."

★ ★ ★

In 1975, the summer before the girls' senior year, the Indiana High School Athletic Association took over the administration of the girls' basketball program and announced that the first girls' state tourney would be held that March. It would be just like the boys' tournament, with all teams in one tourney regardless of enrollment.

That same summer Cindy's dad, Bill Ross, died suddenly of a stroke. He had been a part of the team, a constant source of encouragement and cheer since they were freshmen. Shattered, Cindy decided to quit the team. The others wouldn't hear of it. Cindy was the center, their rebounder, their enforcer, their intimidator.

But it was more than that: losing Cindy would be like losing a limb. "Judi and those guys said I couldn't quit because I was part of them. They said, 'We wouldn't know how to act without you.' We each knew what the others could do.

They said, 'You gotta stay, for us.' So I decided to stay, and we started thinkin' that we could go to state and prove to people that we were legitimate athletes. We knew that having a dream wasn't good enough unless we worked and got it. My dream was to win the tourney to honor my father, because of the time he'd given me and what we'd done together." Together, they decided to win the first state championship for Bill Ross.

As the tourney approached, Cindy's life became even more complicated. She had fallen in love. Mike Knepper had asked her out that summer and they knew it was real almost from the start. But she had little time to see him and she wouldn't skip practice. It was a classic Hoosier conflict: love vs. training.

Faithful but lonesome, Mike would wander over to the Rosses' house and hang out with Cindy's mom and brothers until she came home from practice. Then they'd sink down onto the living room couch or go out for a quick drive. "This basketball is getting old, Cindy," Mike would say. "You never have time for us." And Cindy would throw an arm around him and soothe him with the words that Hoosier boys have whispered to Hoosier girls for nearly a century. "Mike," she would say, "the season won't last forever."

* * *

The Warsaw Tigers were good, and Judi was the spark plug. She may have been short but she was also aggressive, an intuitive passer, and jet fast. She had the quick hands of a pickpocket, constantly smacking the ball away from dribblers and picking off passes, which led to Warsaw layins. The team's strategy was simply to outrun and wear down everyone else. They pressed from end to end and fast broke at every occasion, with Judy penetrating and passing the ball off to Cindy, Lisa, Cathy Folk, or a gifted sophomore athlete named Chanda Kline. In seven of their fourteen pre-tournament games, Warsaw scored more than twice as many points as their opponents.

They entered the tournament undefeated, barely known and pitted against 359 other schools. Fifty or so relatives and close friends watched them win the sectional final against Plymouth High, 52–38. As sectional champions, they again demanded better uniforms and cheerleaders. The administration consented to let the junior varsity cheerleaders go with them to the regional tournament.

When they won the regional tournament the following week, the school began to take notice. Posters appeared in the halls. Classmates began to stop at their lockers to wish them good luck. It felt weird but good. Judi was dating a guy already in college, and they all got a little misty when roses arrived after the regional title. "He was a jewel," recalls Judi's mom.

The fifty Warsaw fans became 1,500 for the semistate final in Fort Wayne. Hoosiers were Hoosiers, and this was one fine basketball team, and it had been here right under their noses all along. Most of the Warsaw fans wore orange tee shirts. The team won the semistate, too, making them one of four teams remaining in the tourney, and now there was real, high voltage excitement. This was the first girls' tournament, after all, and the Bicentennial year. Warsaw's girls could be pioneers.

One afternoon, in the week before the state finals, the school held a pep rally for them. Lisa, Cindy, Judi, Chanda, Cathy, and the others sat in folding chairs in the middle of the court, staring self-consciously at bleachers filled with their schoolmates, students who just a few weeks before wouldn't have passed up a dogfight to see one of their games.

Near the end of the rally, Ike Tallman rose to his feet and walked slowly across the polished floor to the microphone. The gym was silent. The girls had no idea what he was doing, unless he was going to steal their moment to remind everyone that the boys' tournament was just around the corner.

For a moment he said nothing. Then, looking at Lisa, he began, "Some of you have been after me to share this gym and I said no, not until you can fill it. Well, I owe you girls an apology." He paused and swept his hand in a slow arc around the room. "Because now I see you can fill this gym." Cindy Ross's voice breaks in telling that story. "After that," she says, "we got a whole lot of respect for him. It took a lot for the head coach of the Warsaw boys to say he was sorry to a team of girls."

* * *

Their first game in the state finals in Indianapolis was to be against East Chicago Washington, all of whose players except one was black. This was a totally new and forbidding prospect for small town white girls who rarely encountered African Americans in their everyday lives.

The players on the boys' team, now eager to help, reported that the typical East Chicago crowd was a crazed mob given to tipping cars over and setting them ablaze. Even more sobering were accounts from the Rochester High girls who had lost to them the week before. "Rochester told us that they would probably draw knives on us," says Cindy. "We really believed it." But there was more. The Rochester girls reported that the East Chicago players didn't just knife you right away. They cussed you out first. Every dirty word in the book.

Knives were one thing, but coach Janice Soyez was not about to let her players become unnerved by dirty words, not having gone this far. So they created an

Judi Warren drives against a defender from East Chicago Washington.
Courtesy of Indiana High School Athletic Association.

obscenity drill in practice, to simulate a game situation. Two girls, an offensive player and a defender, worked their way down and back up the court, with the defender cussing out the offensive player. "We didn't know what to say," recalls Cindy. "We were all church girls. But we figured they'd call us 'honky' all the time. So one would dribble and the other would say, 'You bunch of damned honkies.'"

"Never having been around that many blacks, we didn't know how to handle it," says Judi. "We had always looked upon blacks as pretty rough people. We walked into the game and we were thinkin', 'Oh, my God.' They were big and they were black." They were also unarmed, businesslike, and very good. One of East Chicago's forwards, freshman LaTaunya Pollard, was a skilled shooter who was later named the outstanding woman collegiate player in the United States. East Chicago jumped off to a quick eight-point lead, and Cindy committed three fouls in the first two minutes. "I was astounded," Cindy says. "I thought, 'This has got to be wrong. This isn't how it was written.' So we dug in deeper."

In the second quarter Judi ignited the team by stealing the ball again and again, threading her way through defenses and hooking passes over her head for easy baskets. Chanda was hitting every shot she tried. Warsaw turned the game around and opened up a big lead in the fourth quarter.

"They turned out to be good, aggressive players, nothing short of that," recalls Cindy. "They really didn't talk to us at all. . . . Color didn't make any difference at all." After the game, Warsaw tried to walk over to shake hands, but officials intercepted the girls from both teams and herded them downstairs and into their locker rooms.

Over 5,000 people had seen the game, nearly half of them from Warsaw. Just as important, thousands more had watched the game on TV. Probably many viewers had intended to watch for just a moment or paused to watch between other programs. Given the strong ratings that game drew, quite a few must have taken their hands off the dial and sat down to watch it. Many in the Indianapolis area decided to drive out to Hinkle Fieldhouse for the championship game.

That night, when the team burst out of the dressing room and up the stairs, down through the hall behind the bleachers at Hinkle Fieldhouse where Oscar Robertson had run before taking the floor against Gary Roosevelt, where Bobby Plump had hit his shot, the tradition of it all, the cameras, the 3,000 orange-shirted fans who had caravanned from Warsaw to see them go for it, gave them gooseflesh. It hit them all. This was it. This was for the state championship.

That night there were more than 9,000 people in the stands and a huge prime time TV audience. The game, against Bloomfield, was close until the final min-

Judi Warren splits the defense in the 1976 state finals.
Courtesy of Indiana High School Athletic Association.

ute. But once again Judi took over at the end, slashing again and again down the lane, scoring or passing to Chanda for assists, drawing fouls and shooting free throws.

Though Judi Warren was the smallest player by far, she somehow magnified herself in concert, as all great performers do. It was plain to see that here, too, was Hoosier Hysteria, packaged differently but radiant and authentic. At the end she was on the line, hitting free throws one after another, pulling her hair, jumping up and down and clapping, embracing her teammates, thrusting her fists in the air, shimmering like a hummingbird. This wasn't palm slaps and whacks on the butt, this was something new. These girls were excited, and they showed the emotion of the moment. They led their own cheers during time outs. That night Hoosierland melted.

When it was over and they had won, and Judi had won the Mental Attitude Award, and the last strands of the net had been snipped and all the cameras packed away, they slipped on their coveralls, climbed back into the Winnebago

Tigers face their jubilant fans after winning the first girls' tourney.
Courtesy of Indiana High School Athletic Association.

van and headed home for some sleep. They hoped someone would stay up to meet them and drive them home.

The van pulled into the school lot at 3:00 AM. When they drew the curtain back, they were looking at a cop. When they opened the door, he said, "Better run, I don't think we can hold them back any longer." They were slapped on the back and borne into the gym, which people had again filled for them, but this time completely, the stands, the floor, and the halls leading in. No one in Warsaw had gone to bed. When Judi and Cindy hoisted up the trophy, a mighty cheer filled the gym. "You know what I was thinking?" says Cindy. "I was thinking I wouldn't get to play ball with these guys next week."

★　★　★

On an early November afternoon in 1994, ten high school girls run through a half-court scrimmage, blue jerseys against yellows, at Carmel high school on Indianapolis' North side.

The yellow team's best shooter, Lisa Williams, sprints beneath the basket from one side to another, blond ponytail streaming straight behind her. She runs her defender into a pick, and bursts free, waiting, wide open, body squared for a shot, fingers aching for the ball. No teammate sees her. "THERE SHE IS!" screams Carmel varsity coach Judi Warren. They freeze. Coach Warren slowly drags her fingers through close-cropped, feathered brown hair and steps forward. She takes the ball so that everyone will focus on her. "It floors me, ladies," she says slowly, "how you can play this game without talking. And I know you will start talking the minute practice is over. HELP! BALL! PICK! These are the words we've got to use. You've GOT to talk to each other."

Twenty seasons after she led her team to the first girls' state championship, Judi Warren is now the coach of a major girls' program in Indiana. She is one of a growing number of Indiana women who are returning to their game. After games, opposing coaches sometimes confide that she was their girlhood heroine. She thanks them and feels old.

Some of the problems that Judi and her coach at Warsaw, Janice Soyez, grew up with are behind her. While Soyez coached for next to nothing, Judi earns about $7,000, roughly what the boys' coach makes. Carmel High provides both boys and girls practice jerseys, uniforms, warmup clothes, and shoes. Each year, Judi and the boys' coach work out a schedule to share after-school practice time on the varsity court, alternating weeknights.

At least two Carmel girls will receive full scholarships to major colleges this year. One of them is Lisa Williams, bound for the University of South Carolina after balancing forty scholarship offers. "I started thinking about playing college ball when I was a kid," she says. "Now I can move on to bigger dreams."

Lisa says that at Carmel no one calls her a "dyke" or a "jock" because she's an athlete. "I remember when I was seven or eight, my brothers and sisters said they didn't want me to play basketball because that was a 'dyke' sport. I think that's gone, now. For a while we all kept our hair long just so the comments wouldn't get made. Now it doesn't matter anymore. Some of the best looking girls at Carmel are on the ball court."

Some hurdles remain. One is game scheduling. Girls play on school nights while boys play on weekends, which allows them to sleep in the next morning. "But we've learned good time management skills," Judi says. "In the past few years, only two or three of the girls on our teams have not been honor roll students."

About three-quarters of the coaches of girls' teams in Indiana are men. Inability to find or pay for child care remains a major obstacle for women who want to coach. Judi, a single mother, gets up at dawn to eat breakfast with her fourteen-year-old son Andy, then drives off to teach physical education to as many as 550 elementary students in a week. Then it's practice, and games and supper with Andy, and then often his games. Sometimes even then the day isn't over. Her players turn to her with their problems. Often they come over to talk. "Coach Warren is important to me," says Lisa Williams. "I trust her. She cares about me as a person, not just as a ballplayer who's gonna be gone soon. She'll know what I'm doing in five to ten years. She'll be there for me if I need her."

Each year Judi is honored as a pioneer at one event or another, which means she has to endure once again the film of her 1976 championship game. She sits in the dark, sometimes covering her eyes, mortified by their matador defense and the passes she didn't see and the layups they all blew. She thinks the level of play has progressed so much in twenty years that she could no longer start on the team she coaches now. Her players, who have also seen the film, disagree. "She'd still be tough," says Lisa Williams. "Even in practice, she sees the floor well. She had the moves and she was really fast. Everyone I've talked to says she was good. Everybody knows who she was."

Lisa is asked if the members of the Carmel Greyhounds' girls' basketball team think they owe their coach anything. She pauses. They haven't even played their first game yet and it seems too early to be talking about doing anything for anyone. "Well, mainly our goals are personal," she says, pushing a blonde strand back into place. "But we've talked. There is something we'd like to do for her, and for all of us. We'd like to be the team that takes Coach Warren back to the final four."

* * *

One hundred and twenty days later, they did, and then nearly won the state championship. "Don't ask me how we did it," said Judi, still hoarse a week after the final game loss to Huntington North. "They just decided to do it and no one could stop them."

They grew into each other week by week. Around Thanksgiving E. B. Larson settled in at point guard. By Christmas they had all decided in a team meeting to attack with a controlled offense than trying to win by running. "Around the holidays we got closer as a team," Judi says. "I'd see them together more, and staying after practice to shoot with one another."

They went into the tourney unranked and having lost their last three games. But they were adaptable and determined, led by experienced players and a fine coach. Every game in the tourney had a different script. They nearly blew a

22-point lead in their sectional final but staggered to a one-point win. They used three players and nine fouls on Anderson Highland's best scorer in a regional game and shut her down. They held the ball for the final two excruciating minutes to protect a slender lead against Ben Davis in the first semi-state game. Then E. B., Lisa, and Betsy Palicek poured in free throw after free throw against Rushville in the semi-state final and Judi was back in the final four.

Judi feared they would have nothing left for the finals, which were held at Indianapolis's Market Square Arena. She was nearly right. Dead on their feet, they fell behind by 19 points and somehow found the energy to surge back and win by a point in the afternoon game against Washington. "One sportswriter told me it was the best game he had ever seen," says Judi.

Almost 15,000 attended the final game. Among them were nearly all of Judi's old Warsaw teammates. Judi asked Cindy Ross to speak to her players in the locker room before their championship bid. Cindy told them that she had been through a lot of ups and downs in the 20 years since she had played, but that she always carried in her heart the love of her teammates. Though she rarely saw them or spoke to them, it was always there. It was a bond she would never forget and that could never be broken. "It was just a wonderful speech," Judi says. They hung in well against Huntington North, but lost the championship by four points. They were exhausted, and proud. "I really liked the way they were after that game," said Judi. "They cheered while the winners got their awards. Their heads were up."

A week later Judi's phone was still ringing with calls of congratulations and interview requests. These were gratifying conversations, full of the flattering questions that all coaches hope to be asked at some time or another. Except for one. "You know what drove me crazy?" Judi asks. "Almost everyone said, 'Well, now that you've won it as a player and made the final game as a coach, are you gonna retire?' I couldn't believe it. I mean, I'm 36. I love kids and I love basketball. My mother still thinks I'm unbalanced, and maybe I am, but I've never found a better way to help young people. No, I'm not gonna retire . . . I might do this till I drop."

• •

It is not exaggerating to say that, with the exception of the pros'
Jerry West, there is no one in all of basketball who has the
quickness and accuracy at long range that Rick Mount has.

Frank DeFord, *Sports Illustrated* cover story, February 14, 1966 off was Prairie Creek; thus the name was evolved in his mind—he shouted "Lebanon!" The name was fixed. Lebanon it has henceforth been."

Lebanon is within an area of perhaps a thirty-mile radius that was Indiana's first basketball hotbed. Schools from within this area won the first eight Indiana high school basketball tournaments. In 1911, the Lebanon High School Tigers finished second to despised Crawfordsville in the first tournament but then won three of the next seven. Lebanon can stake some claim to being Indiana's first real basketball power.

Those vintage teams played their home games in the second floor of a hotel. The games took place in a small square room with a potbellied stove in the corner and a few hundred seats around the court. The instant the doors were opened, townspeople stampeded in out of the cold, stomped and brushed the snow off, and huddled together until the room became warm enough for shirt sleeves and coveralls. One house painter named Tom Dawson watched from outside the hotel, perched atop his stepladder, propped against the building. There he would remain for an hour or two, nose pressed flat against the window, wiping the panes clear of steam with a kerchief, and cheering into the winter wind.

John Mount, born in 1885, arrived in Lebanon from Kentucky around the turn of the century. He tried his hand at farming for a while, then found a better living pouring cement and smoothing out the streets and sidewalks of the growing town. Like nearly every other male in Lebanon, John lived for Friday nights. When he had sons of his own, he walked them to the gym and told them how he wished he could afford a car to follow the Lebanon Tigers on the road.

Pete Mount, born in 1926, walked to the games by himself from the first grade on. "You didn't want to sit too close to my dad in a close game," Pete later recalled. "You were liable to get a rib full of his elbow all night." Young Pete saw it all: he was there the night the Zionsville fan went at the referee with a whiskey bottle. He was there when the Frankfort Hot Dogs came to town and the fighting began in the runway to the dressing rooms and spilled outside into the parking lot. It was most exciting when big teams like Lafayette Jefferson and Muncie Central came through. He loved to sit around afterwards with his dad and hear Doc Porter and Butch Neuman and the others tell the stories of the glory days, when it was really tough. He wanted to be a Tiger.

He grew up tall for the times, 6'1", lean at 145 pounds, and a terrific shooter, the kind who could always find the basket even through a tangle of arms. Pete Mount played constantly, shooting at peanut cans and goals nailed to barns and garages and telephone poles. Looking back, he said later, there really wasn't much else to do.

When the time came, Pete started on the Lebanon High basketball varsity as a freshman, a rare privilege granted historically only to a precocious few. Given his slender build, it helped that he was older than most of his classmates, having repeated the second semester of third grade. To maintain turf, Pete found he had to "let an elbow slip every now and then."

Pete broke all the Lebanon High scoring records and nearly led the Tigers to the state championship. Once he outscored the opposing team all by himself, an event which was recorded as an "incredible feat" in a comic book with Dagwood Bumstead on the cover. In Pete's junior year, 1943, Lebanon got to the Indiana championship game for the first time since 1918 but lost by five points to Fort Wayne Central. Tiger fans, enthusiastic even in defeat, ripped apart the steps of buildings along Courthouse Square, and snake-danced through town. For his effort, the *Indianapolis Star* named Pete "Star of Stars" for the 1943 state tournament. A local paper called him, "the greatest prep athlete to dribble n' shoot in modern times."

Pete never got another chance to play. He was called for active duty on March 1, 1944, three weeks before the state finals. As it turned out, Lebanon was upset in the sectionals anyway—and off to war he went, or at least so he assumed.

There were few foxholes and shells in Pete's war stories: When he reported to Fort Harrison, he learned that his sergeant had already signed him up for a basketball tournament in Indianapolis. He played in California, then at Fort Riley, Kansas, then at Fort Sill, Oklahoma, where he once scored 43 points in a game.

They shipped Pete's unit to Germany, but the war in Europe had ended by the time he got there. They were sent home for 30 days to rest up for the final assault on Japan. While he was in Lebanon, Pete married his high school sweetheart, Katie McLain, with whom he had gone steady since he was a freshman. A few days later Pete was back with his unit, ready to leave, when they heard that something called the atomic bomb had changed their schedule again.

In April 1946 Pete was discharged. He and Katie took the Pullman together from Fort Jackson, South Carolina, to Indianapolis, with plenty to talk about. Teams of all kinds were tugging at Pete. Indiana, Purdue, and Clemson wanted him to play college basketball. The Indianapolis Indians wanted him to play minor league baseball.

Pete began the summer laying cement with his dad. Butch Neuman, his old coach, hounded Pete to stay near home and go to college at Purdue. But Katie was pregnant, and the couple needed money. One day when Butch happened to be out of town, Doxie Moore, coach of the Sheboygan Redskins of the new

There were all sorts of opportunities. One afternoon between Rick's sopho-more and junior years, Miami University's basketball coach Bruce Hale showed up in Rosey's office with a gentleman who introduced himself as Aldo Leone, the nephew of the famous Manhattan restaurateur Mama Leone. He said he knew pretty near every basketball coach and player in the New York City high school world, which he kept calling "the prep scene." One of Aldo's friends was Jack Donahue, the coach at Power Memorial High School, who had a towering young center named Lew Alcindor. Rosey and Aldo started bantering about who would win a dream game between Rick the Rocket from the Hoosier cornfields and The Next Wilt. Aldo said he could get the ball rolling, and sure enough Donahoe called a few days later.

They agreed to try it in Indianapolis, where the crowds would surely be mammoth. They almost pulled it off. Tickets were printed, Butler Fieldhouse was rented, there were oceans of ink in the papers—and then the Indiana High School Athletic Association abruptly backed out, claiming the game would have been billed as a "national championship." To this day, Rosey thinks Lebanon would have won.

★ ★ ★

Rick's world at the time was circumscribed by the boundaries of his home-town. He had rarely been outside of Indiana, and he spent almost all his time alone or with his teammates, coaches, hunting pals, and the downtown mer-chants who sought to bask in his spreading fame. He had no brothers or sisters; his best friend was his special girl since early grade school, Donna Cadger.

Pete and Katie's marriage came apart before Rick's freshman year, and Pete moved out. All the hours of games in the driveway had not made Rick and Pete close. "He never would let me come to his junior high games," recalled Pete. "I think he was afraid I'd start yelling and make a scene." "I didn't really know my dad," says Rick. "I looked at his scrapbooks, but it wasn't till I got older that people told me how good he was. I don't know why he didn't tell me. Maybe he didn't want to put any added pressure on me."

Rick seemed shy, withdrawn, and often aloof to those outside his circle. He felt everyone's eyes upon him. "It's like you're in a little glass and everyone's peeking in at you," Rick recalls. "Anything I would do, people would say, 'Oh, that's terrible,' or 'That's okay.' It makes you kind of a loner."

Rick's summer habitat was an outdoor court in Lebanon Park, a couple of hundred yards from a pool where he worked as a lifeguard. Every few hours he'd whistle everyone out of the pool, drop down from the tower, pull on his sneakers, and head for the court. "Hey, kid," he'd say to one of the boys who hung around him, "want an ice cream cone? Rebound a hundred shots and I'll buy you one."

Nights and weekends were for games. As his reputation grew, more and more players, especially black kids from Indianapolis, drove out to try their luck. Though they invited him to the city, Rosey kept Rick on his own court, where the rules were shooter's rules. At Lebanon Park the offensive player called the fouls.

Saturday night was date night. But if Rick had a date, he'd always drive past the court. "I remember once a date and I drove by the court on the way to the drive in and I saw five or six black players out there. I didn't know them. I looked out there and thought, hey, those guys are pretty good. So I told the girl, 'I got to take you home.' I took her home and she got out of the car and slammed the door. I got home real quick and got my shoes and went back. I never had another date with her but I got in some good games. How many guys would do that?"

★ ★ ★

Few Hoosiers who have become famous have made their mark in Indiana. Abraham Lincoln, who spent his youth in southern Indiana, made it big in Illinois and Washington, like Dan Quayle. The Jacksons left Gary to make it in Detroit and California. James Dean, Halston, David Letterman, Cole Porter, and Hoagy Carmichael became famous in New York. Among resident native Hoosiers, maybe only Wendell Wilkie's presidential candidacy, John Dillinger's jailbreak at Crown Point, Larry Bird's senior year in Terre Haute, and Eugene Debs at the peak of his fame received the national attention Rick Mount attracted as a senior at Lebanon high school and a collegian at Purdue.

One event in particular changed Rick's life and briefly thrust Lebanon into the national spotlight. Midway through Rick's senior year, Rosey got a call from Frank DeFord, a writer for *Sports Illustrated*, inquiring about a story on Rick. Rosey cleared his calendar and soon, to hear Rosey and Rick tell it, Lebanon was like a movie set. For two weeks DeFord and photographer Rich Clarkson followed Rick everywhere. Clarkson snapped hundreds of pictures in the classroom, in the gym, in the town square. Rick says that once he saw Clarkson behind him as he entered the restroom at school. He turned around. "Anywhere but in here," he said.

"One of the shots they wanted to take, I don't know why, was with Rick downtown and by the poolroom," says Rosey. "He was standin' right out in the middle of the street with cars comin' by. I was standin' down on one end of the street makin' sure no one ran over him and DeFord was on the other end. Suddenly Pistol Sheets, the guy who owns the poolroom, came runnin' outside, wavin' a gun around, yellin', 'I'll shoot the first guy that hits him!'"

On February 14, 1966, Lebanon merchants gathered around the delivery truck that pulled up in front of a drugstore and tore at the string that bound the magazines. There was Rick on the cover, profiled from the waist up against a farmhouse, wearing his Lebanon High warm-up jacket, his lips parted in what appeared to be a bashful smile, the Cobra perfectly in place. It was the first time a high school basketball player had ever appeared on the cover of *Sports Illustrated*. Lebanon was on the map.

They devoured the article. Deford proclaimed Rick to be perhaps the best high school player of all time, as good as Oscar Robertson had been. He was said to possess the moves of a cat, the eyes of a hawk, and the presence of a king. That sounded about right. On the other hand, he sent them up as hicks, which still leaves a bad taste in Lebanon whenever the subject of the article comes up. For his part, Rick, while suitably honored, wished maybe they could have left Oscar, his ultimate hero, out of it.

The state tournament started the following weekend. As usual, Lebanon easily won the sectional and regional tourneys, but they began the afternoon game of the semistate heavy underdogs, billed as a one man team against a tough Logansport squad.

No one who saw it will ever forget the Logansport game. Down 51–39 with eight minutes left, Rick decided he was at least going to go down shooting. He scored twenty points in those minutes, hitting seven bombs in a row in one immortal stretch. When the smoke cleared, Lebanon had won by a point, and Rick had scored forty-seven of his team's sixty-five points. Leg cramps destroyed Rick in the night game just as cramps had sidelined his father in the tourney—and Lebanon lost by a single point.

The following morning, sports editor John Whittaker wrote in the *Hammond Times*: "I've seen a few great things in my time. I was there when Red Grange went wild against Michigan. I saw the famous Dempsey-Tunney title fight. I watched the Babe call his home run shot . . . and now this performance by Mount."

★ ★ ★

When the headlines appeared announcing that Rick Mount had signed a letter of intent to attend the University of Miami, the people of Lebanon, and Indiana, were stunned. "People on the street wouldn't even speak to me," says Rick.

Given the reaction, Rosey advised Rick that, just to be safe, maybe he'd better also sign a letter of intent with a Big Ten school. Before long, Rick told Bruce Hale he had changed his mind and signed with Purdue. Lebanon was jubilant. One of every nine residents—including infants and the elderly—bought season tickets to Purdue's schedule in Rick's first year.

West Lafayette, Indiana, home of Purdue University, is just thirty miles from Lebanon. Rick never really took to college life. His girlfriend, Donna, was enrolled, too, and soon they were married and living in student housing, driving back to Lebanon on non-game weekends.

Lebanon never seemed to change. The downtowners were always coming up with some crazy scheme. There was still the sign with Rick's name on it at the town line, and now there was a life size cardboard cutout of himself in uniform at the bank. The court at Lebanon Park had been dedicated to Rick, with a sign of course, and Rosey now had a booklet out about jump shooting which featured the shooting statistics of every game Rick had played in.

Purdue coach George King built an offense around Rick, with his big men leaping out like muggers to set picks. That was fine with Rick, just like Lebanon. And Purdue had real talent. Bill Keller and Herman Gilliam, both of whom later had fine professional careers, kept the defenses honest and set up the plays.

Rick was an even better collegian than a high school player. Three times he was an All American, and, as a senior, he averaged about forty points per game in the Big Ten Conference. Such scoring was unheard of. It was then that Al McGuire, John Havlicek and others started calling Rick the best "pure shooter" they had ever seen. For some reason, when you saw Rick Mount shoot, there was no need to explain what an impure shooter was.

The best night of his college career came as a junior in the NCAA Mideast Regionals against Marquette. Purdue, an underdog, found itself a point down and with the ball in the closing seconds. George King set up the obvious play, and it couldn't have worked better. Rick got the ball, drove his man through one deadening pick and into another, and found himself sky-blue free in the corner with four seconds left. He swished his jumper, and Purdue was off to the finals.

It was after that intoxicating game that Purdue fans carried his highway sign from Lebanon up to West Lafayette and transplanted it near a fountain on a campus hill. Maybe on that night, too, Rick Mount, like his billboard, was liberated from Lebanon.

Early in March of 1971, after UCLA had throttled Purdue in the NCAA finals, professional basketball teams came panting after Rick Mount, just as they had come for his dad. This time the money was better, mainly due to a bidding war between the NBA and the newly formed American Basketball Association. Two days after his final college game, Rick signed with the ABA's Indiana Pacers for what was reported as a million dollars, chopped up into various investment schemes and deferred payments. The signing was televised live at six o'clock throughout Indiana.

At the time it was one of the biggest contracts ever. A physical education major, twenty-six credits shy of graduating, Rick quit school. He explained matter-of-factly to the press that he had gone to college not to learn to be a tennis coach but to play pro basketball.

Rick's pro career turned out to be every bit the disappointment Pete's had been, in part because the expectations had been so high. It took five years for the end to come. The Indiana Pacers were a championship team whose offense was concentrated in the front court. Tough, veteran players like Roger Brown and Mel Daniels resented Rick's fame and did not feel that they required a savior. For the first time in his life, Rick was not the center of the offense. Very few plays were set up for him. Often he wasn't a starter.

His confidence faded. He became convinced that his coach, Bobby Leonard, was out to ruin him. He badgered Leonard to trade him, and finally Mike Storen, the man who had signed him from Purdue, got him traded to Dallas and then on to Kentucky. There was one more trade, to the Utah Stars. When the Utah franchise's bankruptcy was announced, Rick was offered $16,000 for his fabled investment plan, into which few contributions had been made.

The end had come too soon. He was 28 years old, a man who had devoted his life to a single, highly valued pursuit—jumpshooting—and who could do it as well as anyone else ever had. It was hard to understand or accept. Like his dad, he went back to Lebanon. He too had a son.

★ ★ ★

"There was a big void in my life after I got out of basketball," says Rick. "You think to yourself, 'No more organized competition.' Boy, it's an empty feeling for a long time."

Rick and Donna Mount have remained in Lebanon ever since Rick left the ABA. There has been no reason to leave: both extended families are there, and they prefer a small town atmosphere.

Rick invested some of his Utah settlement in a sporting goods shop that went under in a few years. Since then, Rick has sold various athletic products

Richie Mount, Pete Mount, and Jim Rosenstihl, mid-1970s,
after a Lebanon Tigers game. *Courtesy of Pete Mount.*

and taught jump shooting at camps and clinics, while Donna has held a job as
a pharmacy technician at Lebanon Hospital.

Rick was once offered a head coaching job at a Lafayette high school, but
his decision to leave college early came back to haunt him when the Indiana
High School Athletic Association (IHSAA) disqualified his contract. He talked
to Purdue officials about making up the credits but came home discouraged.

Rick loves to work with young players. He can teach almost anyone to shoot,
adjusting an elbow here, shortening the stroke there, making sure the guide
hand falls away so the shooter doesn't end up "thumbing" the ball. "I'm 47
years old and these kids still know Rick Mount because their dad told them,"
he says. "It really gives me a thrill if I can help kids shoot the basketball and get
confidence in themselves."

Along with all the regular students, there was one special apprentice. Rick started his son, Richie, born in 1970, with the traditional family peanut can. As Richie grew, Rick schooled Richie in the guide hand and the planted foot, the subtleties of backspin and arch.

Rick had more free time to work with Richie than Pete had for Rick, and there was far more technical structure to this apprenticeship. But its essence was the same: intense competition between father and son. They played thousands of one-on-one games, as Pete and Rick had, in driveways and in Memorial Park. As Richie grew, and the day of his first victory approached, their expressions and voices hardened, and the action became rougher. A grimness set into the competition.

In the summer of 1984 the Mounts decided that Richie should repeat his eighth-grade year. "There are four reasons," Rick said at the time. "It gives him an extra year of maturity. It helps his schoolwork. It helps him mentally, 'cause he's my kid and he's probably feeling a lot of pressure. I had more publicity than my dad did, and now there's more emphasis on athletics. And it'll help him get a college education, an athletic scholarship." The Mounts reasoned that the extra year had helped Richie's dad and granddad, so why deprive Richie of the same chance? But Rick and Pete had repeated a year in early grade school, and both had been at best average students. It had just worked out that way. This was different: Richie was a good student, and this was a calculated family decision.

Richie started his second year of eighth grade in Connecticut and returned home about two months later. Rick took Richie into the principal's office and tried to enroll Richie as an eighth grader. The principal refused. The Mounts hired a lawyer and took their case to the school board. They argued that "red-shirting," as the practice is known, is an Indiana tradition. Rosey was able cite seven kids who'd stayed an extra year at Lebanon High during his coaching career, and everyone knew of kids who had repeated grades for basketball in other Indiana towns.

By a 3–2 vote, in a packed and emotional hearing, the board granted the Mounts' request, citing the absence of a statute or policy forbidding such a move. The state educational bureaucracy asked the Lebanon board to reconsider, but the board held firm. Several months later, the IHSAA ordered schools to draw up rules and penalties against red-shirting in high school.

Rick Mount was news again. The school board's decision was featured on the front page of the *Indianapolis Star*. Television cameras rolled in for Richie's eighth-grade games. The Lebanon Reporter, the local newspaper, backed the Mounts editorially, again citing the absence of policy, and published about a week's worth of letters—mostly unsigned—before announcing a moratorium on Richie Mount mail. Excerpts from some of them show the depth of feeling in Lebanon:

> It absolutely amazes me that in our society it has become acceptable for parents to consider the primary function of going to school to be the enhancement of their child's athletic abilities. . . . As a graduate of Lebanon High School, I am utterly embarrassed.

> I wonder why the practice is so wrong all of a sudden. Is it red-shirting that is wrong suddenly or is it wrong now because it involves a youngster named Mount?

> I have known Rick, Donna and Richie Mount for many years. They are basically good people, very interested in their son's well being.

> Is it fair that Richie gets this whole year to mature when almost every other basketball player does not? And if it is fair, who makes the decisions on which player can repeat eighth grade and which cannot? What if every eighth grader did this . . . would anybody ever graduate from Lebanon?

While the attention did not seem to bother Richie, the experience heightened Rick's sense of estrangement from his neighbors. He believes, and probably with good reason, that had Richie been anyone else's son, or had Richie had belonged to an earlier generation, the people of Lebanon would barely have noticed. Richie Mount made the Lebanon varsity team as a freshman, with Rosey as his coach, and averaged more than seventeen points per game. In one early game against the Frankfort Hot Dogs, rival fans wore red shirts and waved red towels whenever Richie got the ball. Richie hit thirteen of fifteen shots from the field, scoring 34 points. He thrust his fist in the air after every basket and Lebanon won by three. "That crowd really pumped me up," he recalls.

Resentments born in the mid-sixties flared up again in the Lebanon bleachers whenever Rick attended Richie's home games. Several of Rick's classmates had sons on the team, and the parents sniped at each other constantly. "I could hear them," says Richie. "I'd have the ball and someone would stand up and yell 'Pass it, Mount!' and I would stick one from the corner and my dad would get up and yell 'There's your pass!' He'd get so into the games that he'd have

Richie Mount puts a move on his dad, 1985, in one of countless, sometimes rough one-on-one games. *Courtesy of Shoshana Hoose.*

the brightest the sky ever got around Lebanon. They often talked about when the carnival would come to the County each Fourth of July, and how Rick would wipe out the basketball shooting event every year, arching shot after shot through the small hoop until the carney ran out of teddy bears.

In the mid-eighties Rosey put together the "Boone County All Stars"—seniors from county high schools—and took them to Clinton County to play against their best. With fifteen seconds left to play, Rosey stopped the game and sent Pete, Rick, and Richie out together on the floor, along with Brian Walker and his dad. "I'll let you play," he whispered to Pete, "but I don't want to see you runnin' up and down that floor." Pete nodded solemnly, then trotted out and called for the ball. He let fly a long one-hander as the buzzer sounded. No one on earth, Rosey thought, had ever been able to stop Pete Mount from getting in a shot.

Richie Mount is now an officer on the Lebanon Police Force. He rarely plays basketball, preferring instead to patrol the streams of Boone and Montgomery Counties for smallmouth bass. Weightlifting is a special passion. Richie can bench press nearly 350 pounds, and Rick takes pride in showing visitors snapshots that feature Richie's powerful upper body.

In 1994, Richie almost married a woman he met in Lebanon after a workout and dated for most of a year. The relationship dissolved, but it gave him a chance to consider the prospects of a fourth-generation Mount someday pouring jumpers through the hoops for the Lebanon Tigers. "Well," he mused, "just about anything could happen. I wouldn't pressure a son to play basketball. He could turn out to be a football player and that would be fine. So the line could end with me. But if I ever have a son, whatever he wants, I'll help him. And my dad'll be around too."

That much seems assured, at least as long as deer and pheasant can still be found in Boone County and turkey still scratch through the stubbled fields. Rick Mount, still trim at 47, with not quite enough blonde hair remaining to fashion a Cobra, bursts out laughing when he considers the next generation. "Another Mount?" he repeats. "Well, I'd like to see a grandson play, but I don't know if Lebanon fans would. I don't think Lebanon is ready for another Mount." He leans back in a lounge chair in the living room of his modest yellow house, less than a mile from where he and Donna both grew up, savoring the idea. "Another Mount . . . another Mount might just short this town out."

· ·

Located in a white suburban neighborhood, but blacks come anyway.
As a result, there's some latent racial tension, but nothing serious.
Watch the overhanging tree branches on your J from the corner.

From *The In-Your-Face Basketball Book: A U.S. Atlas
of the World of Pick-Up Basketball*, 1974

8

MEADOWOOD PARK

Speedway, Indiana

· ·

STEVE WOOLSEY REMEMBERS THE BEGINNING LIKE THIS: "WE WERE sitting on basketballs, me and Mike Alma, resting between games, when a car pulled up way on the other side of the baseball diamond. These two guys got out and came walkin' through the woods like they were lost. It was the Van Arsdales. They looked so much alike it hurt your eyes. I literally thought I had been injured. A *Van* walks up to me and says, 'Is this Meadowood?'"

It was the summer of 1961. The Van Arsdale twins had just graduated from Indianapolis Manual High School, way on the other side of Indianapolis from Speedway. As famous in Indiana as film stars, they were relentlessly identical, redheaded, freckled, built like fortresses. Their names were Tom and Dick. Their father's name was Harry. After four years of high school, Dick had scored only a few more points than Tom. Dick was the valedictorian, Tom ranked third in the class. Their cheerleader girlfriends ranked second and sixth.

When it came time for the *Indianapolis Star* to name Indiana's "Mr. Basketball" of 1961 there was no choice but to crown them both. Likewise, judges issued two Arthur Trester Mental Attitude Awards. So what if it had never happened before? What Solomonic fool would stand up and say Tom had a better mental attitude than Dick?

After a while, people quit trying to tell them apart and treated them instead as proper nouns, as Vans, for example, "A Van was over at the Big Boy—I forget which one it was" or "Lebanon Hardware's team had Carl Short, John McGlocklin and a Van—I forget which one it was." They were perfect gentlemen off the court and pure mayhem on it. A Van didn't just pluck down a rebound, he tore it from the air, seizing it with both hands, elbows splayed.

They were the boys of that Hoosier summer, having just lost the state tournament to Kokomo in a heartbreaking overtime. Both played valiantly. "There's what you could be if you studied and turned that darned record player off," said everyone's parents. It got old. They were both 6'5" and there were two of them.

What Steve Woolsey saw next was truly revolutionary. More cars skidded into the lot behind the Vans, and out spilled a dozen of the best black ball players in Indianapolis, the cream of Attucks and Tech and Shortridge.

Until that very moment in 1961, Speedway, Indiana, had been all but innocent of experience with nonwhites. Not a single African American lived among Speedway's 11,000 residents that summer. Race relations in Speedway had mainly had to do with fast cars. Speedway, as its residents are hair-trigger quick to point out, is the true home of the Indianapolis 500 race track—not Indianapolis, which lies east of the 16th Street bridge and therefore quite outside the town's limits. The Speedway High School athletic teams were naturally called the "Sparkplugs." Truancy increased in May as the drone of engines at the track, a mile away, beckoned to the boys through the school's open windows. Speedway's four grade schools were named after the engineers who founded the track and her streets were named after the cars, first touring autos of the day and then post-World War II "drives" named Buick, Crosley, DeSoto, Nash, and Lincoln.

Speedway grew rapidly. In the late 1950s ground was broken on a housing development called "Meadowood" on Speedway's west side. An oak forest was cleared, with a few acres left uncut for a neighborhood park. Developers poured a basketball court in the middle of the forest and planted four standards with backboards and rims.

Playground basketball in the Indianapolis area was a movable feast in 1961. There was no single outdoor court that attracted the best competition. Players were like surfers who followed the best waves from beach to beach. They telephoned each other early in the day and agreed on a court for the evening, driving in caravans on summer evenings to Ben Davis or Warren Central. There was a glut of talent that year, as four of the top ten teams in 1961 season-long polls were from Indianapolis—Arsenal Technical High, Manual High, Crispus Attucks High, and Indianapolis Cathedral High. The players from these four teams had battled each other all winter long and knew each other well. The only real surprise was that somehow, when the weather warmed, the summer's hottest court was out in Speedway.

As words got around that there were great players at Meadowood Park, crowds grew larger night by night. Soon Speedway residents encircled the court, two deep in places, cheering. The battles were furious, often pitting Van against Van. And then one night the Van Arsdales failed to show and they were gone the next night too. They never came back. Crowds of spectators dwindled, then disappeared. But black players, properly introduced, remained and the court developed a reputation as a place where blacks and whites could play together. Over the years dozens of ABA and NBA players made their bones at the forested court called Meadowood. There the competition—though ever after Vanless—remained elite.

★ ★ ★

Meadowood Park was a special delight to those who grew up on parched, hardscrabble courts. "It was surrounded by trees, and, you know, Indiana gets so humid in the summer," remembers George McGinnis, an NBA all-star forward who spent his adolescent summers there. "I had been used to playing in areas where, Jesus, if it got hot, that was it. Meadowood had that nice drinking fountain. The cement was nice and smooth, there were no cracks. The buckets were true, just the right height. But what I remember most is the competition. We had some hellacious games out there."

There were two adjacent full courts, but they were only about two-thirds as long as a regulation court, too short for cherry picking, as the habit of hanging around your own basket and not playing defense was called. The court was unlit, but in midsummer you could shoot by firefly until 9:30 or so. Importantly, there were johns. In short, it was heaven. In the summers, players would start to show up about 6:00. The worse you were, the earlier you'd show, because the good players would come later, get picked, and hold the court. Speedway High School players always tried to keep playing until Morris Pollard, the Sparkplugs' coach, arrived. At the time, high school coaches in Indiana were not allowed to coach students in the summer but could stand around the playground margins and watch, the way ejected baseball managers linger in clubhouse tunnels. On the last day of the season, Pollard would advise each of his returning players to "give me a good summer at Meadowood."

Two full-court games were played simultaneously. The north court was the showcase court. If you lost that game and you were halfway decent, you might get picked by someone forming a south court team. This was an invitation to consider carefully. If a player with a big name played on the south court he'd get dissed all the way home, but playing beat watching. And to ditch one's team-mates in the middle of a south court game for a call to play on the north court was a serious breach of etiquette.

Sunday was prime time day. Jim Price, who spent most of the '70s in NBA back courts, usually showed up with his brothers Mike—who played awhile with the Knicks—Jesse, and Henry. The Price family could hold a court for a long time. "On a Sunday," says Jim Price, "my brothers and I wanted to play the whole day and never get beat. Only a couple of times did anyone stay in all day. I always liked to guard the person who had the name. It got my adrenaline howlin'. I hated for someone to score on me. It was pretty brutal out there. You could knock heads all day with someone and then leave the court together and go have a Dairy Queen."

Steve Woolsey—white, wide-hipped, slow afoot, and a profoundly indifferent defensive player—has probably scored more points at Meadowood than anyone else. There, he is best known as a banker. "Meadowood was Woolsey's home court," recalls George McGinnis. "No matter who came in there, Woolsey was gonna get his points, and he could hit them from thirty feet off that backboard. The backboards were perforated, full of little holes. You got the feeling that if he shot it too hard the ball would just stick there."

Woolsey was a successful local high school player and had a taste of the col-lege game, but Meadowood Park became his domain. Besides being the master of Meadowood's backboards, he is the court's historian and a keen observer of its dress code. "Shoes for whites? When I was young and we first went there—this was before the era of tube socks and leather shoes—we wore high-cut Chuck Taylor cons. We're talking about the early '60s.

"First leather shoes we ever saw, Rick Mount had 'em on. They were Adidas Super Stars. Some salesmen gave them to him to try them out. They looked like wrestling shoes. Rick said they were made out of kangaroo skin and came from New Zealand." [Mount, remembering the incident, says they felt like bowling shoes. "I tried 'em one game, only got twenty-six points and never put 'em on again," he recalls.]

Woolsey continues up the anatomy: "We whites wore Wigwam socks, a wool sock that stayed up the best of any sock you could buy at the time. The tee shirt was the plain gray 'Russell Southern,' it's the one like coaches wear. No names. The trunks? West Point Pepperell."

Blacks could get away with anything. They'd show up with eyes hidden behind shades and under wide brims, wearing bright-colored floppy shirts, or clingy tank tops. Often they wore several layers of sweat clothes, which they peeled off very slowly, layer by layer, as if they expected to hold the north court for a week or so and didn't want to peak early.

Some players just wore street clothes. "The greatest humiliation at Meadowood was getting beat by people wearing street shoes," says Woolsey. "I remember one time we were playing over there and these four guys came over wearing trench coats. They had been to a picnic in the park and one of them was wearing wing tips, one guy had Hush Puppies and another had on penny loafers. We were playing four-on-four, me and Keller and Alma and someone, and they beat us. I said, 'We'll take you again,' and they beat us again."

Unlike the playground rules elsewhere, which adapt freely to local circumstances, Indiana playground rules seek always to imitate real game conditions. Indiana is, for example, a last bastion of "loser's outs." This means that in Hoosierland, when your team scores a basket, the other team gets the ball, just as in a real game. Most other places it's "make it/take it," meaning if you score, you keep the ball.

Indiana playground rules encourage outside shooting, even in the hearts of the state's biggest cities. In Indiana the ball is always taken back behind the free-throw line to start a new play. In some other places, like New York, kids play "straight up," meaning a missed shot can be tapped back in by either team. This has the effect of compressing the area of play, breeding great rebounders but poor shooters.

In Indiana, you choose up sides and settle disputes by "shooting for it" (it is said, "the ball never lies"), and you keep score by twos, just as in a real game. A Hoosier and a Brooklynite may play a game to eleven baskets, but if they play in Indiana, the winner will have twenty-two points and, in Brooklyn, eleven.

The differences are jarring when Hoosiers first play outside of Indiana. "When I played in the service," says Woolsey, "it was like learning a foreign language. We played by ones and my mind was still converting to twos. It's like kilometers to miles. I'd get in the middle of a game and I couldn't think of where I was at."

* * *

Before black basketball players appeared at Meadowood Park, race relations in Speedway, Indiana, had meant keeping cars off your lawn during Memorial Day weekend. *Courtesy of the author.*

When dusk would gather over the Meadowood court, black players would motorcade out of Speedway, driving eastward back to the city, leaving the court to the white kids who lived nearby. They shot in the dark, navigating by the sound of the ball against the rim and the net, talking mainly about girls or the best games of the night.

Sometimes the conversation would drift into the differences between blacks and whites. There was constant speculation about why blacks did so well at basketball. The prevailing view was that they enjoyed some physiological advantage. There was no denying that almost any black could out-jump almost any white at Meadowood.

The notion that black kids cared more and played more because basketball was the road out of the ghetto was widely debunked. How could anyone care more or play more than they did? You couldn't play more than every day. On the other hand, it was true that almost all the Speedway kids, at least, were bound for some college. That was taken as a birthright. Maybe that made basketball mean a little less.

Black players learned as much about whites at Meadowood as whites about blacks. George McGinnis grew up in a depressed area on Indianapolis' west side. As an adult, George played for Indiana, Denver and Philadelphia as a 6'8", 235-pound forward. Even as an adolescent, he'd been big and heavily muscled.

McGinnis remembers his first trip to the park very well. "I first came out to Meadowood in my eighth-grade year. I can't remember who drove me out. I drove past Speedway High School with its swimming pool and that big parking lot and past the nice houses and well-kept lawns. I was nervous. I thought, "What am I doing here?"

But McGinnis, who has an open and adventuresome personality, quickly found friends in Speedway. Sometimes when he got really thirsty, he walked across the street to Parks Commissioner Fuzzy Jordan's house and asked if he could drink out of the spigot. Often as not, Fuzzy's wife, Marge, would bring out a pitcher of ice water.

"I remember a really nice kid, Tom Gilbert," recalls McGinnis. "He played for Speedway High and his family lived by the Meadowood court. I'd play so hard and get real hungry and I'd go home with Tom and say, 'Mrs. Gilbert, can I have a baloney sandwich or something?' and his mother would fix me one. "That family was so nice to me. They had a little place on a lake, and the Gilberts would take me down there and let me stay the weekend. They got me into water skiing. My dad worked two jobs and really didn't have time to teach me to drive. Mr. Gilbert taught me how to drive down at the lake in his three-speed jeep."

Blacks and whites alike seem proud of the court's tradition of racial harmony. Most fights of all kinds are broken up quickly. But the games are rough, and the suburban setting produces a background tension that has from time to time erupted into violence. Steve Woolsey's skull was fractured once in an interracial brawl that escalated from a casual remark. That evening, Woolsey regained consciousness in a hospital bed, looking up at the minister of his church. "I thought I was ready to bite the dust," he recalls, "but it turned out my minister was there visiting an old lady upstairs when he happened to run into my dad and then came down to see me. The other thing I couldn't figure out was why I was dying with my jock on."

★　★　★

If Meadowood had a king, it was a short, stocky white player named Bill Keller. He started showing up at the park as a chubby seventh-grader, always

Three ex-Speedway High Sparkplugs, left to right, Jeff Niemann,
Tim Hoose, and Craig Hoge, on a Sunday afternoon at Meadowood.

in the company of five or six older boys. His escorts—they seemed more like
chaperones—got a kick out of watching young Billy dismantle those who underestimated him, which, until his reputation grew, was everybody.

Keller had started playing basketball as a young child, tagging along behind
his brother Bernie, seven years his senior. He couldn't see why they didn't want
him. "Bernie's friends used to call me 'tubby' and 'meatballs,'" he says, still
miffed. "He'd take me over to School 67 to play and ride my bike home and
make me run behind him. They would usually let me in their games when they
were tired and it was dark and you could barely see the rim. I was always too
young or too short . . . you develop a real sense of pride when people won't let
you do something."

As Keller outgrew his baby fat, he began to develop a big reputation, both at
Washington High School and at Meadowood Park. He was quick, strong, intuitive and a great shooter. He had a death-before-dishonor approach to losing.

Los Angeles Laker star Jim Price has a clear memory of guarding Bill Keller at Meadowood: "I think I was a freshman when he was a junior, but he already had a big name. It was like playin' against a rock. He never backed down. He outhustled you. When the smoke cleared, he was ahead."

The Kellers lived one block away from the Speedway town limits, maybe a hundred feet east of the 16th Street bridge. The town would gladly have paid to move their house that one block, especially in Bill's senior year, when he led Washington High to the Indiana state championship and was named "Mr. Basketball," the State's outstanding player.

Most of America's major colleges thought Keller, who stopped growing at 5'10", was too little to help them. The Citadel, a military school in Virginia, was one of the few colleges that went after him earnestly. They flew him down for a visit, and the guys at Meadowood waited breathlessly for a trip report, hoping he had been offered a car or some money. Instead, he came back with several packages of Fruit of the Loom underwear, courtesy of a Citadel alum associated with the firm.

Bill Keller accepted a scholarship to Purdue, where he starred for an NCAA tournament runner-up team. In his senior year he was named America's best player under six feet tall. In the summers, he brought his Purdue teammates to Meadowood for, he promised, some real competition. One summer evening, Portland Trailblazer guard Herman Gilliam, one of Keller's Purdue teammates went along. They happened to arrive at the court during a between-games dunking contest.

The typical Meadowood contestant, rather than trying to decide between a helicopter jam or a windmill was standing in line, licking his fingers and trying to get the ball to stick in his palm, wishing he had bigger hands, and thinking about getting his steps right. The most common results were either that the ball would slip out of the leaper's hand on the way up or slam into the back of the rim and out into the woods.

Gilliam, a slim 6'2½", took his place at the end of the line, unrecognized in shades and a wide-brimmed straw hat. When his turn came, he picked up a second ball, took three outlandish strides, soared into the air, and slammed both balls, wham bam, through the hoop and onto the cement. Steve Woolsey rates it as the most exciting moment in Meadowood's history. "The brothers went crazy. A guy named Al Fox ran through the park, just yelling, "Two at a time, two at a time!""

* * *

Meadowood's soft perforated backboards spawned
bank shot artists. *Courtesy of the author.*

Bill Keller pushes away a bowl of chips. "You know what I really miss?" he
says. "The money has been pretty good, the opportunities were good, but I miss
the conditioning. I watch the pros on TV, and I think, 'I used to be in that good
of shape.' It would take a lot of work to get back."

Keller is mulling this over in the sunken living room of a lovely split-level
home "right next to Bob Macintyre of Bob Macintyre Chevy" in a community
north of Indianapolis. He is the only male in a cheerful, sports-oriented family
of four.

Keller's wife, Joyce, is opening mail orders for "Billy Keller's All-Star Summer
Basketball Camp." When things get too quiet, Jeannie, his elder stepdaughter,
slips down to the trophy room and cranks up "The Ballad of Billy Keller," a song
that sold quite well in Indiana several years ago, on the stereo console Keller
won as the Most Popular Indiana Pacer. He won the award so many times the

club discontinued it for a while. Hearing the song, Joyce shrieks in what is probably mock agony.

After a nine-year career as a high-scoring guard with the Pacers, a knee injury cut short Keller's career one year before the ABA merged with the NBA. All those years he'd continued his struggle to prove he was big enough to play basketball.

Ironically, he was adored throughout Hoosierland in large part because he was short. Watching Billy Keller zip through the giraffes and greyhounds, firing up three-pointers on the dead run, and scooping the ball over their giant limbs and into the net, it was easy for the thousands of ex-high school players to believe that if they had just stayed in shape and wanted it a little more, they could have been out there. Had he been 6'7" and 220 pounds, Bill Keller might have been all-world. At 5'10" and 185, he was a friend.

George McGinnis, who last played in the NBA in 1982, now lives with his wife, Linda, and son, Tony, in a very large mock-Tudor home in Denver. Cedars flank the front steps and fan out to a privacy fence not quite tall enough to conceal a basketball goal. "How many rooms do we have here?" he repeats. "Oh, God, I don't know. I never counted." He says he has invested his basketball earnings well, and that for a kid from Haughville, as his neighborhood was called, he's done all right.

"You know, when I first started playing my dad was totally against it," George says, "because he thought I should be working. He used to scream at my mother for buying me tennis shoes. But then I got better and better and we won the state championship and in my senior year he was all gung-ho."

The last game McGinnis' father saw him play, just before he died in a construction accident, was a high school all-star game between Indiana and Kentucky in which McGinnis scored fifty-three points and took down thirty rebounds. It was the greatest performance in the history of the half-century-old interstate series, on which much Hoosier ego rests.

"Maybe God just had it that way," says McGinnis, "because it was probably the best game of my life. He was hugging me on the way back in the car and I can still remember him saying, 'You're going to be a pro, and do you know what I want when you get that first big piece of money? I don't want a car, no way, what I want is a helicopter.'"

After briefly dominating the Big Ten at Indiana University McGinnis became an all-star as a professional player. Then, after three fine seasons with the Philadelphia '76ers, he was traded to Denver. A proud and sensitive man, he was

George McGinnis, ABA and NBA star, spent many weekend
afternoons in fierce combat against Indianapolis's best players
at Meadowood. *Courtesy of Indiana Basketball Hall of Fame.*

bitterly hurt, and the experience sent him into a tailspin. "It was the first time
I was ever rejected," he says. "I started questioning, questioning, questioning,"
he says, eyes closed. "I never really was the same."

"In pro sports, "he says, "I never really felt the glue I felt at IU or in high
school. About the minute you got to know a guy, within a week he was gone
and they bring in another guy the next day like nothing ever happened. It was
hard for me to accept that."

His mood lightening, McGinnis takes a basketball down from the mantel-
piece and begins to bounce it. "When I was in eighth grade, Billy Keller showed
me this drill at Meadowood, and to this day I show it to kids and they can't do
it. See, you take the ball right here between your legs, you drop it, catch it with
the left hand, go around this leg, drop it and catch it with your right hand." The
ball is a blur between McGinnis' legs. The percussion echoes in the marble of
his living room. Beads of sweat appear on his brow.

"You know," he says, "coming from where I did, I thought all the people in Speedway were millionaires, and I thought most people were unapproachable because of that. They were just basically hard-working middle class, but I don't think we were able to understand that. To us, middle class was like rich. I thought wealth separated people, and I've learned a lot differently since then. People at Meadowood were nice and receptive to me, and I've never forgotten that."

Steve Woolsey now lives in a three-bedroom ranch house in a small town north of Indianapolis with his wife, Jeannie, their 17-year-old daughter, Lori, and their 5-year-old son, Scott. He drives a feeder truck for United Parcel, the job he has held ever since he came home from a brief stint at a junior college in Wyoming. "I could have done just about anything I wanted to," Woolsey says, "but here I am out driving a truck. I make more money than any high school coach in Indiana, but money doesn't necessarily mean success."

He has come to regard his boyhood obsession with basketball as a poor investment. "I played five, six, seven hours a day, knew every statistic, read every book, knew every ball player that ever played. I dreamed about basketball at night. It never occurred to me that I would have to work for a living."

Still, old habits are hard to break. On summer Sunday afternoons, Steve drives Jeannie into Speedway, drops her off at the Speedway Shopping Center, and heads for the park. Now 39, balding and slower than ever, he still knows the perforated backboards as no one else ever has. "There is just something about that design, the aluminum-and-steel backboards. They just . . . boom . . . you can just hear it."

Steve is recounting the experience of watching Scotty enter the world. "Yeah, the miracle of life," says Steve, "you can't put the feeling of seeing your child born into words." Up to now, Jeannie has been listening quietly. "Do you know what I said to Steve when he saw Scotty on the delivery table?" she asks. "I said, 'Now you have someone to take to Meadowood.'"

★ ★ ★

It's late, and Bill Keller's thoughts are drifting. "When it got dark out there, it really got dark with all those trees. There was one light by the parking lot and you could kind of see the light coming through the trees. You could just hear your voices and the balls bouncing and the nets when you hit.

"Sometimes when we're on that side of town, I've taken Joyce by Meadowood, just driving by. I try to explain to her what the place is all about. We park in

Bill Keller, who starred at Purdue and with the Indiana Pacers, got his chops at Meadowood. Here he lofts a running hook over Willis Reed of the New York Knicks. *Courtesy of Indiana Basketball Hall of Fame.*

the parking lot out there and watch the guys playing, just sit back and watch. Nobody knows I'm there, and I think about all that went on there. Then she'll say, 'Have you seen enough?' and I start the car, but I always take the longest way around so I'll catch a glimpse of Meadowood from all angles."

· ·

I don't know if I practiced more than anybody, but I sure practiced enough. I still wonder if somebody— somewhere—was practicing more than me.

Larry Bird

9

LARRY BIRD

The Guy Down the Road

• •

LATE ONE EVENING IN AUTUMN 1994 JIM JONES CAME HOME FROM A coaching clinic in Louisville. As he was catching his wife up on the days' events, she handed him a small UPS package. It had a Florida postmark. She was smiling and looking right at him. He tore the tape and opened an envelope. A ring fell into his hand. He looked at it, puzzled for a moment. It was huge, a gold ring with the number thirty-three fashioned in diamonds across an emerald face. There were thirteen diamonds in each three. There was also a note written in a familiar, loopy handwriting, thanking him for support that came a nearly a quarter-century ago. It was from the best player he ever coached. It concluded, "I hope I made you proud. Larry."

Jim Jones was the high school coach of the best basketball player who ever grew up in Indiana, with the arguable exception of Oscar Robertson. For years Jones picked Larry Bird up at dawn each morning, took him to the gym at Springs Valley High, fed him donuts and milk, unlocked the door, and gave him a chance to excel. He often told Larry Bird, as he has told hundreds of others, that no matter how badly he wanted to succeed, there was a guy down the road who wanted it more. If you're shooting a hundred shots, he said, the guy down road is shooting a hundred and one. And now, after thirty-two years of coaching, Jim Jones has a way to prove it to the kids he still picks up at dawn: he has a ring from the guy down the road.

Now that Larry Bird's basketball career is over it seems somehow easier to consider what he meant, and means, to Indiana. To people around French Lick he is a source of pride. He honors them whenever he comes home. The early risers among them glimpse him running at dawn, and they see him in town, ballcap over his eyes, taller by half a head than anyone in any room. They still love to tell the stories about how he picked up his first MVP trophy wearing jeans and left it on his mom's refrigerator, and about the time he told the brass from "The American Sportsman" to call him back when they decided to feature the farm ponds of southern Indiana.

To Hoosiers statewide he is among many other things a throwback, an image from Indiana's past, a reminder of times when basketball was all there was in the winter and when it was played best by white players from small towns, boys who played a more earthbound form of the game. "I really don't need anyone to boost my ego," Larry Bird said during his NBA days. "I've already proven that a white boy who can't run and jump can play this game."

That had always been assumed in Indiana, at least until the 1950s, when black players began to transform the game into a faster, higher-flying form. Within a few years, most of the game's major stars were African Americans, even in Indiana's high schools. Deep down, few in Indiana ever expected the world's best basketball player to look like Larry Bird again.

And yet, for a while, before Michael Jordan raised the standard perhaps beyond reach, and before Magic Johnson found the peak of his game just as Bird's health began to decline, there was no better basketball player anywhere than Larry Joe Bird, from a town of about 2,000 in Orange County, Indiana. Three times he was voted the most valuable player in the National Basketball Association. He led his Boston Celtics teams to two NBA championships and barely missed several others. When the US Olympic Committee agreed to allow the best basketball team ever assembled to represent the country in the 1992 games, Larry Bird stood tall as its co-captain.

But how did it happen? He played against competition mainly from small hill towns in southern Indiana. Growing up, the only blacks he played against were the staff members at the local hotel, though he ended up playing in a league in which he was the only major white star. He became a superb rebounder without having superior leaping skills. Defense? Jim Jones chuckles. "Even then, he couldn't guard anybody one-on-one. But he was the best team defensive player, the best anticipator, I had ever seen."

During his playing days, Hoosiers poured their hearts out to the man who put Indiana back on the basketball dollar. Streets in French Lick and Terre Haute were named after him. Days after he held up the NBA championship trophy on national TV and said, "This is for Terre Haute," fans tried to wipe the donor's name right off the Indiana State University Field House and replace it with Larry Bird's. He stopped them with a modest but firm letter to the local newspaper.

But no one could stop Hoosiers from asking, as they still ask, how could a small-town boy whose team never even got out of the Bedford regional, who barely made the Indiana high school all-star team, become LARRY BIRD?

Parents wonder what, besides the value of hard work, they can teach their children by holding up Larry Bird as an example. How do you teach your kid to be a basketball savant, to play like a great pool hustler who has already run the entire table mentally while his pigeon-like opponent tries to figure out the next shot? Maybe there are some things that simply playing all the time can't explain. In the slow, sifting dust of his retirement of Larry Bird's retirement Hoosiers still wonder, who WAS that man?

★ ★ ★

French Lick and West Baden, Indiana, are two sides of the same road sign, planted along Highway 56, in a valley to which Indians and white settlers alike were drawn by three springs of rank-tasting, foul-smelling waters that their animals seemed to love. This is the hill country of southern Indiana, springs and limestone quarries and fossil beds, the part that was piled up by the last glacier to come through.

In 1904 Thomas Taggart, mayor of Indianapolis, a genial Irishman who was doubtless cheered by the few cents he and his cronies made on every barrel of beer sold in Indiana, built a 600-room resort hotel and mineral spa in the valley and named it the French Lick Springs Hotel. Located at the junction of the Southern and Monon railroads, it became one of America's preeminent resorts.

Twenty-one trains a day carried socialites and industrialists, politicians and entertainers, and prizefighters and gamblers and gangsters through southern Indiana and right up to the portico. There they were met by some of the more

French Lick Springs Hotel waiters in the 1930s. Hotel staff members and their children were the first black players Larry Bird ever played against. *Courtesy of French Lick Springs Hotel.*

than one hundred black porters and busmen, who wheeled their trunks over the sawdust walking paths, past the Japanese gardens and into the great hotel itself.

They checked in, found their rooms and padded down to the baths, Turkish baths, Russian baths, electric baths, mud baths, expensive baths full of the same stuff the Indians' horses had lapped up. Taggart called it "Pluto" water, after the king of the underworld.

Taggart built a bottling plant across the street and soon was selling Pluto water hand over fist. Pluto's twenty-two minerals were said to soften skin, cure rheumatism and arthritis, and clean the pores. And, especially after even more salts were added, it won rightful acclaim as a laxative. Guests found a jar of Pluto outside their doors each morning. "If nature won't," said the label, "Pluto will."

Leaders from all professions gathered there. Al Capone, the Pluto of his day, was a regular guest; he was perhaps the only one who relaxed with five bodyguards. It is a Bird family story that Big Al once tipped Larry Bird's grandfather a hundred dollars. The hotel was a popular site for political conventions. In 1904, Democratic National Chairman Tom Taggart ran Judge Alton B. Parker's faltering campaign against Teddy Roosevelt from the hotel lobby. In the same grand setting, the nation's governors squeezed Al Smith out in 1931 and brought in FDR as the party's new standard bearer.

Tom Taggart took womb-to-tomb care of valley residents. Almost everyone who lived in the valley worked either at the hotels—a rival sprang up in West Baden—or at the Pluto plant. Taggart built separate housing for the black workers who came up from Evansville and Louisville. They had their own church and school, their own restaurant and bar in the "Brown building." Even Joe Louis, who trained for several of his fights at the West Baden Hotel, was not allowed to stay in the rooms, although he alone among blacks was allowed to play on the French Lick Springs golf course.

Whites ran the grounds, the kitchen, the golf course, and the casinos. They worked year-round, nine hours a day. In the winter, they stayed outdoors, clearing ice off the trees. During the summer, the women who did not work in the dining halls got ready for winter, freezing meats, canning, getting the apples in. Three generations of people in the valley slipped out of their beds and into uniforms each morning and made ready to coddle the richest people on earth. It is small wonder that Larry Bird, the grandson of Tom Taggart's people, seems content to pick up awards in the world's finest hotels in jeans.

The winter rivalry between the West Baden Sprudels and the French Lick Red Devils was red-hot even by Hoosier standards. Both towns were poor and small, and there was no breathing space between them. "They just despised each other," said Jack Carnes, 61, a lifelong valley resident and long-time kitchen manager of the French Lick Springs Hotel. "You were just liable to get beat up if you went to West Baden or a West Baden kid went to French Lick. They fought over that basketball *all* the time."

"When I was a kid growin' up, there probably wasn't a ball game when there wasn't a fight afterwards. Our teams weren't that good, but whether you won or lost, you *had* to agitate the other team. The old West Baden gym had a balcony with four or five rows of seats, and I've seen people jump off of that balcony and onto a player. It was just *violent*."

In the mid-'50s the two towns began to face pressure from the State Board of Education to consolidate their schools. West Badenites could see the writing on the wall from the start, for theirs was the smaller school.

In a series of rancorous public hearings, they first resisted the whole idea, then fought for a new building which would straddle the town line. But French Lick had almost 80 percent of the valley's people and almost all the power.

One thing was sure. West Baden parents refused to let their children play for, root for, or date French Lick Red Devils. So it was that in the fall of 1957, when the West Baden students crossed the line into French Lick, they went not as Red Devils, but as Springs Valley High Black Hawks.

The first Springs Valley basketball team must have been sent from heaven. Even today, valley residents invoke the boys of '58 as the Irish recall cherished rebellions. They won twenty-five games in a row. In the tourney, they massacred three teams from big schools, teams ranked among the top ten in Indiana. It actually looked like they might go all the way, until they were martyred in the state finals by a Fort Wayne team with a 7'-tall center.

Residents make it clear that it was the *team*, not the board of education, that consolidated the schools. They buried the hatchet in the skulls of common foes. Some of the players were from French Lick and some from West Baden, but when sharpshooters like Bob McCracken and Marvin Pruett started lobbing mortar from the corners and the fast break was on, there were no Sprudels or Red Devils, only Black Hawks and enemies. Such was the heat that Coach Rex Wells, who had come from West Baden, spent much of his time calming his players. At halftime, he would sit the boys down, pass out oranges, and read them poetry.

Tickets became harder to come by as the undefeated string grew longer. The shortage became a drought, a matter that naturally engaged civic leaders like Shorty Reader, a midget who owned the poolroom downtown. "We was all in there one night, gripin' about how we couldn't get into the Shawswicke game," recalls Jack Carnes. "Next night Shorty had tickets for everyone, good seats, too. He said, 'Only thing is, be there when the doors open.' We thought it was funny that he didn't wanna go.

"Well, we got in first thing and before long some people came in wantin' our seats. We got in a big fuss, the police friskin' everybody, and finally they set up new seats for us on the floor. When we got back we told him all about it and Shorty said, 'I knew I didn't get the color quite right.'"

Today a great banner celebrating the team of '58, one of the best teams ever seen in southern Indiana, hangs from the rafters of the Springs Valley gym. "If we'd had a losing season that year," says Jack Carnes, "we'd probably still be fightin' today."

* * *

The Birds, Kerns, and Nobles settled into the valley mainly from Ireland and Wales. Joe and Georgia Bird, married when Joe came back from Korea, produced six children, five boys and a girl.

Larry, born in 1956, was the third of the five boys. Like lots of younger brothers, Larry grew up fast, tagging along, younger and smaller, burning to play too. "When me and Mike were 8 and 9, Larry was 4 or 5," says Larry's brother Mark. "Every time we went some place, we had to take him along. We used to beat him up every day. He was a little smart butt. We used to send him home cryin' and then Dad'd come down there and beat me 'n' Mike up for beatin' up his baby. He'd come down with a switch or somethin', and me and Mike'd get it. Even if we just told him he couldn't play, he'd go home and tell Dad we hit him, and it'd be all over for us."

"Those brothers were so competitive, and they just pounded on the kid," says Jim Jones, who started coaching basketball at Springs Valley high in the early '60s. "Boy, he'd fight them tooth and nail, and he'd stay around and play after they'd leave. His will to win was the biggest thing. I remember in Little League, when he'd get beat he'd cry. They were just great, competitive kids."

Larry started his career on a basketball team in fourth grade. He is remembered locally as a skinny kid with a good eye and a quick temper. Once in junior high he was sent home from practice for fighting. On Friday nights while his brothers played for Springs Valley High—Mike as a part-time player and Mark as a high-scoring star—Larry stayed home.

The family had a hard time making ends meet. Joe Bird, Larry's father, was a laborer with a drinking problem and Georgia Bird, his mother, worked at a variety of jobs, often as a waitress. They moved around a lot, sometimes living with relatives. Joe was sometimes in the household, sometimes not. When Larry started playing for the school teams, he moved in with his grandmother, as Mike and Mark had done when they played. She lived only a block from the school, and, better still, she let the boys stay out as late as they wanted. Larry would play in the gym at night until they locked the doors and then play outdoors near a street light. "I used to drive by the park, and he'd be out there with a couple of friends until one or two in the morning," says Gary Holland, then Jones's assistant coach. Even after the others went home, Larry would stay out, whipping the ball against a concrete wall.

It was the way he practiced, as much as the amount of time he spent at it that made him good. "Most kids are afraid to fail," Jones says, "but Larry wasn't.

Most kids keep practicing what they're good at but Larry practiced on his weaknesses. He spent one whole summer doing things left-handed. He was obsessed."

Larry made the Springs Valley team as a sophomore, wearing Mark's old number, 33. A guard, he stood 6'1" and weighed but 135 pounds. He was mainly a passer and rebounder on a team of good shooters. Slow afoot, he developed his own ways to help the team on defense. "He would let his man go and steal the ball from someone else," recalls Jones. "Or he would leave his man to steal the ball or block a shot. Somehow he could just anticipate what someone else was going to do."

In the season's second game, Larry broke his ankle in a battle for a rebound. He practiced shooting with the team, balanced on one crutch, until his cast wore off and then begged Jones for a chance to play again. "We told him if he could play up to a certain level, we'd take him to the state tournament," says Jones. "I didn't tell him we'd already decided to take him. I said he'd have to run the suicide drill every day within a certain time, and he couldn't do it and get frustrated and almost cry. He practiced very hard, and dragged his leg around until he beat the time." He went to the sectional, got himself in at the end of the first game and won it with two free throws. Springs Valley was defeated in the second game.

Larry had a fine junior year as a 6'3" guard, averaging about sixteen points, ten rebounds, and six assists a game. He spent much of the season feeding the ball to a senior named Steve Land. In the season's final game, Land entered the fourth quarter needing a few points to break the school scoring record. Springs Valley was far ahead, so Jones pulled the starters except for Land, who was supposed to stay in until he broke the record. But the subs couldn't get the ball to him. Pass after pass was intercepted as time ran down. "I remember Larry saying, 'Put me back in, coach, and he'll get it,'" Jones says. "I did. Bang. Bang. Bang. Three or four passes later, the kid has the record."

A week later Springs Valley was upset by Paoli in the first game of the sectional. Still, Larry Bird had made an impression. Around town some people were saying Larry might even have a future as a small college guard. No one was prepared for what happened. Over the summer, he shot up to 6'7" and increased his strength by working out each day on the football team's new Universal weight machine. Somehow he lost none of his exceptional coordination; instead, overnight, he became a guard in a center's body.

"I had been away at college, and I hadn't seen him play," recalls Mark Bird. "Once between his junior and senior years I was workin' with our uncle up in

it in without breaking stride. The next morning, Holland, Beezer, Larry, and several others ran the film clip over and over. "We just sat there laughing," says Holland. "Even Larry had to laugh."

Larry's self-confidence increased by the game. "Frankly," says Beezer, "I always figured Gary wanted me to be the leader, but after the second or third game it was clear who our leader was. Larry liked to joke around, but it was always *after* practice. He'd get his work done first. He could come down on you out there, too. I might be standin' around and Larry'd come over and say, 'You tired? Then why aren't you workin' to help us win?'"

On the days when the team had a 6:30 A M free-throw practice, Jones would swing by Larry's grandmother's house and try to wake Larry and Beezer up. "Larry probably didn't look too favorably on it, but he'd roll out and put his pants on and we were off." Beezer, on the other hand, often rolled back over.

It came back to haunt him in the tourney their senior year. After Springs Valley had won the sectional, Beezer found himself on the line for four last-minute free throws against Bedford with the regional championship at stake. He missed them all, and Springs Valley lost by three points. "After the game," Beezer says, "we went back to Shorty's, and Larry just laid it out to me. He said, 'Beezer, you should have got up and shot them free throws in the mornings.'"

★ ★ ★

It didn't take long for Gary Holland to realize that there couldn't be many better players in Indiana, if any, and he owed it to Larry to spread the word. In Indiana, the greatest honor a boy can get is to be named "Mr. Basketball," and, after that, to make the twelve-player all-star team that has played a group of all-stars from Kentucky each summer since 1939. The selections are made by the *Indianapolis Star*, particularly by a promotions man named Don Bates, now retired. "When you die," explains Bates, "that's in your obit, that you were an Indiana All-Star. And it's usually in the lead paragraph. It's like your pedigree."

Bates and his advisory committee always had a tough job. Half the coaches in Indiana were out to convince him they have an all-star. The lobbying is to this day year-round and intense, with letter-writing campaigns and violent fan reactions when their boys don't make it. Always, fans from both northern and southern Indiana have believed the Star has slighted—maybe persecuted—them.

With Larry, Holland knew he had an uphill fight. "Mr. Basketball" was out of the question—no one would believe he was that good. Larry had been a guard the year before, the number-two scorer on a team that hadn't even won its sectional. Now he was a 160-pound center on a small, rural team, light-years from Indianapolis.

Holland called Jerry Birge, a respected sportswriter from nearby Jasper, who had seen Larry enough to know. Birge responded by printing hundreds of fliers and glossy action photos. He sent them to every newspaper and radio station in Indiana and hounded Don Bates and his colleagues at the Star. Birge had the feeling he was getting nowhere.

But early in the season Indiana University coach Bobby Knight began to show up at Larry's games. He'd slip in quietly, after the game had started, sit up there eating popcorn for a while and slip out again. He rarely spoke to Holland, or to Bird, but he sent three of his players—Steve Green, John Laskowski, and Kent Benson—to talk up IU over dinner at the Jones' home. After the tourney, when he made his pitch, Larry signed, though his first choice was Kentucky. "We were all IU fans," says Mark Bird. "My dad was probably the biggest IU fan ever. He'd say to Larry, 'Boy, I seen this red jacket the other day, and I sure would like to buy it and wear it to one of your ball games.'"

"When he signed with IU, it really caught my attention," says Don Bates. "I thought, I'd better drive down and take a look at this kid. They were playing at Mitchell. I got there and they were warming up. Right away you could tell which one Bird was, shooting layups and jump shots. He had great hands, big hands. He scored about thirty-five points and had about twenty rebounds that night."

Larry made the all-star team, but, even after spectacular practices, he played less than half the time. When his coach summoned him for action at the end of the second game, he refused to play, stating that he wasn't a mop-up player. Deeply proud and certain of his abilities, he was burned by the insult, and the memories still linger.

Asked by writer Ray Didinger in 1985 to explain "What do you think it is that drives you?" Bird replied, "I'm sure it dates back to Indiana . . . I didn't even make all-state my senior year [he didn't make the wire service teams] . . . I heard what they said about me. Too slow, can't jump. Country kid, never had the big-city competition. I went to the state all-star game my senior year, and I got in the first five minutes. I wondered if I was really that bad.

Indiana high school all-star Larry Bird dunks against a Kentucky counterpart. Note the placement of Bird's right foot. *Courtesy of the* Indianapolis Star.

Larry Bird debuts as himself in the 1994 Hollywood film *Blue Chips*. The car is driven by Nick Nolte. *Courtesy of Kevin Swank, the* Evansville Courier.

"I look back and I realize I was the best player in the state. No one gave me credit for it. But maybe it worked out for the best. It kept me practicing four or five hours a day in the summer, and now it's a habit."

★ ★ ★

In the autumn of 1974 Bird travelled to the IU campus at Bloomington with seventy-five dollars in his pocket. Overwhelmed by the campus ("33,000 students was not my idea of a school, it was more like a whole country to me"), he hitchhiked home after 24 days. Bob Knight, who later expressed regret for not supporting Larry, saw him play only once, briefly, at an informal scrimmage. Within the next two years Larry found himself in turns married, divorced, fatherless, and a father. Joe Bird, divorced from Georgia and unable to keep up support payments took his life in 1975. The same year Larry married a high school sweetheart and months later, convinced he had made a mistake, broke it off. The couple conceived a child during a brief reconciliation, then divorced. A daughter named Corrie Bird was born in August of 1977. At first Larry claimed the child was not his, but her mother went to court and won a paternity and child support judgment.

Bird enrolled briefly in a local trade school, dropped out, then entered at Indiana State University in Terre Haute. Mark was nearby, as was an ex-Springs Valley teammate, Tony Clarke. Bird was ineligible for a year, then suited up for ISU, making an immediate and overwhelming impact. In those years he met Dinah Mattingly, a student at ISU, whom he later married. In his final year of play, he led Indiana State to an undefeated season and the final game of the NCAA tournament, where they lost to Magic Johnson's Michigan State team. He was voted the nation's outstanding collegiate player and drafted by the Boston Celtics, for whom, in a thirteen-year career, he won international fame as the greatest forward ever to play basketball.

During each of his Celtic years, Bird returned home in the summer, staying with his mother in West Baden. He would play golf and fish and relax as he could nowhere else. His old friends grew accustomed to his impulsive calls, sometimes at odd hours. "I only got to see Larry once last summer," said Beezer Carnes, now a pipefitter, in 1984. "He just called me up and said, 'Let's go.' We just went out and drove around till four in the morning. I had to get up at five the next morning and I wanted to get one hour's sleep, anyway. He tried to talk me into cuttin' work the next day, but I have a mortgage on a new house I'm tryin' to pay off and I really couldn't cut . . . I told him, 'If you'll pay for the day,' and he just laughed."

★　★　★

Years after Larry Bird's classic matchups with Magic Johnson and his final minutes with the Olympic Dream Team, Hoosiers, including those who know him best, still reach back, trying to remember games and shots and passes that might have foreshadowed his greatness. But at heart it's still something of a mystery. "He'd make passes that you didn't even see were possible," says Jones. "You wondered, how'd *he* see them?"

Some think the explanation lies in where he grew up. Larry had only about 300 classmates at Springs Valley High but there were sometimes 3,000 fans in the gym when he played. Maybe it could only happen in small town Indiana, goes this line of reasoning, where basketball was all there was to do and everybody cared so much . . . but then nobody else got that good.

The former Monon Avenue, French Lick, IN. *Courtesy of Tom Roach.*

Mark Bird holds to at least a partial genetic theory. "We were all good shooters," he says, "everyone in our family. They say that grandad Bird was just a tremendous baseball player. Dad quit school early to join the Navy, but Shorty Reader knew our dad real well, and he'd say, 'You kids *ought to* be good, as good as your dad was.'"

Gary Holland offers something quite different, something that speaks to Larry's success in the NBA. "Larry just seemed like he could adjust to the character of other people," he says. "Really, the game of basketball is getting along with other players. After he got out of high school here he signed at IU, and then he dropped out and enrolled in Northwood Institute up here for a while. We never had any blacks in school for him to play with, but at Northwood there were a few, some good players. I was amazed by how he could adjust to their style of play. It was rough play. He fit in real good. They really respected him."

Finally, Jim Jones just laughs. "How did Larry Bird get so good? . . . He just has a God-given talent for the game. He loved it so and he worked so hard. There'll never be anyone just like him." Maybe the only explanation for Larry Bird is that somebody had to be the guy down the road.

· ·

I don't know if I practiced more than anybody, but I sure practiced enough. I still wonder if somebody—somewhere—was practicing more than me.

Larry Bird

10

THE EDUCATION OF
STEPHANIE WHITE

· ·

Author's Note: Only once in my 30-plus-year career as an author have I ar-
rived at a bookstore for a signing event to find a mob of readers waiting for me.
On this occasion shoppers had formed a line from the bookstore door around
the corner of a supermarket to someplace I couldn't see. Some had been wait-
ing for hours. Most were women and children.

The magnet was eighteen-year-old Stephanie White—and she wasn't even
present. Why? The day before, a review of the second edition of this book had
appeared in the Lafayette, Indiana, newspaper. The review featured a photo
of the book's cover, which depicted Stephanie's sculpted face on a Hoosier
Mt. Rushmore, along with Larry Bird, Oscar Robertson, and Bob Knight. Her
adoring fans loved the idea that she had been so recognized.

The bookseller unlocked the door and Steph's Army surged toward me. I
signed books without even looking up for the next couple of hours. I felt like a
Beatle.

Two hours before tip-off everyone agreed that the line behind the school at Benton Central High was at least two football fields long. People blew into their hands and passed along thermoses full of coffee and jiggled from foot to foot to stay warm. Moments after the doors mercifully opened, 4,000 people surged into the gym and packed themselves into the bleachers, shoulder to shoulder, as high as the eye could see. The crowd was a thousand more than the fire marshal's posted order permitted. Of course the fire marshal was there, too, trying not to be noticed and praying nothing would happen.

They were there to see the most exciting player to hit the Wabash Valley in many years, a player who had scored 66 points just the game before, nearly outscoring the other team. Now the player need 23 more points for the career state scoring record for girls. Everyone wanted to see her do it.

In 1994, her senior year at Seeger Memorial high, enrollment 399 students, Stephanie White was widely regarded as the best female high school player in America, and maybe the best in Indiana's history. The summer before she had been one of only three high school girls in the nation selected to play in the US Olympic festival, a proving ground for future Olympians. In the four years she had played for Seeger, the Patriots had lost only seven games. She was averaging 40 points a game.

Male scouts and coaches spoke about her as if she were a new hybrid or a technological breakthrough, The Girl Who Played Like a Boy. "Stephanie White is the first girl that people have talked about like they did Damon Bailey or Glenn Robinson," observed Garry Donna, publisher of *Hoosier Basketball* magazine. "You know, where they say, 'I've just got to see her play.'" At 5'10", she could spring up and grab the rim. Her movements were strong and fluid. She was an amazingly creative passer and a tough, intuitive defender. She was pretty, and feminine, well-proportioned, but not bulky; just by looking at her it was hard to see how she could be so strong. She did startling things nearly every game, especially as a passer. To those who had worked to build the girls' game in Indiana, Stephanie White was the popularizer who was bound to come someday, the girl who would be so good that hard-core basketball fans throughout Indiana would become excited.

★   ★   ★

An hour before game time, Stephanie brushed back her shoulder-length black hair and tried to look into the bleachers through the crowd of children surrounding her. Behind her she could see her parents, both sets of grandparents, aunts, uncles, and cousins on both sides, half her congregation, and many of the people she had grown up with. They were all looking at her. She told herself for the millionth time not to lose it in front of them all when she broke the record. Television crews bathed her in a circle of hot light. Already she was drenched. Two boys came up and raised their tee shirts to show that they had smeared her number 22 across their chests in Patriot blue paint. She smiled. A friend came down to show off her baby. Children lined up to offer her various objects to sign as a trainer taped her ankles. One was a jacket. "Are you sure you're not gonna get in trouble?" Stephanie asked, hesitating with her marker. A girl nodded solemnly. Stephanie signed.

In the locker room a few minutes before the game she drew back her jet-black hair and fastened it with a red holder, pulled on her red, white, and blue uniform and thought about her opponents, the Turkey Run Warriors. The main problem would be a set of twins who fancied themselves as intimidators. A couple of years ago they had almost exchanged blows outside the locker room door after a game. She was glad her sister Shanda was with her in the lineup. Shanda would have her back against anyone or anything.

When at last the game started Stephanie quickly reminded the fans why they had come. She gave them wraparound passes, feather-soft three-pointers, bone-crunching picks to spring teammates for open shots, and powerful moves to the hoop. At one point Stephanie raced around a screen and smashed into one of the twins, who pushed her to the floor. She bounced up, smiling inches from the girl's face, and returned the favor sweetly a few plays later with a forearm shiver that sent her sprawling. Shanda advanced, ready to rumble. Stephanie told her to forget it and they ran back up the court. With several seconds remaining in the first half, Stephanie needed only one point to break the record. She sprinted from beneath the basket in a tight, counter-clockwise arc, received a pass, and drove for the hoop. She was fouled hard as she rose to shoot. She stepped calmly to the free throw line, thinking about using her legs to support the shot, and tossed the ball softly through the iron ring for the record.

The game was halted. Kids poured down from the upper reaches to be near her as everyone stood and cheered. One by one, her teammates gave her lingering embraces, each taking time to say something special. She had given them big games and big crowds and adventures that they wouldn't have had without her. The other team's players were applauding, too, even the twins. Her game face was disintegrating and it was becoming impossible to hold the tears back. When Kelly Fink, her four-year teammate, gave her the ball to keep, she took it into the stands and handed it to her red-eyed parents, who themselves were trying to remain composed as television cameras closed in. "I love you guys," she whispered, embracing first her mother, then her father. "It made me feel so good," Kevin White said later. "We've been so busy headed toward goals for so long. 'I love you' are words we haven't stopped to say enough to each other."

* * *

From the early years it was clear to Kevin and Jenny White that there was something unusual about their first born. It wasn't so much that she loved to play ball games. Everyone loved to play in their family. Grandma Henry had been a basketball player in the six-girl days, and both Jenny and Kevin had been varsity athletes at Seeger. But Stephanie seemed driven to play. One evening when she was five, Kevin had hit her a milk crate full of balls after his baseball practice. She fielded them all and threw them all back and remained in position. He hit her another crate, and another. She was like one of the broomsticks in *The Sorcerer's Apprentice*. She wouldn't stop, even when her father was worn down. It was hard to wear Kevin White out; he was 24.

Injury meant nothing to her. One day she broke her wrist playing basketball and was out playing soccer the next day. She explained that you didn't have to use your arms in soccer. By second grade she was playing baseball with ten- and twelve-year-olds and then asking to be taxied straight to soccer. She often complained that her leg hurt, but she wouldn't rest. One evening Kevin and Jenny noticed that she was dragging the leg behind her as she ran, and seemed to be in some pain. They drove her straight to a bone specialist in Indianapolis, who diagnosed bone cancer. Kevin broke down in tears a few evenings later while rocking Stephanie on the porch. Stephanie was looking up at him through clear blue eyes. "Don't worry, Dad," she said, "I'll beat it." Luckily the problem turned out to be a stress fracture that had become badly infected from constant wear. The real struggle was getting her to rest it long enough to heal.

* * *

The closest town to the country acre on which the Whites live is West Lebanon, population 900, one of a group of farming communities that straddle the Wabash River near the Indiana-Illinois line. Thirty-five miles south of West Lafayette, West Leb is in the heart of Purdue country.

When the Indiana state basketball tourney came around, West Lebanon High played in the sectional at Attica, a town a few miles upriver that had the biggest gym around. At least that was the case until 1951, the year that the citizens of Covington, the next-biggest town, built a bigger gym and took Attica's home-court advantage away. It took them all winter to draft the blueprint in Effray Harden's downtown barber shop and, then, when warm weather came, they all went outside and built the gym together, as volunteers, on shifts after work and on weekends, the way you raise a barn or rebuild a flattened church after a tornado. Unskilled laborers worked side by side with carpenters and glazers and masons until finally the welders welded the baskets to the standards and the painters lined the floor. In the end it held 3,200 people—400 more than Attica's gym.

West Lebanon High closed in 1959 as part of a consolidation with Seeger High, but the old schoolhouse, which looks much like Hickory High in the movie *Hoosiers*, still stands. The West Leb gym has been open a night or two a week for people in the community to play basketball ever since. It is here, on Wednesday and Sunday nights among men three and four times her age, that Stephanie White learned to play basketball.

At first she begged just to tag along with her father to watch, but soon wormed her way into the full-court games. She joined a formidable lineup. Besides Kevin White, who works as a laborer in the shipping department at Quaker Oats, the regulars included Rex Cronk, a burly, bearded 6'1" highway worker, Tom Miller, a football coach in Lafayette, Mike Miller, whom they called "The Hacker," and Doc Greenwood, the local veterinarian, a highly competitive ex-Seeger High guard. And now a ponytailed girl in fourth grade.

She was appealing and tough. She wanted so badly to learn the game they loved that they could hardly stop themselves from teaching her. "They showed me how to set screens to get other people open and myself open," she recalls. "And they taught me to see things before they happen; to anticipate a cut before someone goes. Over and over they kept saying, 'Throw the ball HARDER . . . You're playing with guys, not girls."

They soon learned that Stephanie White meant business. "The worst thing was when they tried to baby me. It made me so mad. Once when I was in fifth grade one of them blocked my shot clean and called a foul on himself. I wouldn't take the ball from him. I said, 'look, I'm here to improve. How am I going to get any better this way? DON'T BABY ME.' As I got older they grew out of it. They would pound me and not call a thing. That helped and I never got hurt."

The education of Stephanie White became a community project. Improvement was continual, but from time to time she did things that surprised them all. There was the night when she was twelve that she stole the ball twice in a row from Doc Greenwood and laid the ball in at her end. "Dammit, Steph," Greenwood had muttered, "The second time I was ready."

Stephanie's mom, Jenny White, contributed countless of hours of outdoor labor. She had postponed a career as a teacher to stay home with her three daughters, each of whom had her own needs. Often, it seemed, Stephanie's greatest need was rebounding. "Hundreds of times I've heard her say, 'Mom, will you go out and rebound for me while I shoot?" Jenny says. "I usually go, except in really cold weather. I've learned to throw the ball back to her just the way she wants it."

Kevin White was the project manager. Though he had blown out his knee before he could play on the Seeger varsity basketball team, he had an analytical mind for the game and tried to learn enough to keep up with Stephanie's growing talent. Along the way he developed a few techniques not normally found in instructional videos and clinics, such as firing a shotgun in the air to try to distract her as she shot free throws.

For the first year or two Kevin was the only one at the gym who would push Stephanie down to get a rebound or charge into her. He said he did it to make her mentally tough, but she thought he was showing off in front of his friends. After a while she found a way to get him back. "I learned that if I didn't react it would make him mad. It got to the point where he just couldn't take it if I'd bounce back up and not say anything. I would just smile."

Stephanie developed ways to assert her strength without losing her temper. Her composure could be disarming. "Once we were playing out in the yard and I tried to intimidate her to see how tough she was," Kevin recalls. "She was working on dribbling with her left hand and she made the same mistake three times in a row and I grabbed her basketball and kicked it as far as I could and started yelling at her. She kept eye contact with me and waited until I finished. She said, 'Are you finished?' I said 'Yeah.' She said, 'Don't EVER kick my ball again. It's not a soccer ball.' I felt so low."

★ ★ ★

Kelly Fink first met Stephanie White, her future teammate at Seeger High, when they were in fifth grade in a YMCA basketball program that Kevin had organized. To the girls who lined up in shorts to learn a new game, Stephanie seemed almost like a different species. "I remember she was trying to teach us how to set picks," says Kelly. "We didn't know what she was talking about. We sort of stood there looking at her. She was so advanced, we didn't know what to think. We couldn't do it."

After their games, the girls were invited to dress up as cheerleaders for the fifth-grade boys' games. All but four did. Kelly and two others who didn't want to just sit down and watched the boys. Never one to sit still, Stephanie developed her own alternative. "She dressed up in this warrior costume and ran in circles around the gym whooping," Kelly says. "She got everybody psyched up. People loved it."

By the time Stephanie reached adolescence, she had given herself to the game. When she tested the limits of her parents' authority, the issue usually involved basketball. She begged them to let her ride her motorcycle to an outdoor court in the dark so she could shoot at night. No, they said, pointing out that her bike had no headlight. Well, how about if she taped a flashlight to her helmet? No. And then there was the night Stephanie announced that she could no longer do the dishes because, as she put it, dish water 'removes the natural oils in my hands.' That, she explained would ruin her shooting touch and destroy her chances for a scholarship. Kevin bought her a pair of Playtex gloves.

Stephanie entered the Seeger High starting lineup in her second game as a freshman and immediately took over as point guard. Point guard meant passing, and passing was her love in life. After five years at the West Leb gym, she could now whip the ball through a blur of arms and legs and make it spin right up into a cutter's hands. She could throw a bounce pass diagonally the length of the court. Working alone, she had invented her own passes, with side spin and top spin and back spin. She could throw behind her back off the dribble with either hand and hit an X she had taped to the basement wall. Stephanie knew passes.

The only problem was that her new teammates couldn't catch them. "They were like bullets," says Kelly Fink, who joined Stephanie on the varsity as a freshman. "I thought I was strong, but my fingers were like butter with her sometimes. I worked one whole summer on being able to catch her passes. I started playing with the men, too. After their games I would have them throw me hard, long, baseball passes. I waited till Steph wasn't around because I didn't want her to know I couldn't catch them. I was determined to do it."

Stephanie was a team leader from the beginning. She led mostly because she was so good and also because she seemed to have been born with the software of the game in her head. Everything was possible to her; she saw cuts her teammates could make, and recognized new defenses the instant they formed. Her teammates also soon discovered what the men at the West Leb gym had known for five years now: that Stephanie White was a perfectionist, impatient with mistakes, especially her own. Her dedication was contagious. With Stephanie averaging nearly twenty points per game, the Patriots lost only three times her freshman year and did not lose at all until the tourney the following year.

In both seasons they advanced to the Lafayette semistate before they were defeated by schools with much greater enrollments.

She set her sights on a college scholarship and being named Indiana's "Miss Basketball" as a senior. While not wanting to discourage her, Kevin White wondered how college scouts would ever even hear of a girl from West Leb. The newspaper that covered Seeger's games was printed across the river in Illinois; few people in Indiana read it.

Kevin and Jenny tried their best to help her realize her dreams. They paid to enroll her in a national Amateur Athletic Union tournament and drove to Texas one summer and Utah the next, so she could play in tournaments with girls from around the nation in games witnessed by college coaches. "That's what really woke us up to her talent," says Jenny. "We wondered whether she was just a good player from a small town but she was a good as anybody at those camps. She won MVP in her age group one year." After her freshman year letters from colleges began to appear. Within two years there would be letters from more than 200 schools.

By Stephanie's junior year, nearly every Seeger girls' game was a sellout, at home or on the road. It didn't matter that girls played their games on week-nights, or really where the games were. Hoosiers love a hot team, and this was a hot team. On game nights, hundreds of people from all over the Valley piled into vans and cars and pickups and trailed them wherever they went. The guys from the West Leb gym were among the Patriots' biggest fans. Rex Cronk signed on to drive the team bus and sat as near as possible to the court so Steph would be sure to hear him yell, "Throw it harder!" Ministers wove the Patriots into sermons and announcements, usually praising the way they carried themselves in a big game. "Sometimes our team even makes the Praise List at our church," says Kelly Fink. "That's the list of things to be thankful for, like recovering from surgery or a new baby."

It was about this time that the starters, and particularly Stephanie, began to attract a permanent swarm of children who attended all her games, imi-tated her every move and asked her to autograph whatever objects they could produce. Stephanie loved the chance to matter so much to younger kids but it took a lot of time. The local McDonald's helped by sponsoring autograph nights when the Seeger girls could all just sit together and eat and sign things for an hour or so. Success brought the Patriots closer together. Often they would play-ing hide-and-seek in the locker room before the games to break the tension. On weekends they drove around together, often in the Whites' blue Probe, to catch games around the Valley.

It was not always easy for the boys to stomach all this. Stephanie's boyfriend was fine—he went to another school and played three sports himself—but Seeger High is a very small school. Especially in Stephanie's junior year, when the girls were undefeated and the talk of the Valley, an atmosphere of tension set in at school. "They'd say stuff to us when we walked down the hall, or in class," Stephanie recalls. "Stuff like, 'The girl's team isn't really that good.' They thought they were getting cheated because we got more recognition than they got. We thought the behavior was immature and we let it go. We've worked for this. If they had worked that hard they would have got there too."

★　★　★

In Stephanie's junior year the Patriots were eliminated from the tourney in the Lafayette semistate by Lake Central High, a talented, well-coached, and nationally ranked team from a school near Chicago. "They were intimidating," recalls Kelly Fink, who was by now a starter. "They were much bigger than us. The younger players were really scared." Seeger had led by six points with two minutes remaining, but then took hasty shots and lost the ball again and again. "It slipped away so fast at the end," says Stephanie. "I tried to get people together at the free throw line and say things like 'let's be patient' but it didn't work. It's frustrating to watch the tape of that game. I gave the ball up sometimes when I shouldn't have. I keep saying, 'Why did I pass then, why didn't I just keep it?' I was silly."

The next year they dedicated themselves to getting through Lafayette and on to Indianapolis in the tourney. They were closer, and stronger, and better balanced. Kelly and Stephanie had been playing together for four years, and by now she could catch any pass Stephanie could throw. Stephanie continued to improve on her own as well. Each morning she got up to lift weights before school with the swim team. She still played twice a week with the guys in the gym, and by now they had trouble keeping up with her. She startled them all again one evening by swatting one of Rex Cronk's shots out of bounds. It was the first time they could remember her having blocked a shot with such authority. "I was back on my heels," he explains. "Otherwise, she'd have never got it."

Perhaps best of all the White sisters seemed to have worked out their differences. Shanda, two years younger than Stephanie, was the only member of the team that Stephanie would criticize in front of the others. Shanda hated it. "She was always saying I wasn't trying hard enough, or that I didn't want it badly enough," Shanda says. "I would tell her, 'Look, Steph, I just don't see all those cuts like you,' or 'I'm not fast enough to catch that pass,' but she wouldn't listen."

At Purdue, Stephanie earned the Wade Trophy as the nation's top female basketball player and led the Boilermakers to a national championship. *Courtesy of Indiana Basketball Hall of Fame.*

At home, Shanda had adapted subtle ways to defend herself against Stephanie just as Stephanie had learned to overcome her father's mind games. The best was sweetly simple. "When we'd be playing outdoors," Shanda recalls, "sometimes I'd just walk off the court and go in the house. That'd really get to her."

In the last ten games or so of the 1994 season, Shanda became a much more aggressive player, averaging about twenty points and ten rebounds per game. Shanda says she just grew into it, while Stephanie says she seemed to 'want it more,' but neither quarreled with the result. The new Shanda helped make Seeger a statewide power. During the regular season, Seeger was able to beat Lake Central in a close game on their court. Going into the tourney, the Seeger girls believed this was their year.

Practically speaking, it probably came to an end when, during the sectional final, Kelly Fink put all her weight on one knee as she was trying to save the ball from going out of bounds and felt something pop. She had torn her anterior cruciate ligament and faced surgery. They braced her up so she could play the following week in the regionals, but she was more like a mummy than the old, athletic Kelly Fink.

The season died on a single play the next week at Lafayette, and, of course, against Lake Central. With Seeger behind by three points and less than a minute remaining, a Lake Central player missed a free throw. It clanged off the rim on the opposite side of the basket from Stephanie, and a Lake Central player knifed in and stole the rebound. That was it. Stephanie fouled out with fourteen seconds remaining in the game. She had scored 39 points, collected 14 rebounds and stolen the ball six times against a team that had been ranked third nationally by *USA Today* at one point in the season. Stephanie had scored 17 of Seeger's last 20 points.

When she walked slowly off the court, despondent and exhausted, 6,000 people rose to their feet as if jerked up by a puppeteer, in a final tribute to a great player. "That ovation was the one of the most thrilling moments I can remember in decades of having watched sports in Indiana," says Patricia Roy, a commissioner of the Indiana State High School Athletic Association who has dedicated her career to the development of athletic opportunities for girls.

Nearly an hour later, Stephanie was the last player out of the locker room, a ballcap reading *Basketball is Life*, pulled low over her red-rimmed eyes. She answered reporters' questions until they left and the cloud of children surged into the vacuum. The kids seemed to make her feel better. She signed until even they were gone.

A few weeks before, a Lafayette editorial cartoonist had decided to draw what Stephanie White had come to mean to girls' basketball in Indiana. He found himself sketching a mountain, with two puzzled looking boys on the summit. Coming at them was a long chain of girls, being pulled toward the top by a ponytailed player with "Seeger" on her jersey. The mountain was called "Recognition." "C'mon," Stephanie White is saying. "We're getting there."

Kelly Fink, for one, is a believer. "I heard something I couldn't believe this morning," she said a few days after their season had ended but while the boys' tourney was still on. "One of the boys on the team comes up to Stephanie in class and says, 'Did you see our game last night?' Steph says 'yeah.' He says, 'Well they called me for charging into a guy and he didn't have his feet planted. Aren't you supposed to have your feet planted?' It was the first time I had ever heard a guy ask a girl to explain a rule."

Now Stephanie is on her way to Purdue. Her father would have preferred Stanford, but Stephanie had her way as usual. This way the kids from Benton and Warren counties can still crowd up to her after the games, and her grandparents can see her, and so can her Seeger teammates who stay around the Valley. The guys from the West Leb gym can elbow each other knowingly when she rifles seeing-eye passes toward women who know just when to cut and with fingers as strong as theirs. Fans from several counties away are already buying season tickets to the Purdue women's season. A fine student, Stephanie will major in aeronautical engineering. Her bedroom walls are papered with photos of airplanes. Officially she says she may want to be a pilot. Secretly, maybe she'd like to be an astronaut.

But there are other goals first. She wants to coach. And there's a little stretch of that mountain left to climb. "Yeah, there are still things to do," she says. "I want to change the girls' game so it's more like the guys' game. I want it to be more exciting. I want to be a point guard who can rebound and shoot as well as pass. I want to put a little showtime in it. People like Judi Warren started it and molded it. They helped it to become what it is now. We're just adding on to what they did. I want to be one of the people who will help it to be what it is in the future. I think I can."

· ·

What does every boy in this town want to be? He wants to be the basketball coach. It's the dream of the U.S.A.; the prairie wagon and the plains; the unconquerable frontier. That's why you stick with it; that's why coaches stay with the game.

from John R. Tunis's 1944 novel *Yea! Wildcats,*
about life in Kokomo, Indiana

11

COACHES

From the Lady Lions to Bob Knight

. . . .

MARK SIMMERMAN WAS ECSTATIC. HIS YOUNG GREENFIELD CENTRAL team had won the first game of its sectional. It looked like they might even win the whole thing for the first time in over thirty years.

Privately, he hoped the victory had saved his job, too. But given the nature of his one-year coaching contract, it wasn't crystal clear: "They [the principal and athletic director] gave me a list with about fourteen or fifteen items that I needed to meet," says Simmerman. "One of them was that I had to win ten games." He had finished the regular season 9–11. This tournament victory was the tenth.

All season long Simmerman had tried to keep his situation from his players, but you don't keep secrets like that in a small town. Even the kids in the cheer block knew, for Simmerman's wife, Teri, also a teacher at the school, had been their faculty sponsor. "The whole cheer block was crying," says Teri Simmerman. "Our minister was there, and the next day he preached about it. The team captain came up to me afterward and said, 'Do I get a hug?' because he thought Mark's job had been saved."

Greenfield Central went on to win the sectional that evening, and it looked even better. But shortly after Greenfield lost the first game of the regional by three points to a New Castle team that went to the state finals, the principal and athletic director asked Mark Simmerman to resign. Ten wins was ten wins, and Simmerman had won nine. He refused to quit.

When the students heard, ninety-two of them walked out of school, chanting Simmerman's name. They marched to the local newspaper and asked for an investigation. Anguished, Simmerman tried to figure out what to do. Mostly, he thought about his coaching future. "In Indiana," he says, "some people think if you get fired there is something the matter, that there is something to it.' Finally he scribbled "I quit" on a scrap of paper and handed it to the athletic director. Shortly after, local sportswriters named him County Coach of the Year.

At least the ordeal was over. "On nights when he would lose a game," says Teri Simmerman, "we'd be up till three or four in the morning because we knew what it meant. You see, I wasn't married to him when I first saw him coach. I didn't know what a coach went through. He was only 27 years old and he had higher blood pressure than my mother, who's on medicine."

"What it boiled down to," says Simmerman, "I'd made two or three bigwigs upset. I'd made enough enemies because one kid didn't make the ball club or didn't play enough, and his dad would go and complain to the administration and they would listen to these people. The simplest thing [for them] was to make a change." He echoes a very familiar theme. "If they would just leave it up to the kids, there wouldn't be any problem. When the parents step in, there are problems."

The average high school basketball coach in Indiana lasts less than three years with a team. Two Indiana high schools began this season with their seventh head coach in the last eleven years.

Some Indiana school boards have the power to hire and fire only two individuals, the principal and the head basketball coach. It is common for Hoosiers to run for the school board for no other reason than to fire the coach.

"Corydon was the damnedest town I ever saw for hiring and firing coaches," says former Indiana High School Athletic Association (IHSAA) Commissioner Phil Eskew. "I remember talking to the superintendent down there, who said, 'I think we got Wall fixed up now. We're going to rehire both the football and basketball coach. I think I'll get that done tonight.' I had breakfast with him the next morning. He said, 'Damnedest thing happened last night. I went into that meeting and someone made a motion: 'I move, we fire the basketball coach.' It was carried. Then someone else said, 'Well, I move we fire the football coach,' and he was gone. That was the school board."

The tenure is shaky, the pressures volcanic, the pay minimal, and the hours eternal. And yet, each vacancy is eagerly sought in Indiana. Why would anyone want to coach? Same reason someone would want to be a rabbi in Williamsburg, a cowboy in Wyoming, a guide in the Adirondacks, a county agent in Iowa, a conductor in Vienna, or a claims adjustor in Hartford. Coaching is the operative profession in the community, the way to participate most directly in the experience of Indiana.

A good basketball coach is a conspicuous, respected, consulted, and admired community leader, a source of power. The rewards are visibility, respect, and a chance to shape the most vital aspects of a community. For some, it's a chance to stay young, to stay with a game you love and played and don't want to leave. "If you're good, a coach is just another minister," says Howard Sharpe, who has coached Indiana high school teams for forty-seven years. "The coach is the most crucified man in the community. You got to win. People don't know that every time there's a game there's a loser. The wife can't even go to the store if you don't win."

Indeed, a coach's wife has a lot in common with a preacher's wife. Mary Jo McCracken, wife of the late Indiana University coach, Branch McCracken, recalled her awakening to writer Ray Marquette. "When Mac and I were first engaged, my father called me into his office one day and asked me point-blank what qualifications I had to be a good coach's wife. He told me that the university had a fine young basketball coach and he didn't want his career to be impaired. So we sat there for four hours and discussed how I could help Mac in his profession. I honestly believe that my father was more interested in Mac's future than he was in his daughter's ability to be a wife."

Coaches dread the day the son of the principal or superintendent tries out for the team, but even more harrowing can be the debut of the coaches' own progeny. "They booed our son one year," says Susan Held, wife of Anderson High Coach Norm Held. "I'll never forget that, although my son says he never heard it. I couldn't believe people would do such a thing. The year before, he had made the winning basket in the regional. It really bothered me."

A good coach can mean a great deal to a teenager. Coaches get a chance to make difficult things fun, to dramatize the value of cooperation, to attack self-doubt. The mere act of unlocking the gym early in the morning or late at night or in the summer can mean worlds, especially to poor kids. "I've fed my players, bought them clothes, put teeth in their heads," says Howard Sharpe. "I'd give 'em my own money, tell 'em, go buy shirts and socks. Some of 'em could buy and sell me now."

The ones who go to college come back at Christmas to show off boyfriends or girlfriends, and then, later, some settle down in town and lend their voices to the chorus in the bleachers. Coaches come home to cold meals and roll stiffly into bed, having offered up their own aging bodies for teenagers to slam up against in practice. When observers portray community high school basketball as the last breath of fresh air left in the game, it is here, in the bond between good, caring coaches and their players, that the observation seems most true.

★ ★ ★

Skip Collins is in the beginning of his annual worst day of the year. He looks it, too, bleary-eyed, pale, unkempt. Twelve hours ago his Valparaiso Vikings lost the opening game of their regional and were eliminated from the tourney. A couple of key calls went against him down the stretch, to his mind fouls that went whistled. He has been up most of the night with his distraught players.

At 9:00 AM, having already finished his morning radio show, he appears for coffee at the local Big Boy. The shades are drawn and Collins is wearing sunglasses, but still the sun seems to hurt his eyes. A teacher of English literature, Skip Collins is melancholy this morning. He speaks softly.

"I've just finished my twentieth year as a head high school basketball coach, and that's all I've ever done," he says. "Every one of those twenty years, I lost my last game. I've spent a morning like this every year for the last twenty years, feeling sorry for myself, knowing that I was cheated badly the night before and so on. I feel miserable. I feel like anyone who has spent twelve months working for something and I had a chance at it and the chance didn't work out. It's an empty feeling.

"It's very hard to accept. Every year I sit down and decide whether I want to start over again. This wouldn't be a good time to make a decision, not after the last game. I always plan to quit after the last game. I think, 'Hey, this is crazy,' they need someone younger to do this, I want to go into the shoe business, I can't stand this anymore. So far every year I've been crazy enough to try it again. You may know intellectually that to put so much of your life and happiness into a game is a little nutty, and yet you do it anyway."

His coffee arrives, but he doesn't seem to notice. "I'm 41 years old, and I always thought I would coach till I was 60, but that's not true any longer. Most people don't realize the time that goes into it. Running on the track at 6:30 AM, starting in September, nights full of films and scouting. I spend most of my summers in camp work, trying to make enough money to afford to be a teacher. I make about $4,000 to coach. Financially, it's not a very good deal. I guess I'd do it for nothing."

He is asked about the future, maybe as a college coach. He offers a familiar perspective. "The small Indiana schools would probably be a step down. I have better facilities here. I suppose there are some semi-major schools who would consider someone with no college experience for a head coaching job, but most college coaches wouldn't want a 41-year-old assistant. They want someone who is 25 and looks good in a paisley shirt and with a good tan. I'm kind of between a rock and a hard place."

Asked what he'll do if he decides not to return for a twenty-first year, Skip Collins stirs his stone-cold coffee absently. "If I had enough financial backing, I think I'd like to write. I'd put down a combination of observations and fictional things that roll around in my head. I have a lot of crazy ideas. I would enjoy that."

One official's call sticks in his head. Late in the game the ball was slapped away from a Viking right in front of Collins, who is certain his player was whacked on the forearm. "I never berate the officials," he says, perhaps reevaluating this policy. "I never swear at them or anything, but I was just in anguish that they weren't better than they were last night. It's like, you might spend your whole life learning to play the piano and go to a concert and begin to play and find that one of the three judges has a great ear but the other two have gone tone deaf but they are going to judge you anyway."

Collins gets up to go. Unfortunately, he has rounds today. As he passes out of the restaurant, two geriatric women, waiting on a bench to be seated, follow him with their eyes out into the parking lot. "Isn't that Skip Collins?" one of them asks. "He looks sad." "Yes, who could blame him?" replies the other. "I thought Valpo could beat Michigan City for sure." They fall silent for a moment, then the first brightens. "Well," she says, "I guess we're not going to the game tonight . . . want to go into Chicago?"

✶   ✶   ✶

On a Wednesday night in November, about a thousand fans are in the Warren Central High School gym for the early season clash between the Warren Central Lady Warriors and the Rushville Lady Lions. Nearly half the fans have come from Rushville, thirty-five miles away, many traveling in a caravan of school buses. Elderly ladies are decked out in Rushville red, and men who clearly will discuss this game together somewhere tomorrow over coffee have come to enjoy the familiar pleasure of referee baiting. Guys in varsity sweaters shoulder each other in the top rows of both sides; girls band together in the rows behind the benches, a surprising number of them keeping statistics.

This is the first game of the season for both teams. Warren Central is ranked seventeenth statewide, mainly because of their 6'5" center Linda Godby, whose name appeared on many preseason all-American teams and who is an early favorite for "Miss Basketball.": Rushville, a perennial contender for the state championship, is this year unranked and rebuilding.

This game will pose an unprecedented challenge to coaches Cinda Brown of Rushville and Sue Parrish of Warren Central. Both are vocal and active veteran coaches, and the National Federation of Sports has just passed the "bench de-corum" rule, which requires all coaches to remain on the bench while the game is in session "except for spontaneous outbursts of enthusiasm."

The rule is bitterly opposed as an unnecessary restraint and an impediment to communication with players by almost all coaches in Indiana. The Indiana coaches' association has discussed symbolic protests ranging from having ev-eryone coach in wheelchairs—to symbolize their crippling—to having everyone stand up and get a technical on one wildcat Friday night. "I'm afraid there's gonna be violence," Howard Sharpe has said.

After the national anthem, Rushville's scrambling young guards harass War-ren Central's ball handlers into an early series of mistakes. Parrish, who has a strident, intimidating style as a coach, is beside herself, red-faced, screaming to catch the attention of her players, who, in the heat of battle, have already forgotten to look toward the bench with each change of possession, as was the plan. Every part of Parrish but her very bottom is out of her chair.

As Rushville takes a slim lead into the locker room, the lobby fills with pop-corn eaters, mainly kids in jeans and down vests and ball jackets. No spike haircuts here. Five girls from Rushville, pals, are among the contingent that follows the Lady Lions on the road. Rushville's girls' team actually outdraws the boys'. The main reason is that they rarely lose. Cinda Brown's teams have won seven out of every eight games played during her nine years at Rushville.

Between handfuls of popcorn, the girls are eager to talk hoops. Asked if they have any particular heroes, several answer at once. "Steve Alford," they say. What do they like about him? "His legs," comes the chorus.

As play resumes, it is clear that Parrish has made adjustments. Linda Godby's cuts toward the ball are more direct and the Warren Central guards more

Rushville coach Cinda Brown pours her heart and soul into her
Lady Lions, even if it means testing the "bench decorum rule."
Courtesy of Indiana Basketball Hall of Fame.

creative in getting the ball to her. Warren Central overtakes Rushville and begins to pull away. Midway through the third quarter, Cinda Brown leaps from her chair to scream for the attention of one of her players. It is a reflex formed of many years' coaching. The referee's hands form a T, for a technical foul, as Brown, chagrined, finds her seat. Her lips form the word "damn."

Both coaches, as it happens, are seated in chairs with casters, like office chairs, which allow them to roll. As Rushville's plight deepens, Cinda Brown begins, quite unconsciously, she says later, to roll closer to her players. When she crosses onto the floor for the first time, the girl seated next to her grabs the back of the chair and drags her back. Brown, intent, appears not to notice. This happens all the rest of the game, players hauling their coach back from another technical. Rushville succeeds at this, but Warren Central rolls to an easy win. As they walk slowly to their locker room, the Rushville girls are blinking back tears.

The girls' basketball program has made great strides forward in the eleven years since the admission of girls' teams to the IHSAA. Girls now have equal access to good equipment and, in most cases, to practice gyms. Girls' coaches earn as much as boys' coaches. The stigma against girl athletes seems almost to have disappeared. While Sue Parrish chafed under the slurs and taunts of the day, her young star Linda Godby says, as if the thought is new to her, "The boys don't put us down at all. They support us."

Likewise, while an athletic scholarship was a fantasy for Sue Parrish, a tall and gifted athlete, Linda Godby has been contacted by nearly a hundred colleges. Some observers say it won't be long before a school like Rushville features the girls instead of the boys on Friday nights.

But as the girls' program advances, Cinda Brown and Sue Parrish, women coaching girls' basketball teams, are increasingly rare. Eleven years ago, when the girls' program started, only about 5 percent of all coaches of girls' teams were men. Today that figure is about 73 percent, and—more troublesome to women coaches—the percentage of male coaches has risen in each of the eleven years. Most women in the field originally conceded the need for men to coach technique until women learned to coach—as Sue Parrish puts it, "How were you going to teach girls how to shoot a reverse layup if you'd never shot one yourself?"—but had assumed that the first generation of men would yield to the educated women.

It hasn't worked out that way. Indeed, men, eager to get started in coaching and better qualified at that time than women, filled the scores of new coaching jobs. "It was the only position available, and I was trying to get into the coaching profession," says Bill Keller, a former star player and now a men's coach at a small Indiana college. "Why wouldn't I take it? It was a lot of fun. It gave me a real appreciation for girls' basketball."

But a decade later the jobs are still held by men, and women are getting out. "Coaching is too big a deal in Indiana for men to give up," says Parrish. "Nobody's quitting. So all you have is retirees. Now we see some women coming back [from college programs], but are you going to fire men to give these women a job?"

There may be other reasons. "The boys' program has become so intense that I know a lot of coaches who have become physically ill," says Judi Warren, the first girl heroine as a player and now a high school coach. "It drains 'em, they have to put so much into it. I've heard a lot of men say coaching girls is more enjoyable, that girls are more receptive and eager to learn. They give you feedback, they praise you. If the guys are in this to help our program, I have no complaint. But if they're just taking over a job because it's something to do, and they see it as a step down, that upsets me."

"Most of the women who are in it are single," says Cinda Brown, whose two stepchildren are grown. "It's so demanding, I don't see how anyone could be a coach and raise kids." "Who's going to take care of the kids?" asks Parrish, who describes herself as "unmarried and the mother of twelve." "How many husbands are going to stay home on Saturday for three and a half hours taking care of kids while Mom's coaching?" Parrish's voice is rising to a bench level. "How many men will put the meals on the table, pick the kids up from the babysitter and get all that ready by the time Mom comes home after practice?"

Well, at least one. Jim Rosenberg does well with macaroni and cheese and fried chicken, but his pièce de résistance is scalloped potatoes. "It's not out of the box, either," boasts his wife, Sharon, coach of the Carmel High School Lady Greyhounds.

Sharon and Jim Rosenberg are the parents of one son, Brian, 4. Now in her tenth year as a head coach, Sharon thought about getting out the year Brian was born. But like so many Hoosiers, she loved coaching basketball, and she is good at it, having won about 60 percent of her games at Carmel. After a long search, the Rosenbergs found a daycare provider who could keep Brian till 6:00, and Sharon went back to the bench.

Jim is a restaurateur who is able to arrange somewhat flexible work hours. In a typical week during the season, there are at least two evening games, one night of scouting, and several practices. Sharon takes Brian with her on scouting trips. "He loves it," she says. "He's good for about a half, but that's long enough for me to learn the other teams' patterns."

Meals are the biggest headache. The Rosenbergs try to have a family dinner at least two nights a week. Sharon prepares two or three meals for the week on Sundays and then leaves notes for Jim, who often has dinner waiting on the table when she comes home from practice. "We don't even own a microwave," she says proudly.

"The key is your husband," says Sharon Rosenberg. "Their hours, their patience. Except for having to hear all my frustrations, Jim's happy I'm doin' it. He helps out any way he can. If I practice till 7:00, he'll wait until 8:00 to go in. In the heat of the season it gets hectic. All your holidays are taken up with practices. It's tough trying to be supermom, making sure Brian gets to the zoo. We love him and we feel guilty that we're denying him things."

"There are a bunch of women getting out of coaching," she says. "A man can pack up the family. A woman can't say, 'Oh, honey, I've got a job in Evansville.' Women are being replaced by men. For one thing, I think fathers feel girls respond better to a man. They think men give more discipline. It's always the dads who are in here yellin' after the little girl goes home cryin'. The dads are always in your face, especially the ones who played ball."

Men and women agree that coaching high school girls is completely different from coaching high school boys. "Girls are so emotional," says Judi Warren. "If they've had a spat with their boyfriend just before the game, they're gone for the game. The hardest thing to do in girls' basketball is to keep 'em steady.

"A lot of times a coach really needs to be close to the players. The community won't always accept a guy coach givin' a girl a big hug or smackin' 'em on the butt. I'm not sure a girl would be as open with a guy in talking about personal things as my players would with me. Part of coaching is getting kids ready for society, getting them ready mentally and emotionally."

"Three of my starters were sobbing tonight," says Cinda Brown, "not crying, sobbing tears. They don't handle criticism nearly as well, but they work harder. Big macho guys, nobody can tell them what to do, but girls are ready to do anything you tell them to. I can't remember ever having to tell a player not to shoot so much, I have to tell them to shoot. They emphasize teamwork. They don't care who scores the points, they want to win."

"If you had two guys that didn't like each other," says Parrish, "they're gonna go in the locker room and cuss each other out and more than likely belt each other. Then they'll go out on the floor and pass the ball to each other. But it's just not normal for 14- to 18-year-old girls to confront the people who are causing them problems."

And there's makeup. "They want to know in the morning if we're gonna sweat and how much," says Sharon Rosenberg. "They need to gauge their time for makeup. They're basic Max Factor girls; a base and some blush, mascara and eye shadow. It's water-base; you'll look down during a workout and see white stuff on their sweats."

Judi Warren agrees that matters such as makeup can be a pain, but not as big a pain as the stresses that go with an all-consuming pressure to win. "I'm afraid it's going to change," she says. "I'm afraid that girls' basketball is going to become like the guys'. In a way, I hate to see it. It's getting hard-nosed and very disciplined. In a way, I like that, and in a way, there are some things I'd like to keep for ourselves, the emotions, the femininity."

★ ★ ★

Seventy boys and girls, second- and third-graders, watch the old man. Eyes bright, faces upturned, they listen intently. "Now, pay attention," he says. "Here's the way we do it. Come out on the floor right now and get in a circle around one of the players." Howard Sharpe has all twelve of his North Knox High varsity players out at nine on a Saturday morning to work with the kids. "Now pay attention to Mark Dillon here, Mark's gonna loosen you up." Dillon, a 6'3" junior center, leads the children through some stretching exercises.

"Now. First group, come up to the center. Okay, I want you to dribble the ball around the cone in the center. Okay? Now, you don't slap the ball, you push it. Push. Push. Push. Push." A yellow-haired girl in a red leotard steers the ball around, sometimes with two hands, while Sharpe and his players shout encouragement. Then the kids try to push two balls at once, and then while crawling on their knees, changing hands if they can. "Push. Push. Push. Push," Sharpe says, following them around the cone. When they finish he pats them on the head. "Oh, you're doin' better all the time," he says to one beaming child. "Look how you've got better since last Saturday, even."

An hour later, fourth- and fifth-graders take the court, followed an hour later by fifth- and sixth-graders. At noon, Howard Sharpe starts off for home.

Each day Sharpe, 70, commutes 104 miles to North Knox High from his home outside Terre Haute. He drives alone, often in winter darkness along a hilly two-lane road, morning and night, and back in to work with the little kids on weekends. It is a regimen that would break many younger men, but no one alive could know what it means. For Howard Sharpe is really driving a road of his own. There is only one car ahead, and it is getting bigger every day in his headlights.

Howard Sharpe gets one win closer to the all-time record.
Courtesy of Bob Williams.

Sharpe is closing in on a legend. On a Sunday morning in November 1985, he had won 717 games as an Indiana high school coach, or, as he puts it, "My kids have won 717 and I've lost 327." That's seventeen games shy of the all-time Hoosier high school win record, set between 1931 and 1967 by the late Marion Crawley, mainly at Lafayette Jefferson High School.

Except as master coaches, Crawley and Sharpe couldn't have been less alike. Crawley, who died in 1982, was a model of self-control. "Just by his presence on the bench, Crawley was one of the game's biggest intimidators," referee Don McBride has said. "He didn't have to do or say anything to get your attention."

The vintage Sharpe was a shrewd, driven, combative man, a man who paced the sidelines baiting referees, probing for any angle, arousing and orchestrating the passions of everyone in the gym. "You think Bobby Knight is wild," Sharpe chuckles, "he's a pussycat compared to me before I finally grew up."

Sharpe is a short, compact man, given to suspenders in his few leisure hours. He has a precise, absorptive mind and a phenomenal memory for statistical detail. One of his many inventions is still bringing in royalties. When, at the county fair, you toss a basketball at a rim that seems too small and which offers no backboard against which to gauge distance, you are probably surrendering quarters to the "Sharpie."

He grew up in a rough town in rough times. "I bought my first set of sneakers at Seventh and Broadway in Gary, sixty-two years ago," he says. "I started high school in 1929. There was nothin' to do in the Depression but play. I didn't get this flat nose from watchin' TV." His heroes were his coaches, strong men who in turn made him want to coach. He worked his way through Indiana State Teachers College and coached at three small rural schools before settling for forty years at Terre Haute Gerstmeyer—later renamed Terre Haute North—and now North Knox.

In part, Sharpe's daily journey is a quest for personal redemption. While Crawley won four state titles, Sharpe's marvelous Gerstmeyer teams, four of which made it to the state finals, never won. In fact, Sharpe is best known in Hoosierland for a game his team lost. It is not enough to say that it was a one-point, last-shot loss in the only chance he ever had, or probably ever will have, for the brass ring. You have to know what happened.

In 1953, three members of Sharpe's Gerstmeyer starting five were members of the same family. There were the identical twins, Harley and Arley Andrews, and their younger uncle, Harold. Sharpe made it even more confusing. He gave Arley number 34 and Harley number 43. Angler that he was, Sharpe was forever accused of changing their jerseys at halftime to protect whichever twin was in foul trouble.

Until the final game, Gerstmeyer had had only one real scare on the tournament trail. They fell behind against Evansville Central by sixteen at the half in the semistate. Fans in Indianapolis received the premature announcement of a great upset, something along the lines of Dewey licking Truman.

After delivering a crash course on defensive positioning, Sharpe, wrought up, marched out of the dressing room to begin the second half. Harley caught his elbow. "Coach," he said, "you're gettin' too excited. We're only eight shots behind." Then he went out and made 5 long shots in a row, turning the tide.

Early in the game for the state championship, against South Bend Central at Butler Fieldhouse, a foul was whistled against Harley. The official flashed the hand signal four-three, four-three, but the scorer mistakenly assigned it to Arley, number 34. Sharpe noticed the error and protested furiously, but they would not change it. Saddled with an extra foul, Arley—the team's best shooter—sat out much of the third quarter and fouled out with only twenty-eight seconds gone in the fourth quarter.

Still, they had a chance. South Bend Central led 42–41 with seventeen seconds left. Gerstmeyer forced a turnover. "In those years," recalls Sharpe, the words coming slowly, because this is a memory with some genuine pain left, "the clock still ran on a violation. So we ran over to get the ball and they rolled the damn ball clear across the court. We threw it in and got a shot at it with four seconds left to go."

Indianapolis sportswriter Bob Williams described those four seconds. "If one watches the film [of that game] carefully, a small man is standing in front of the Gerstmeyer bench. He watches the ball, leans with it, almost begging it to score. The shot hits the back of the flange and pops away. The man immediately throws his hands to his head. It is basketball agony at its most painful."

"Well, my God, that's what I lived for," says Sharpe, his eyes wide. "I've tried all these years to win it, that's been the goal. My God, it almost killed me. It's been the most disappointing thing in my life." He is silent for a while, and then he brightens. "I guess it wasn't meant to be," he says. "Actually, people have treated me nicer for it than if I would have won."

In 1982 the Vigo County school board forced Sharpe, then 66, to resign his coaching position of forty years. Former players poured into Terre Haute to battle for their coach, but they couldn't save him. Thirty wins behind Crawley, it looked like the end had come. Months later he was fighting for his life in double-bypass heart surgery.

But someone seemed to be looking after Sharpe. He survived that operation and, later, another. One day the phone rang. It was the athletic director of North Knox High School, fifty-two miles away, wondering if he'd consider coaching their basketball team as a lay coach, without pay, and teaching the region's children how to play. He had his teacher's pension and Social Security, money didn't matter. "They gave me the title 'Athletic Coordinator/Basketball Coach,'" laughs Sharpe. This, in Indiana, is like "Altar Boy/Pope."

So Sharpe set out after Crawley again. North Knox is a typical Indiana school with an enrollment of 558 students, a gym that holds 4,400 and some very rabid fans. Sharpe's young team won only three games the first year. There was grumbling. They thought the old man was supposed to know something. Then, last year, he went 10–10, lost the sectional in an overtime and calmed most of his detractors. Now he's junior-loaded and optimistic.

"I got nice kids," he says, "good kids." He begins to tick them off on his thick fingers. "The one big one is a year behind in development, not a blue chipper, but I'll send him to some college, get him part of his education. Then I got a scrambler, shoots every time he can see it. I tell him sometimes I'm going to wring his arm. Another kid, his biggest trouble is himself. He gets down on himself. He's one of those guys who always wants to fake, drive, and take a jump shot. Then I have a real nice kid. They own all the orchards down here. About 6'2", good student, a pretty good team player. Then I have a kid, a real screwball, has a crazy shot. I got a left-handed kid, throws watermelons all summer. He plays better when I let him sit awhile."

He is asked how coaching Indiana kids has changed in a half-century. "Used to be," he says, "you were the leader of your community if your son played on the basketball team. Now, kids'll come up to me and say, I've got better things to do, they'll drop out. Well, that's fine with me. 'Cause when I walk across that line to practice, that floor is sacred."

Maybe there is no one left who can understand what Friday night means to Howard Sharpe. "This is not just a game to me," he explains, his voice filled with emotion, "it's a science. You see, I've got to have the ball 1,460 times a season, with .885 points per possession, or I'm not even in it." Sensing that he is losing his guest, he leans back. "Ah, it's like bakin' a cake," he says, smiling. "You put so much flour in and so much sugar in. Well, you got to put so much rebounding in. . ."

Had he been born a century and a half later, Abraham Lincoln, who grew up a county or two away in southern Indiana, might well have wanted to play for Howard Sharpe. At 6'4" and 180 pounds, smart and strong, Lincoln almost certainly would have made the North Knox varsity basketball team, probably sending Mark Dillon to the bench.

Like all of Sharpe's players, Lincoln's hair would have been cropped neatly. He would have handed the ball to the referee with a polite "Thank you." He would have learned that there is only one way to shoot a free throw, with your index finger on the valve stem. A pouting expression would have meant the bench. And Sharpe almost certainly could have got the kid a scholarship somewhere, maybe at ISD.

"I'd sure be willing to take seventeen and tie him this year," says Sharpe, his thoughts returning to Crawley. "But I can't because God didn't give me the ability. I'll get a dozen."

He is asked how much the record means to him. In an age where others pursuing records drone on about playin' 'em one game at a time, Howard Sharpe is a breath of fresh air. "Wouldn't you want it?" he demands. "Wouldn't you want to be mentioned with the best?" He describes how it feels to walk into a high school gym on Friday night, game night, his night: "Practically everyone in that gym last night came up and shook my hand and treated me with respect. I'm supposed to be a legend. They say there's none better. I like that, wouldn't you?"

★　★　★

A 1984 drive from French Lick to Indianapolis starts with a stop at Sunoco, where a fill-up gets you a copy of *Bob Knight's Basketball Tips*. Just south of Bedford, radio station WFPC reports that "Bob Knight wearing gray slacks, a white, open-collared shirt and the traditional red sweater," had been the very special guest of the Pike County Chamber of Commerce just the evening before.

The "It's Knight Time" bumper stickers thin out north of Bloomington, around Martinsville, but Knight himself surfaces on WIBC in Indianapolis to state flatly that he'd really rather drive a Buick. Likes the way it handles. Something in his voice says that if you're dumb enough not to at least test-drive it, well, there's nothing he can do to help you.

Not since Alfred Kinsey opened the Institute for Sex Research on the Bloomington campus, causing parents to send their kids to Purdue and Ball State and ISU instead, has anybody created so much attention at Indiana University as Bob Knight. Asked by *Playboy* magazine if he ever thought about running for political office, Knight replied, perhaps hinting, that he'd prefer to be appointed Senator.

One reason for his grip on Hoosierland is that his basketball teams win. Indiana has won two national championships in Knight's fourteen seasons as head coach, and an injury kept the Hoosiers from what probably would have been another. Even in the seasons when Indiana University does not have a national powerhouse, Knight's teams, stocked mainly with kids from Midwestern towns, seem to overachieve. His best teams are seamless units of unselfish athletes, inspired players who very obviously value the team above themselves.

Another reason is that his explosive temper keeps Hoosiers on their toes. The cable now delivers the IU games to a statewide audience. Cameras focus obsessively on him, alert for a violent or theatrical reaction to an official's call or a close-up of a player's face as Knight chews him out. With luck, an object might go by, or Knight might snatch a fistful of a player's jersey and draw his face close. It's like watching the Indianapolis 500: get up for a beer and you might miss a spin.

Knight has turned Indiana into his stage. His antics have polarized Hoosiers. You're for him or against him, but you can't ignore him. "Now, I'm a Bobby Knight man, don't get me wrong" is a common Hoosier' prelude. Hoosiers ap-

Indiana University men's coach Bob Knight pulls guard DelRay Brooks
to the sideline for instruction. *Courtesy of John Terhune.*

plaud him for insisting that his players succeed academically and for decrying
the moral slime of big-time college sports. They are prayerfully grateful to
him for restoring Indiana basketball to national prominence after a period of
decline.

Still others wince as they watch Knight loom over a seated kid, flanks shaking like a great bear, ripping into him as the boy looks away. Tension builds around the screen: I'd never let my kid play for him, someone'll say. I wouldn't hold my breath until Knight comes after your kid, comes the reply. Rimshot. One thing's for sure: nobody would like to be the kid on the screen.

Knight has become the State Dad. An IU game has become a referendum on discipline, a debate on corporal punishment. Indiana families gather in the den for the games, often bickering in front of the set when Knight explodes, hawks versus doves, bleeding hearts against hard-liners, positions calcifying as the season wears on.

Knight cultivates a master/warrior relationship with his players, creating a militant world in which a coach is necessary to make players be all that they can be. A team is an elusive, half-mystical connection of undefeatable individuals, an organism that changes shape and density to accommodate any challenge.

Indiana University practice sessions, which are closed to the press and public, are presumed to be a form of boot camp, a place where Special Forces are trained. Not all recruits can take it; more than a few have dropped out. "Veteran players did a good job of preparing me," says Steve Alford, Knight's current star, "like what to expect and how many practices there would be. But I don't think you actually realize what it's like until you go through it. He brings the most out of you as a player and as an individual. He's not going to tell you a whole lot, you just have to understand what he wants to get done."

Not surprisingly, Knight came to Indiana from West Point. In 1971, after fielding a series of unyielding defensive teams for the Army, Knight decided to move on if the right opportunity came. Indiana hired him in the wake of a near-mutinous turmoil with racial overtones. They needed a disciplinarian.

The beginning was rocky. Trustees, alumni, players, and fans had come to identify Indiana University basketball with Branch McCracken's high-scoring pack of thoroughbreds. McCracken had believed that part of his team's duty was to entertain the fans. Win or lose, IU fans were usually chanting "we want a hundred" at the end of the game. It was a source of statewide pride.

By contrast, Knight gave them probing, patient opportunists, content to pass the ball and cut and screen until they could create a likely shot. Knight dismisses the tension, saying, "I just said, this is the way we're gonna play, and that's the way we played." But for a few weeks Hoosierland was in turmoil.

They lost their first four conference games, and the crowds booed. "I saw the first conference game he ever played at Indiana," recalls former IHSAA Commissioner Phil Eskew. "Some guy stood up behind me and said, "Can't we just have one fast break?" At the end of one game, with the score 59–40, fans started chanting, "We want a hundred."

But Knight turned it around. Indiana won nine of its last ten games and went to the National Invitational Tournament. In 1975 and 1976, Knight built beautiful teams, consisting of strong individuals who shared a common vision of excellence, his vision.

The success of those teams and the power of their coach revolutionized the high school game in Indiana. It's a high-tech, slow-paced, half-court game now in Indiana high schools. Knight and his assistants fan out each summer into a network of camps and clinics, briefing high school coaches on optimal screening angles, offensive rotations, and help-side, man-to-man defense.

High school coaches most often describe Knight as a fraternal man, a man who returns calls, makes his assistant coaches available, helps personally if asked. Like fans and parents, some feel ambivalent about his approach to discipline. "I don't like his aggressiveness toward players," says Carmel girls' coach Sharon Rosenberg. "But he keeps them working and gives them a cause. He creates discipline. There is no woman to compare him to."

"I've heard coaches say, 'Well, I wouldn't let one of my players play for Bobby Knight,'" says Bob Collins, sports editor of the *Indianapolis Star.* "But when Bobby Knight knocks—"

The 1984–85 year was especially eventful for Knight. He led the Olympic team to an easy victory, but the Ultimate Conflict didn't materialize. The Russians chickened out. He challenged them to a game anytime, anywhere, but the goad got lost in a vast Siberian silence. Then his Indiana team went into a deep tailspin. He tried all sorts of things to pull them out. Once he started all freshman; later he kicked a starter off the team for missing classes.

The crash came during a game against Purdue, when, enraged by a referee's call, Knight hurled a chair onto the court. "I was going up to the free-throw line and a chair went by," said Purdue guard Steve Reid. "I didn't know what to do."

Neither did anyone else. Assembly hall was riotous. The state was apoplectic. Supporters and detractors flooded the newspapers with letters. Lapsed IU fans declared on all-night talk shows their intention to defect to Purdue. Hardliners closed rank behind him. "Like General Patton in World War II, Knight knows how to shape boys into men and naturally this bothers all the people who would like men to be wimps asaend sissies," wrote a woman in the *Indianapolis Star.* "They would prefer someone more like Alan Alda, who is sensitive, caring, supporting and vulnerable. Sorry, wimps."

Sensing a heroic opportunity, a legislator from Elkhart trumpeted his intention to introduce a resolution in the Indiana House condemning Knight's conduct. A volley of hate mail from as far away as Texas sent him diving for cover.

Hoosiers reacted as strongly to the punishment as to the crime. Knight—the disciplinarian—got away with a one game suspension and a coy little apology, which he turned into another broadside at the referees. Later he skipped the Big Ten coaches' meeting, offering the explanation that he had been quail-hunting.

"I thought he had matured tremendously until last season," says Collins. "He kept divin' into empty swimming pools. There's no excuse for some of the things he does. He seems determined not to let people see him the way he really is. If the people who dislike him the most could, see the Bobby Knight that other people see, I wouldn't say they'd like him, but I think they'd be more tolerant and not so derogatory."

For Hoosiers, the event was an occasion for self-examination: it was embarrassing. As *Indianapolis Star* writer John Shaughnessy put it, "Does it ever seem to you that we take Knight too seriously?"

★　★　★

I've been trying to interview Bob Knight for a year, placing dozens of calls and messages to his assistant, Mary Ann Davis. She finally relays the word that he'll see me at Williams Arena in Minneapolis after the 1984 US Olympic basketball team, which Knight is coaching, has finished practice. BUT . . . under no circumstance am I to watch the Olympians practice. I must sequester myself somewhere out of sight of the court and wait to be summoned. I can't peek: I'm on the honor system. Don't worry . . . someone will find me. And sure enough, on the appointed day, team trainer Tim Garl climbs to the arena's upper reaches to fetch me and leads me down to the courtside bench where Knight is seated, his back growing bigger with every step. Garl mumbles my name to Knight and vanishes.

I sit down beside Knight and introduce myself. He does not reply. He stares straight ahead. No handshake is offered and no eye contact is established. I plant a tape recorder on the bench between us and click it to a start. He continues to fix his unblinking attention on something in front of him, maybe a spot on the floor. He is a huge man with a whitening mane and a hulking posture. His voice, when he finally uses it, is forceful and direct.

It is soon clear that this is going to be a lecture on Indiana basketball, not a conversation. He cuts off my questions as soon as he feels he has grasped their intent, and answers with speeches that end abruptly, almost leaving holes in the air. Players, hair still beaded from showering, walk by. Knight hails them, artfully interrupting my questions. Or he controls the interview's tempo by shouting at his son, who is absent-mindedly shooting at an empty basket, to get him a Dr. Pepper, *goddamnit.*

He seems to grade my questions. There are no A's—probably A's are unattainable—but the ones that allow him to demonstrate his impressive knowledge of the history of high school basketball in Indiana might draw a B–/C+. Even though Knight grew up in Ohio, he still can tell you where Bobby Plump was when he hit the shot for Milan, the score when he hit it, and how long he held the ball. He says he can even remember the first time he heard Indiana high school basketball was special. "A friend of mine named Wilbur Burkey who coached at Smithville, Ohio, had, seen Crispus Attucks High School play. He told me that Oscar Robertson might have been the best basketball player he had ever seen. That was in 1956."

It is a common belief in Indiana's dens and rec rooms and bars that Bobby Knight is the one man who can win without a preponderance of black players. I've heard this dozens of times during the year I've been interviewing Hoosiers about basketball. I decide to ask him what he thinks. Deck guns come swiveling around. "What a bullshit question," he says. "Anyone can play basketball, black, white, blue, or green. You can think of a better question than that."

I try. Asked if the Indiana High School Tournament has an NCAA feel to it, one that gives a native Hoosier player an advantage in post-season college play Knight rises, looking around for someone with whom to share this priceless moment. "Boy," he says, beseeching palms raised to the heavens, "you goddamn writers come up with more *euphemisms* and more phrases that you try to attach to things, it's un-goddamn-believable." With the adversary clearly in disarray, he makes eye contact for the first time.

"I gotta go," he says. "Did you get everything you needed?"

. . . .

I remember sitting on a bench with my father when he was a high school coach at Monroe County when I was three and since then I can't remember a day in my life that I haven't picked up a basketball.

Steve Alford, 1984

Basically, he owns all of Indiana.

IU teammate Dan Dakich

12

STEVE ALFORD

All In

• •

"I'VE GOT THE MOST UNUSUAL STEVE ALFORD STORY THAT YOU'VE EVER heard," says Norm Held, coach of the Anderson Indians. "We had a game here in the Wigwam against New Castle. We're one point ahead with five seconds to play, and Alford gets fouled. He has two shots. We call time out to let him think about the first one. We really weren't letting him think about it 'cause you know he's gonna make it. Actually, we were worrying about how to score when we got the ball again.

"So we go back out there and he *missed* the first one. So we call another time out. We were thinking about the overtime. We went out again and he missed another one. He probably can't remember a game in his life when he missed two free throws in a row. Mike Chappel, who writes for the newspaper, had the best line the next morning. He wrote, 'Well, I'd 'a lost my farm, how about you?'"

Shaking his head, Steve Alford confirms the story. "That's the only time I've ever missed two in a row in a game. The first one hit the back of the rim and the second one was in and out. I don't know what happened. . . . At first I was shocked, and then I got very upset. I told Coach (his father, Sam Alford) I was going to stay in the gym all night and shoot free throws."

Steve Alford is known to basketball fans throughout America as the star of Bobby Knight's Indiana University basketball team and throughout the world as the youngest member of the 1984 US Olympic basketball team. But he became an immortal in Indiana as a high school player.

In his senior year, Steve averaged over thirty-seven points per game and was named the outstanding player in the state. Always double- and triple-teamed, he hit over 60 percent of his field goals and 94.4 percent of his free throws. In that year he was the best free-throw shooter on planet Earth—high school, college, or pro.

For connoisseurs, the Steve Alford game came in the semistate round of the state tourney in his senior year. Against a physical team from Indianapolis Broad Ripple, Steve drove again and again toward the hoop, stopped, spun away, and faked his jump shot. Bodies rocketed into the air, fingers splayed, ready to slam the ball into Illinois. As the first defenders came down on him he floated shot after shot through the hoop, got up, and walked to the free-throw line.

He shot twenty-five free throws that game. They all went in. Only one nicked the rim in passing through. When all was done, he had scored fifty-seven points, the most ever in an Indiana tournament game. At the beginning of the game, people were talking "Mr. Basketball," in itself a form of sainthood. When they flicked their sets off, he was sitting at the head table, dining with the likes of Oscar, McGinnis, Mount, and Bird.

★   ★   ★

As he describes his elder son's early childhood, a tone of wonderment is present in Sam Alford's voice. "He started sitting on the bench with me when he was three. From then until he graduated from high school, he only missed two of my games—one to go to a free-throw shooting contest in Kansas City with his mother and once when he had chicken pox."

Sam Alford, 42, the head coach of the New Castle Trojans, has been coaching high school players in Indiana more than half his lifetime. Here in the Vienna of basketball, it is easy to imagine him as the father of a musical prodigy, describing perhaps the first time he heard a scale creep from his infant son's fingers on the drawing room piano.

"He learned to count by watching the scoreboards," Sam says. "He used to sit on the bench with me, holding a clipboard and a piece of paper. Every time

Steve Alford drives for 2 of his 57 points against Indianapolis Broad Ripple in the 1983 tourney's semi-state round. *Courtesy of Frank H. Fisse.*

Mr. Basketball, 1983: sainthood, Hoosier style. *Courtesy of Frank H. Fisse.*

the scoreboard would change he'd draw a line through the old numbers and write down the new ones."

And it was never hard to shop for Steve. "He never asked us for a gun or a holster. He never wanted to play cowboys. He always used to throw blocks at Tinkertoy cans and shoot Ping-Pong balls at bowls and glasses. I never had to force basketball on him," says Sam, almost apologetically.

Unlike the urban players whose game evolves in Darwinian playground competition, Steve Alford developed his skills in isolation. The New Castle gym was his monastery. He purged his game of imperfections each day in exacting private sessions that lasted long after regular basketball practice. A missed free throw warranted an act of mortification, namely twenty-five fingertip pushups. Each summer when the Alfords went to Florida for a week or two, the basketball went along. They looked for motels with basketball courts.

"He punished himself," says Sam Alford. "On the court in our driveway other kids would come in for a bottle of pop between games. Steve would rest by shooting free throws." When they heard the ball thumping at midnight, the Alfords knew Steve couldn't sleep. He allowed no one to interrupt his private sessions. "When I am working out individually, I don't want a girlfriend, I don't want a mom, I don't want a dad, I don't want anybody to bother me, and if they do I get very nasty and upset with them because I find my time in the gym is to do what I want. Each new day I wanted to do it right after I woke up," he says. "It was so fun I wanted to do it over and over again.

"I competed within my own body, within my own mind . . . it wasn't until high school that I wanted to play against good competition. I did all kinds of imaginary things. I'd line up twenty chairs on one end of the court and work on my dribbling. I'd dribble between each chair, one behind my back, one between my legs, spin move right, spin move left, then I would put the chairs in a circle and put a ball on each chair and I'd have to hit two shots with each chair before I could move on to the next.

"I'd set up a chair and put a broom in it, shoot over a broom, just like it would be a hand in my face. I dreamed that the brooms were Oscar Robertson or Jerry West, and I was playing against the Bucks or Lakers."

The real Oscar Robertson, the one whose strong hands swatted NBA defenders away as if they were clouds of gnats, prefers education by fire. "Shooting and dribbling, you can do a lot of that alone," Robertson says, "but I think the most improvement comes when you get into competition, in the battle. Because no matter what happens, you know that chair does not have a hand and a person may not move the way you planned. Basketball is reaction to different situations. You have to react to what happens to you . . . after a while it becomes automatic."

Told of Oscar's opinion, Alford replied, "Oscar had some ability that I didn't have and I think he could go out in alley ball and do those sorts of things. I had to become a great shooter. I agree with the pressure bit, but now that I've developed the shot I have, it doesn't matter who is up in my face. Pressure doesn't bother me, because I've worked that out on my own."

At 19, Steve Alford comes across as an obliging and unusually controlled young man. He is 6'2" and slender—about 160 pounds—with a well-proportioned upper body; he looks like a tall gymnast. He is an ad for clean living and good grooming. His hair, carefully layered and parted in the center, lies perfectly.

He has long been used to being interviewed. Answers to questions can sometimes seem a little canned, with more "cherished moments" and "youngsters" than you would expect in the typical 19-year-old's vocabulary.

But then Steve Alford, like every member of Sam Alford's New Castle Trojans basketball teams, has been groomed for life as a public figure, for a basketball player in New Castle represents the town. "Our players can't have beards or moustaches, hair is kept off the ears," says Sam. "When we go on the road, we wear sport coats or sweaters with ties. When we eat, the seniors go first. We won't let our players wear earrings"—there is something unsettling about the image of Steve Alford with pierced ears—"we try to be very polite with everything we do. We want every young boy growing up in New Castle to say to himself, I want to be a Trojan when I grow up."

★ ★ ★

As a basketball hero from a basketball town in a basketball state, Steve Alford has come to represent idealized Indiana. He manages his time carefully, for the demands are incessant, from celebrity golf tournaments to television talk shows to requests for autographs, which he signs "Yours in Christ." He prays before and after each game. "I talk to God whenever I get the chance," Steve has said. "It's like when I dedicate myself to basketball, I do the same to Him, because He has given me all that I have today."

Very occasionally, the 19-year-old boy pops out for a moment, a hair that won't lie down. As Sam tells the story of the adolescent Steve hiding in the closet with a tape recorder, imitating a baseball announcer's play-by-play style, Steve scrunches up in his chair and begins to giggle. The giggle turns to laughter, and soon he is blushing furiously. At another point, Sam mistakenly calls Steve by his younger brother's name. When the interview is finished, Steve walks to his father's side. "Dad," he says softly, "you called me Sean again."

Both Sam and Steve admire Sean Alford, two years younger than Steve, for his adjustment to Steve's celebrity. "He'll answer the door and people'll walk right past him, looking for Steve," says Sam. "This past year, he's had the toughest job in the US."

* * *

"When we came here I was 9 years old, and Dad thought it would be tough to get me to move from Martinsville," Steve says. "But when New Castle offered him a job and I first saw this place there was no question this is where I wanted to be."

Steve is speaking from the bottom row of bleachers in what a banner stretched across one wall proclaims to be "The largest and finest high school field house in the world." The basketball floor is set in the bottom of a giant crater whose 9,325 seats (New Castle High's enrollment is 1,150) begin in a wide circle at street level. From courtside, students jogging around the track at the top look like mules working their way slowly around the South Rim. To visiting teams, this must seem like the pit of Hell.

"My junior year we played Cincinnati Moeller here," says Steve, referring to a high school best known for its nationally ranked football teams. They walked into the field house on Saturday morning, while we were practicing. They were huge, 6'6", 6'7", all football players. I remember looking up and you could just see them thinking, 'Oh my God, what is this place?'

"They took the floor that night, and Dad said, 'Okay, they've never played here before and the place is a scllout, so let's pick 'em up full court right from the start.' The first twelve trips down the court they didn't get past midcourt line. At one time it was 20 to 0."

Old-timers in New Castle say the gym was needed to break the "Muncie syndrome," a spell alleged to have beset the New Castle Trojans when they played the regional tourney in the Muncie gym. There was the time the lights went off in the middle of a shot and the buzzer went off in the middle of a rally—or did the lights go off in the middle of the shot?—oh, whatever, there was a half-century's worth of bad calls.

So the Monday Morning Club, as the civic leaders that meet for coffee at Kresge's every Monday morning are known, decided to build a gym big enough to host their own regional. Consequently, almost everyone in New Castle can find a "Gym Now" bond in an old scrapbook. When the dust cleared in 1959 the world's champion high school gym stood in a town of 19,500.

Steve Alford squints up at the joggers. "The first thing I told myself, ten years ago," he says, "was that I wanted to fill this place. My junior and senior years we filled it pretty regularly."

"You expect me to remember a third grader?" says Bobby Knight, glancing sideways at the clown who had asked him to recall his first impression, of Steve

Alford. Steve, while more indulgent, is equally vague about their first meeting. "It was such a long time ago," says Steve. "I went to his basketball camp nine straight summers."

Knight's courtship of Steve was brief and to the point. First he sniffed the air for rivals; he thought he caught a whiff of Purdue. "He was teasing me," recalls Steve. "Dad had a player named Jerry Sichting and Jerry ended up going to Purdue. Jerry was sort of a hero of mine. So whenever I went to camp Coach Knight would ask me if my dad had convinced me to be a Boilermaker fan yet. I told him, 'Well, I'm sure a Jerry Sichting fan.' Coach Knight says now he made a mistake in not recruiting Jerry."

Then Knight popped the question. "At the end of my sophomore year, late in the summer, I went down there [to Bloomington]. He just said, 'If you're interested in coming here, we're interested in having you, so let's make a verbal commitment now and forget about the recruiting.'"

And the marriage. "You don't actually realize what it's going to be like until you go through it," said Steve after his freshman year. "It's something I'll be able to cherish, and hopefully someday I'll be able to write a book about my four years at Indiana. There'll be some great times and there are going to be some bad times when things don't go as well. I think the bad times are probably better learning experiences than the good times."

Steve's freshman season could surely be likened to a honeymoon. Defenders behaved like broomsticks as Steve broke ancient shooting records at Indiana University. In the NCAA tourney, he gave an inspiring performance in a nationally televised upset of top-ranked North Carolina, in the game's closing minutes he was treating the likes of Michael Jordan and Sam Perkins as if they were Broad Ripple High again, drawing fouls and swishing free throws. At the end of his storybook season, Coach Knight selected Steve as the youngest member of the US Olympic basketball team. Steve played impressively and his team won an easy gold medal.

As his sophomore season began, he was a member of most of the preseason All-America teams, ranked as one of the best two or three guards in America. He started strongly, but then, for the first time ever, the baskets seemed to have shrunk. During one six-game stretch, Steve shot only 26 percent from the field. Indiana quickly fell out of the Big Ten race.

He was exhausted, having played competitive basketball for nearly three years without a break. His legs felt like lead. Because Indiana's forwards were not scoring threats, opponents ganged up on Steve and center Uwe Blab. After holding Steve to seven points. Illinois guard Doug Altenberger, 6'4" and 200 pounds, explained the secret of his success: "I made sure everywhere he went he got bumped and that when he got open he was too tired to shoot it."

"There are some things he can't do," Knight told the Indianapolis News during Steve's slump. "When you've got a kid like Steve who is not quick, then taking the shot away from him is really going to affect the way he plays . . . we've got to do some things better in other ways than we have with Alford."

★ ★ ★

"I'd like to settle down and play pro ball," Steve Alford says. "It's a longer season and I like playing basketball as long as possible. I've worked so hard and worked so long. It seems like I've been playing forever. I'd like to start getting paid for playing."

But Steve is smart enough to know that NBA basketball is a different game, a realm where even the best shooters tend to be tall and physically imposing. "I know there's a chance that I might not even get to play pro ball," Steve says. "But nobody else knows how hard I've worked; only I know that. I like people to say, 'He's not good enough, he doesn't know what he's getting into.' When I left high school, everyone said I was too skinny, too light, that I couldn't take the Big Ten season. But [in his freshman year] I was third in the league in scoring and I did most of the bruising. I hope that by the time I'm a senior, my stock is really going to be good."

According to Marty Blake, director of scouting for the NBA, he'll indeed have to wait till then to know the value of his stock. "He's gonna have to get stronger, although Jerry West only weighed about 170. He's got speed and quickness, he's a very smart basketball player and he can get his shot. He has good range. I don't know if he's gonna be a great player, but he has the tools. He did a terrific job on the Olympic team."

Blake agrees with Bobby Knight that having made the Olympic team put unnecessary pressure on Steve as a sophomore. Knight has said that picking Steve did not mean that Steve was necessarily one of the best dozen players in the United States. He needed a shooter, and Alford was the best shooter in camp, no more, no less.

And after the NBA? "I don't want to leave basketball, I can't leave basketball. I want to do it as long as I possibly can. I'd like to coach at the college level. I would only coach high school in the state of Indiana."

And romance? "Basketball is number one to me and nothing is going to interfere with that," Steve says. "I had a date for the prom but I found out that I was invited to go to the Dapper Dan [a high school all-star game] in Pennsylvania

Steve Alford signs for young fans. *Courtesy of Frank H. Fisse.*

the same night and I went to the tournament. The girl took it well, she's in athletics so she understood. But if I have a girl, she has to be understanding."

Asked if he feels Steve missed anything of childhood by devoting so much of it to a single pursuit, Sam Alford replies quickly, "I certainly do, but I don't think he knows that. Maybe when he has children of his own he'll realize what he has missed.

"I think a lot will depend on the next few years for him. Up to this time basketball has been the number-one thing in his life, but he'll learn that each year from now on it will become tougher and more of a job. If he can keep it fun, keep in the right perspective, that would be good."

Wanting is an art. Desire is an art. An average player who wants to win will beat a great player who doesn't.

Damon Bailey

13

AN INTERVIEW WITH DAMON BAILEY

. . . .

DURING INDIANA PACER TIME-OUTS IN THE 1994–95 SEASON, FANS sometimes caught sight of Damon Bailey in the margin of the camera's eye. Respectfully dressed in slacks and a sweater or jacket, he was often craning forward from a seat behind the bench or standing at the outer fringes of the huddle to listen in on Coach Larry Brown's strategy. He had the look of a man who did not wish to intrude, who did not presume to claim something he had not yet earned, and yet who wanted to be seen.

In the madhouse excitement of the Pacers' post-season run for glory, it took such sightings for fans to remember that Damon Bailey was on the roster. After having been chosen by the Pacers in the second round of the 1994 NBA draft, Bailey played in three pre-season games and then was offered a one-year contract during which it was agreed that he would undergo surgery on both knees. It was an unusual arrangement but Damon Bailey is a special case. "It wasn't really a very hard decision," said Larry Brown. "I liked what I saw of him. Obviously he had been very well coached and versatile. I look forward to a chance to coach him."

But there was more to it than that. Damon Bailey had been a legendary high school player and a four-year starter at Indiana University, and he had not been forgotten by Hoosier fans. More than 20,000 had attended the 1994 NBA draft, held in Indianapolis. Many of them were there to see that Bailey landed with the Pacers.

Though there had perhaps been a very few high school players in Indiana's history as good as Bailey, no one had ever been so loved. Pat Aikman, who directs the Indiana-Kentucky All-Star game for the *Indianapolis Star*, remembers the moment when he fully understood. "It was the week before the game in Indianapolis in 1990," he recalls. "After practice we took the team to the Indianapolis zoo. There was a dolphin show, and Damon was just hounded. People came up to him constantly and kept shoving paper in his face for him to sign. It was distracting and his teammates were being ignored and he seemed embarrassed. I asked him what he wanted to do. He said, 'I just want to get out of here.' So we got up and headed for an exit door. Damon pushed it open and right outside was young couple strolling a baby. As soon as they recognized him, they picked up their baby, thrust it in his arms and started snapping his picture. It was like he was one of the Beatles."

Growing up in a tiny town south of Bloomington, Bailey scored more points than any other Indiana high school player, played before bigger crowds, and led his team to almost unprecedented success. Patient with fans and writers, he proudly and politely represented the forgotten hamlets of Indiana whose schools were lost to consolidation a generation before. Songs were written about him, paintings of his jersey and shoes were commissioned, fans plucked blades of grass from his front lawn as souvenirs. His college coach, Indiana University's Bob Knight was once asked if Bailey had become as popular in Indiana as had been his former star, folk hero Steve Alford. "There's no comparison" Knight said. "As popular as Alford was, he wasn't even close to this kid."

★ ★ ★

Damon Bailey was born and grew up in Heltonville, population about 300. It is a crossroads community of shingled houses with one general store, set in the limestone country of south-central Indiana whose giant quarries produced the stone for New York skyscrapers and Washington monuments. Its residents are timbermen, stoneworkers, farmers, and factory workers. Until the fifties, a railroad line backed up to the Heltonville Limestone Company, a mill that employed hundreds. Freight cars were loaded with slabs of freshly planed stone and hauled off to Indianapolis and the world beyond. In those days Heltonville boasted three saloons, a hotel, and, most importantly, a high school basketball team of its own.

The Heltonville High Blue Jackets had at least one Bailey in the lineup during most of the years from 1925 on, including Damon's grandfather, great uncles, uncles, and cousins. Damon's father, Wendell Bailey, class of '68, was a three-year starting forward for the Jackets, and his mother, Beverly Case, was a cheerleader for rival Tunnelton High.

Heltonville and Tunnelton were among group of tiny towns in Lawrence County whose residents were united in their burning resentment of Bedford, the county seat. Bedford was the home of the giant Indiana Limestone Company, which had been formed in the mid-1920s when Chicago bankers put up the money to buy out most of the small independent mills and quarries of the area. It was a source of pride in Heltonville that their mill had been large and prosperous enough to avoid the merger. The Bedford Cutters, as their basketball team was called, played in a gym that seated 4,500 fans and drew team members from a town of 15,000. They always hosted the sectional. They were the ultimate Goliaths.

In 1974 Heltonville and six other little towns were forced to consolidate their schools along with Bedford High School into a regional monolith called "Bedford North Lawrence." Though Heltonville High had never won so much as a sectional tourney in half a century, the loss of their school and its team was a mortal wound. The Blue Jackets had been the soul of the town in winter. Even today, many still remember commencement night in 1942, when the Heltonville school caught on fire and collapsed before the fire department from Bedford arrived. After everyone was evacuated, a few brave souls went back in to try to rescue the things that meant most to the community. Among the first items they pulled out were the basketball uniforms.

The consolidation meant that their children would go to school with Bedford kids who viewed them as hicks. Heltonville parents feared that their sons and daughters would become immersed in Bedford's faster culture and lose their identity. Worst of all they feared for the town's very identity. What did it matter that twelve grades had studied under one roof at Heltonville High? They had been family; aunts in the upper grades had walked down the hall to straighten the jackets and smooth the dresses of younger nieces on school picture day. Now, they wondered, without their school, without a team to anchor them, would Heltonville simply blow away?

* * *

From the beginning, Damon Bailey was not only bigger than other boys his age, but unusually well coordinated. After high school Wendell Bailey had continued to play basketball in local industrial leagues several nights a week. He took Damon with him down gravel roads and two-lane highways to old backroads gyms, still standing. Damon was devoted and attentive. He could heave the ball up against the backboard and down into the net at five. A few months later he could do it with his left hand. By third grade he was playing on his school's sixth-grade team.

At ten, Damon was regularly playing with his father in games against working men three times his age. They understood they were not to baby the kid. There was no praise from Wendell Bailey. Criticism was necessary. Sickness was not tolerated. Toughness was valued above all. The transformation of Damon into a finished basketball player became a family enterprise; each day his mother and later his sister Courtney rebounded the hundreds of shots he launched toward a driveway goal. Each morning began with weightlifting and running before school.

By the time Damon entered junior high he had played on several national championship Amateur Athletic Union teams. Word spread rapidly among coaches and basketball writers that a new Larry Bird lived somewhere south of Bloomington, not far from where the original had grown up.

Damon's life was changed forever by a single event in the late winter of 1986. One Monday evening Bob Knight, upset with the play of his team and particularly that of his guards, decided to drive twenty-five miles to see the eighth grader he had heard about. Locals first froze in the shock of recognition when Knight entered the Shawswick junior high gym, then shyly pressed around him and finally left him alone as he absently munched popcorn and studied the boy. At 6'1", Damon Bailey was half a head taller than anyone else on the floor, powerful, insightful and fluid. The following morning Knight told his coaching staff, straightfaced, that, "Damon Bailey is better than any guard we have right now. I don't mean potentially better, I mean better right now." The remark was overheard by journalist John Feinstein, who reported it in his book, *A Season on the Brink*.

It was as if a television crew had happened upon Christ educating the elders at the temple. Overnight the Indiana basketball world flocked to see the child from backwoods Indiana. Unlike Larry Bird, who had escaped public attention until college, Knight's comment served up Damon Bailey as an adolescent.

Bob Knight enters the Shawswick Junior High gym to watch eighth-grader
Damon Bailey play. If Indiana were a church, this would be a scene on a
stained glass window. *Courtesy of Sanford Gentry.*

Game after game, 1,500 fans packed into the stuffy little gym. As he entered
his teen years, Damon Bailey began to sign autographs and his parents quietly
took out an unlisted telephone number.

Somehow, the attention made Damon, an already sturdy individual, even
stronger. He learned to zone out the distraction of fame and became a better
and better player. He led Bedford North Lawrence High—or BNL, as it was
called—to four consecutive state finals, the first Indiana player ever to do that.
His peach-complexed face with the wide smile showed up on TV at six and
in sports pages throughout Indiana. He grew to be 6'3" and 190 pounds. The
weights gave him a body of steel. He was a white player who could dunk. He
showed no fear. By the time he was a senior, he was almost as famous as Knight.
He credited his teammates, he flattered his coach. Always, he identified his
home as Heltonville, not Bedford. Signs sprouted at the town line proclaiming
Heltonville the home of Damon Bailey. Heltonville residents who had boycotted
BNL games ever since their school had been erased scrambled to buy season
tickets. They were back on the map.

By the morning of March 25, 1990, when the BNL players arrived in Indianapolis for Damon's fourth and final try for the state high school basketball championship, most of Indiana was absorbed in the story. Anticipating that Damon would bring in a greater crowd than usual, officials of the Indiana High School Athletic Association moved the finals to the Hoosier Dome, a football stadium in downtown Indianapolis. They were astonished when 41,101 fans showed up for the two afternoon semi-final games, pairing first Concord and Anderson, and then BNL and Southport. It was nearly twice as many fans as had ever before attended a high school game in the United States. Damon scored 25 points and grabbed ten rebounds against Southport, giving his team a chance to play for the championship a few hours later. That evening, 41,101 returned for the championship game against undefeated and number-one-ranked Concord High of Fort Wayne.

The last two minutes and eighteen seconds of that game are simply dreamlike. Behind by six points, and with his last chance for a state championship slipping away, Bailey gathered his teammates beneath one goal and urged them to get him the ball and trust him with it. He then scored BNL's final eleven points, leading them to a three-point victory. When the buzzer sounded he fell to the floor with his teammates in a heap of joy, then sprang to his feet and plunged into the crowd, trailing cameras and cables behind him.

For a moment he disappeared into what must have been half the population of Heltonville, then emerged with his family. Organ music swelled throughout the stadium. While his mother dabbed her eyes, and his father's lips moved, and his sister wrapped her arm around him, Damon Bailey calmly began to field reporters' questions. Only one seemed to give him a few seconds' pause. It was about the man for whom he would play the following winter and who had thrust his family in the spotlight five years earlier with an offhand remark. "What about Coach Knight?" someone asked. "Well," Damon Bailey replied, "Up to now I haven't thought much about it. But I'm his boy now."

The spotlight grew even hotter at IU. In his first game, which was played in Hawaii, Damon scored only three points. The next morning's sports headline in the *Indianapolis Star* read, "Bailey has quiet game." To fans who had waited

Damon Bailey first dunked as a seventh-grader. Opponents constantly underestimated his leaping ability. Marion's Jay Edwards (12) and Lyndon Jones (4) are in the foreground. *Courtesy of Sanford Gentry.*

Damon Bailey, here a high school freshman, who restored pride
to forgotten hamlets like his native Heltonvile, became the most
beloved player ever in Indiana. *Courtesy of Sanford Gentry.*

so long and hoped so hard he turned out to be tantalizing and frustrating collegiate player. For long stretches he would seem to disappear, shooting rarely,
then suddenly emerge to take over a game, making Big Ten players look like
Concord High again. No one knew the real Damon Bailey. Knight professed
puzzlement. When it was done, Damon had been a starter on four winning
teams and was the fifth-leading scorer in IU's long history. Playing with injuries,
he was named a third-team All American as a senior and averaged nearly 20
points per game. Had he arrived in Bloomington unheralded, he would have
left a god.

But many Hoosiers were disappointed, though they told each other they
weren't. He hadn't been the second Larry Bird. Bob Knight praised Damon
lavishly in the days after his senior season, calling himself Bailey's "greatest

fan," and proclaiming him "one hell of a basketball player." A year later, Knight seemed to be offering a different appraisal. "I got less out of Bailey than anyone I ever coached," Knight told Robin Miller of the *Indianapolis Star*. "I didn't get it done . . . rarely have I felt that about a kid."

This interview took place in the Indiana Pacers' training room at Market Square Arena in Indianapolis in November of 1994, while Bailey was beginning a program of physical therapy after operations on both knees. Wearing red shorts and a Pacers tee shirt, he answered questions while reclining on a training table. Heat pads bore down on both thighs. From time to time a trainer arrived to adjust the heat and assistants delivered various objects for him to autograph. Bailey is a sturdy, short-haired, clear-eyed young man who considers questions carefully before answering in a voice that is lower and huskier than his boyish face would suggest. The words come through a heavy Hoosier twang. It is a Heltonville twang, not a Bedford twang.

PHIL HOOSE: Growing up, did you get the sense that you were being groomed to be a basketball player?

DAMON BAILEY: Well, I was being groomed, but it wasn't like when I was born my parents said, "We're gonna make him a basketball player." My dad played a lot and as a kid I tagged along and I fell in love with the game. Once I showed that interest, my parents pushed me hard to be a player and gave me a lot of support.

PH: Did your father give you technical instruction? Did he say things like, "Damon, you have to come out to meet a pass, or 'here's a place to move when the ball's on the other side of the court?"

DB: Some, but it was more like on-the-job training. The men my father played with were very good basketball players. They really knew how to play this game. Mine was a hands-on education. I figured things out as I was playing. I would think, "Hell, if I can't get the ball this way, I'll have to try something else." Little kids ask me all the time now, "What do I need to do to become a better player?" I tell them, "I don't know because I've never seen you play." Every player needs to work on different things. But if there's one piece of advice I could offer every kid, it would be to play with people who are older and better than they are. They will make you do things you don't want to do and that you've never done before. When I was young I couldn't jump over those men so I had to learn new ways to score.

The force. *Courtesy of Sanford Gentry.*

PH: What was it like being so young and playing with men?

DB: They didn't cut me any slack. If I was going up for a shot, they were trying to block it, and if they knocked me into the wall, they knocked me
into the wall. They weren't trying to hurt me. They were trying to help
me in the long run. They were trying to help me learn things that most
kids didn't.

PH: Did you play against your father one-on-one a lot?

DB: Yes, quite a bit.

PH: Do you remember the first time you beat him?

DB: (laughs) It was just before my junior year in high school. We were in
my driveway. We went to 24 points, by two. He was an inside player. He
would drive in and find a way to score, however he could. I was taller
than he was by then but he could always find ways to score. I thought I
was a very good player when I was a freshman and sophomore in high
school, but I could never beat him. When it happened, it was a close
game, and it went into overtime.

PII: How did he react to the loss?

DB: He didn't say anything. He just walked inside. I bragged a lot to mom. I
think he was proud of me but I also think it was frustrating for him. He
was very competitive. He was glad that I had become good enough to
beat him but he hated to lose. Even now I don't think I could beat him
very bad. He is a very smart player. People say you can't teach someone
to be a smart player, but I think you can.

PH: How?

DB: My dad was very hard on me when I was a young player. I won't tell
you differently. He wasn't full of praise. He never told me I had played a
good game until we won the state championship. I admire him for that.
I thank him for that. There's no way I'd be the player I am if he wasn't
the way he was. When I was a five or six I played on a Boy's Club team,
and I was bigger than everyone else. I was the best player. I can remember going to the Boy's Club and scoring 40 or 50 points, and my team
winning by 20 or 30, and then getting in the car and being in trouble.
I'd get yelled at for the one time I didn't throw it to the kid who was
wide open underneath the basket, whether the kid could catch the ball
or not. After a lot of that you become a smart player. You understand.
You learn to see things that most players don't see. It can be taught in

a certain way. It wasn't like a classroom for me. My father never sat me down and said, "Here's what you need to do." It was from years and years of playing, and years and years of him getting on me for not making certain passes. After a while you start thinking, "Hey, there's more to this game than just me."

PH: But are there any other lessons that get taught with this type of education? Is there a part of you that says, "Man, I can never please this guy. What's it gonna take?'

DB: (takes his time) I don't want to say no because I don't want to lie, but I don't want to say yes because I really don't know. I won't pretend that there weren't times that I was thinking, "Man, I scored 40 and got 10 rebounds and we won by 25 . . . What else can I do?" But again, I thank and admire him because there is no way I'd be the player I am without him. I have a drive to be a good player, but I needed someone to kick me in the ass every now and then. As a high school player I got up every morning and went to the gym because I wanted to. I thought that playing and running before school would give me an edge. But there were times when I would wake up and think, "I'm not gonna do it today." Sometimes that would last a week. But dad was there saying, "Get up. Go down there." He knew that I wanted to do it, but he also knew I needed a kick. He made me understand that being good was not going to be easy. And that in life I would have to do things I didn't want to do.

PH: Were you having fun?

DB: It isn't fun becoming a good player. It's fun being a good player. I remember one time in junior high I was sick. And maybe by today's standards I was too sick to play. I didn't want to play. Dad made me play. I played very well. I remember him saying, "Do you think Dr. J never played sick?" It gave me an edge.

PH: Did that edge pay off in college?

DB: There were times that I could barely walk. I had a side injury my senior year in college. I could barely straighten up. But I kept playing because I loved to play. If I couldn't play there was no sense in my being around. I had developed the toughness to block pain out. A lot of people wouldn't have got out of bed the day I played against Temple in the NCAA tournament. I had the tunnel vision, the focus to block it out. And it's been worth it, because there are a lot of things in life that you can't control but you have to keep going.

I just went out and tried to do my job the best I could. Sometimes my knees hurt, sometimes I was sick. People think that being a good player is all fun. It isn't. I love being where I am now. But there's been a lot of heartache. And a lot of sweat and pain put in, back when I was eight or nine, and now.

PH: It's surprising to a lot of people how well you can jump.

DB: I used to be able to. One reason my knees are so bad now is that I was doing squats with weights when I was twelve. That was too young. By the time I hit IU my vertical jump went down. I hope the knee operation will put it back to where it was.

PH: Do you remember the first time you ever dunked?

DB: Yeah. It was the summer after my seventh-grade year. I was at my junior high. I could palm a basketball even then but I'd never even been able to even come close to dunking, and then all of a sudden one day I did it in a warmup drill before a game. My friends went nuts. So did I. After that it was a piece of cake. I just needed that one time, and then I could do it over and over.

PH: You said that your dad didn't praise you until your high school team won the state championship. When did he praise you then? After the game?

DB: No, it was the week before the state finals. He told me several times that I had worked hard, and now I was becoming a man, and I could see things now, as a player and a man, that I hadn't been able to see before. He no longer had to point certain things out to me. He said he was proud of me. That was the proudest time of my life.

PH: There was such excitement around Indiana in the week before your last chance to be a state champion. What was that week like for you?

DB: That was the most meaningful time in my life so far. It's hard to make people understand how much this dream has meant to me. I don't just mean playing professional basketball, I mean being able to be an idol to a lot of kids. To have people look up to me. To have my family play the biggest role in putting me in this situation.

PH: Everyone has fantasies of stepping in to snatch victory from defeat. But you actually did it, and in front of forty thousand people. What did it feel like? Was there a voice in your head at the turning point that said, "Hey, Damon, this game is slipping away . . . if you don't act now your dream will die?"

DB: (Sighs) I'm very competitive. There was never a time when I thought we were gonna lose. We were down by 6 points with 90 seconds to go. Even then I didn't think we would lose. I wasn't gonna let that happen. I would do anything. Score points, play defense, knock a guy out. Whatever it took.

But it's hard to imagine having the confidence to feel that you could just personally take over. . . . Those were good players out there. That was an undefeated team. This was for the state championship. They wanted it too. It was their dream as well.

DB: Wanting is an art. Desire is an art. An average player who wants to win will beat a great player who doesn't.

PH: If you close your eyes and think about it, what can you remember about that last stretch?

DB: A foul had been called with about two minutes left. I got my team together underneath the other team's basket and told them, "This is it. This is what we've worked for all of our lives. We're not gonna lose. Get behind me and we'll do this." After that I really don't remember specifically how we won, play by play.

PH: Have you ever watched the tape?

DB: No.

PH: Never?

DB: Never.

PH: Why?

DB: I don't look back. I can do that with my grandkids when I'm sixty. When I'm done playing a game I don't have time to sit back and think, "Boy I was a great high school player." Every step you take is a bigger step than the one you took before. What happened before doesn't matter. The other Indiana Pacers don't care that Reggie Miller went to UCLA, or what he did last year. They care that we have a game against Houston on Wednesday. What matters is what's going on now. I've never watched a film of myself, except to learn. Never for the pure sake of enjoyment. At IU when I was in a shooting slump I watched a film of us playing against Kansas, because I had shot the ball very well in that game.

I don't like watching basketball, I never did. Even as a kid I rarely did. And when I do watch, I try to learn. I watch certain things. I don't watch a Michael Jordan dunk as much as I watch how people tried to prevent him from scoring. The other night when the Pacers played Atlanta I was at home and I watched it. Mainly I focused on what Reggie was doing to get open. I was trying to learn. I was frustrated just sitting there. I wanted to be playing.

PH: Let's talk about Coach Knight. First, the moment when he walked into the Shawswick gym to see you when you were an eighth grader. Did you know he was coming?

DB: No. Actually he came two or three times. The first time I didn't know it until after the game, when the kids started talking about it. It was a thrill, but I wasn't in awe of him. I've never been in awe of anyone. I don't say this to disrespect him. I think Coach Knight is one of the greatest coaches ever. I enjoyed my time with him. But I was never in awe of him. I felt that I belonged there.

PH: When you finally did notice him, surely you knew what he was there for.

DB: Yeah, I knew what he was there for, but I was smart enough to know that if I didn't continue to work hard, that visit wouldn't matter.

PH: How did you find out about the quote in *A Season on the Brink* in which Coach Knight tells others that you, an eighth-grader, were better than the IU guards?

DB: Right after the book came out somebody shoved the part about me in my face and said, 'Here, read this.' I had read about the quote in newspapers. I never read the book. Never read the part about me.

PH: Did you believe what he said? Did you think there was any chance that you were actually better than the IU guards?

DB: I was smart enough to know that it wasn't true. And now I can look back and it's even funnier when I think of how many times Coach Knight says things that he doesn't even mean.

PH: Did another Damon Bailey ever appear at IU while you were there? I mean, did Coach Knight ever say, 'There's this grade school kid in Oolitic or somewhere that's better than any of you?'

DB: No. He never did that to us during my four years.

PH: What was your dad's reaction to the quote about you in the book?

DB: I don't know how he felt. He never said anything to me, but that's not surprising. You'll never see a quote from my dad, or any other member of my family. They've never given an interview. They just instilled in me what was right and wrong. I've made the big decisions in my life on my own. I never talked to them about going to Indiana University. I was the one who would be there for four years, not them. I told them. It would have been fine with them if I had gone to Purdue. They've stayed out of the spotlight.

PH: How did Indiana recruit you?

DB: Coach Knight started recruiting me early. There was no song and dance. He said, "This is what we can do for you and this is what you can do for us. If you wanna come, come."

PH: Did you visit anywhere else?

DB: I halfway went to Purdue. A buddy who was a Purdue fan took me to a football game up there and it was arranged that I would meet Coach Keady and the staff. We talked, but my heart was set on Indiana.

PH: What was Coach Knight like to play for?

DB: You can comb through any sport at any level and you will never find a person who is more competitive than Coach Knight. Pheasant hunting, fishing, coaching a game, he wants to be the best. That's why his players and teams are successful. They will find a way to win. I won't say it was all fun. Sometimes I woke up in the morning and wondered what the hell I was doing there. Sometimes I wondered whether it was worth it. Now I can look back and say I'm glad I stayed. I'm glad I went. Coach Knight made me a better player and a better person. I came to IU with a good work ethic and he drove it home. When I chose to go to college at Indiana University, people kept saying, "How are you going to handle Coach Knight?" I was never a bit worried, and to this day I have no hard feelings toward Coach Knight or anything he ever said to me, because there's nothing that Coach Knight ever said to me or did to me that had not been said or done by my father before I went to Indiana.

PH: There were times when you dominated your college games and then there were times when you seemed to be somewhat passive. You went long stretches without shooting. What was going on?

DB: Fortunately or unfortunately, depending on the way you look at it, I played with some great players at Indiana. Calbert Cheaney, Greg Graham, Eric Anderson. As a freshman, even as a sophomore and junior, I had to play behind those great players. There were times I made a personal sacrifice to make our team better. I could have averaged 20–25 points a game all through my career, even as a freshman, if I wanted to shoot enough. But my first year Calbert Cheaney was our go- to player. Somebody had to get him the ball. Nobody better than I, I thought. Every year I was there I led the team in assists. Coach Knight never told me not to shoot. I just played that way. I was thinking, "If I shoot 20 times a game, how many shots does that take away from Calbert?" Maybe by playing that way I didn't look like as good a player as people thought I was. I think my senior year I showed them. I averaged over twenty points until I hurt my side, and then it was hard to play. You can check me on this, but I think I was the winningest player ever to play at Indiana University. By that I mean I spent more time in first place in the Big Ten and have a better winning percentage. I know I'm close. I feel that I'm a winner. I don't want to be known as a great player or shooter. I want to be a winner.

PH: Are you confident that you can be a good NBA player?

DB: I think I can do whatever Coach Brown asks me to do. I read the other day that Reggie Miller said that if we win an NBA title he would retire. If that happens, and he does, I'm confident that I could step in and fill his role. If that doesn't happen, I'm confident that I could back Reggie up, or play the point and get him the ball. Sometimes success, and how you are judged, depends on the situation you are in. I'll give you an example: Calbert Cheaney was in a great situation. When he arrived at Indiana there was no star player. He was the best freshman and automatically he took over that role. No one else was gonna take that role until he left. And no one here is gonna take Reggie's role until he leaves. He's been here seven or eight years.

PH: Your fame in Indiana is like that of a rock star. When did that begin?

DB: I think that book really kicked it in. I've grown up with it. It's been part of my life for so long it's just there, like brushing my teeth. Every morning when I wake up I know that after I walk out my door people I don't know will come up to me. They will want my autograph. They'll want to talk to me.

PH: Does it ever just drive you nuts?

DB: It gets old. I try to do the best I can to live up to people's expectations. I try to be a role model.

PH: You haven't mentioned your mother in talking about growing up. What's she like?

DB: Very emotional. When you have people like my father and Coach Knight in your life, you also have to have a person who comes along and says, "It's all right. . . . So they're mad. . . . So they've lost it." I think that's what my mom was and I think that's what the assistant coaches at Indiana are.

PH: Moms?

DB: I think so. They're just there for when Coach Knight gets on you really hard. It gets to you. You get down. They are the ones who pick you back up. You can't have one without the other. Same with my mom. I don't think my dad could have been the way he was to me if it hadn't been for my mom, and I don't think Coach Knight could be the way he is to his players if it weren't for the assistant coaches. My mom was always there for me. She doesn't know all about the game. But she would rebound for me, in the driveway, and in the gym. My sister would too. My success is a family success.

PH: When your high school championship game was over you rushed into the stands and embraced your family. Had you decided to do that before the game or did it just happen spontaneously?

DB: It just happened. I had never seen anything like it on TV. I don't know what hit me. We had just won. I was in a big pile on the floor with my teammates when Bam! I just broke away and went to them. I thought, here is a way to really acknowledge my family and all we've done together. It would be better than just saying it to a reporter. Here was a way to show everybody.

PH: You played in a few games against NBA players before the decision to operate on your knees. What was your early impression of the level of play in the NBA?

DB: NBA players understand the game better than collegiate players. They're very intelligent about basketball. I don't think there's a great talent difference—some NBA players are definitely better than college players—but, you don't have to be a great player. You just have to be very smart and understand the game and know what it takes to play at this level.

PH: What's your life like these days?

DB: I live in Indianapolis. I come in, I work out. I'm trying to work very hard, but I can't overdo it. So I'm pushing taking it slow (laughs). It's frustrating. It's hard for me to sit back and watch the guys practice when I want to be out there. I want to be there but I think watching can help me too. I can see what it takes to play in this league, I can understand things. I won't just be thrown into it. This will take a lot of the pressure off me and off the Pacers. No one will expect me to score thirty points or Coach Brown to play me 48 minutes in the first game.

PH: Is that what you think people expect of you?

DB: People expect a lot, both of me and the team. But nobody will expect more of me than I will. I know that I will do whatever it takes to help my team win—score points, distribute the ball, rebound, whatever. The people on the outside won't always understand that. They won't know what Coach Brown is asking of any player. This is a team game. It's not the Reggie Miller show or the Damon Bailey show or the Mark Jackson show. It's the Indiana Pacers show. It hasn't changed. . . . People have always expected a lot of me and I've just gone out to help my team win. I've been a winner everywhere I've played. I think anyone can score points at this level, but only a few people are consistent winners.

PH: Every time you go to your home town, there, on a hill at the crossroads is a monument to you, with an inscription that says it was given with the love and gratitude of your neighbors. And you're, what, 23? How does that feel? Is there any part of you that sometimes steps back and says 'What a strange life I've led?'

DB: Heltonville is a special place to me. It's a place where I can go to relax and I can get away from most of the hoopla. My friends are there, and the people who helped make me successful. You can't find a person that wouldn't enjoy living the life that I live. There have been times that I've hated it. But there's not one thing in my life that I'd change. Everything that has happened, this surgery, even my sister having leukemia, has made me stronger. I'd give anything in the world for her not to have it. At the same time it's made me appreciate what I have all the more. They pain that I go through now is nothing compared to what she goes through with chemotherapy. Imagine what it must be like for a fifteen-year-old girl to lose her hair. I can't imagine how she feels.

PH: Do you think you're special in any way?

DB: Yes. I'm very level-headed. I understood things early. I matured quickly. Some of it had to do with that book and the attention I was getting. . . . My dad never let me get a big head.

Heltonville attractions. *Courtesy of Sanford Gentry.*

PH: Do you consider yourself a chosen person or your success in any way miraculous? Everyone wants what you have, but you're the one who got it.

DB: I think to a certain degree I'm blessed with talent. But it was up to me to go out and develop that talent. It was a dream, but it wasn't a miracle. I've worked so hard. I think that people think I was born and could just play the game or that I woke up one day at thirteen and could play well. It didn't happen that way. It's a dream that my family and I had for many years. We made it happen.

• •

Everything changes a little and it should
Good ain't forever and bad ain't for good

Roger Miller, "Lou's got the Flu"

14

FOUR-CLASS BASKETBALL

Death or Salvation of Hoosier Hysteria?

· ·

ON AUGUST 29, 1996, THE INDIANA HIGH SCHOOL ATHLETIC ASSOCIATION'S (IHSAA) executive board voted 12–5 to replace Indiana's legendary winner-take-all high school basketball tournament with multiple tournaments among schools divided into four classes based on school enrollment. There would be boys' and girls' tournaments for each class, a total of eight tournaments in all for Indiana's (then) 382 schools. The impetus came from small-school principals who had worked their way onto the ISHAA board. "Basically it came down to numbers," said Rob Gardner, then Commissioner of the ISHAA. "All the small schools finally got together and decided to change the tournament. I don't think they felt like they were getting a fair shot under the old system."

The announcement shocked Hoosierland. If this happened, never again would there be a Milan Miracle in which a school from a hamlet would topple an urban giant for all the marbles. Basketball would be graded on the curve.

Students, fans, and coaches voiced their dismay. Opponents formed a lobbying group, "Friends of Hoosier Basketball," convening at Bobby Plump's Indianapolis pub and financing their activities through sales of a tee shirt bearing the message: "Indiana Sports already Have Class." Hoosier basketball legends John Wooden, Steve Alford, and George McGinnis, among others, stepped forward with statements opposing the splintering.

Passionate letters, pro and con, filled the state's op-ed pages. Examples:

Greg Alexander, North Vernon: "If (the proposal) is enacted I will mourn for future generations who will never know of the special, unique institution we have foolishly committed to the grave."

Rudy Williams, Anderson: "So what if (Bobby Plump) hit the shot that beat Muncie Central way back when? . . . grow up, Indiana, and let class basketball to happen."

Mark Bundy, Greenfield: "I write this in honor of my father who was on the Knightstown 1958 sectional championship team. His heart would break if the current system of tournaments were done away with."

Non-Hoosiers following the story in national media scratched their heads. The hit film *Hoosiers* had established Indiana as the place where everyone got a chance but no one a handout. Indiana gave kids big dreams, based on the precept that nothing is more educational than stepping into the ring with a Goliath. Why would they throw that away?

But eight separate competitions were organized that year—four for boys and four for girls. Bobby Plump was among many who felt pangs of loss. "To win a championship in the second or third class won't mean as much in 20 years as winning a sectional in the current format means in 20 years," he lamented "I hope one day I'll be able to say I was wrong but I'm afraid I won't be able to."

★　★　★

Fast forward 18 years, winter 2015. This will be the 18th season of class basketball in Indiana. Nearly all contemporary players hadn't been born yet when the tourney was divided. Back in the first years of the four-class tourney, it was easy to find players who sneered at authorities who felt they needed a crutch to even the playing field. In 1997, the final year before the change, Batesville, total enrollment 589, came within a buzzer beater of knocking off jumbo Newcastle in the semi-state. Batesville's players were bloody but unbowed. "I'd rather lose a game like this to a team like this than win some other state title against somebody else," declared Batesville guard Michael Menser after the game. His teammates nodded their agreement. But the door was shut. Next year Batesville would face midsize opponents in the 2-A tourney, while New Castle would lumber over to 4-A to confront other colossuses.

What is it like for today's Hoosier players compared to the experience of their parents and grandparents? One thing is clear: they are playing before much smaller crowds than the old days. By the divided tourney's fifth year, 2002, the four-class (boys) events combined drew 438,430 spectators—barely half as many as had witnessed the final single-class tournament. Attendance and revenues have continued to decline steadily, for both boys' and girls' tournaments.

One problem seems to be that local rivalries are subdued in the four-class format. The sectional round used to be about settling scores in the neighborhood. Now the sectional round consists of games between like-sized schools from the general region. Some travel great distances for games against strangers. "You can still find hotbeds and good games," says Kyle Neddenriep, high school sports editor for the *Indianapolis Star*. "Last year Westview brought a big crowed when they played for the 2-A championship. But general interest in the tourney has declined. Everyone leaves when their game is over. Nobody wants to stay for the whole thing."

Eighteen years later, while fans voice an acceptance that often feels like resignation ("It'll never go back to the way it was" is commonly heard), there is considerable frustration with the four-class tourney system. In 2012 the ISHAA Commissioner Bobby Cox and fed-up Indiana Senator Mike Delph, who had filed a bill that would have made it illegal for any school to participate in a multiple-class basketball tourney hit the road, sponsored a series of eleven "town hall" style meetings to see what people really felt about four-class basketball after all these years. Of the 514 ballots cast during the meetings more than two-thirds of voters favored a return to the single-class, non-divided tournament. The ISHAA, unmoved, proposed no changes whatsoever to the tourney format. The *Indianapolis Star* headlined their coverage of the event, "11 Meetings, 2,034 Miles and Still no Answers."

* * *

What better place to test the winds of change than my very own high school? I am a 1965 graduate of Speedway High. Speedway is a small town separated from Indianapolis's west side by a railroad trestle just next to the Indianapolis 500-mile racetrack. Back in the sixties, I tried out for the Speedway Sparkplug basketball team year after year and was annually cut. One coach evaluated me "small but slow."

The year I graduated Speedway's student enrollment, grades nine through twelve, was 792. Today it's about 500 students, putting our Sparkplugs in sectional 44, class 2-A. Back in the 1960s our boys' team (there would not be ISHAA sponsored girls' basketball for another decade) frequently squared off against bigger schools, including a few Indianapolis powerhouses. We won our sectional and lost in heartbreaking overtime to Kokomo, a huge, fabled school that had won the state championship four years before. Today, a tourney game between Speedway and Kokomo, two classes apart, could not take place.

In 2013–14 the Speedway girls' team won the Zionsville 2-A sectional thanks to a talented group of seniors and an exceptional junior guard, 5'9" guard Allison Nash. It was the first time the Speedway girls had won a sectional since 1985, back before the tourney was splintered into classes. The point guard for that team? Allison's mom, Julie Nash.

Julie Nash was a hard-driving, scrappy point guard; a leader in a leadership role. Let the others shoot, was the way she looked at it, her game was defense. She was the one who stole the ball and raced down to lay it in, got fouled, reached for her teammates to peel her the floor and canned the free throws. She still loves to talk about the Speedway Sparkplugs of 1985. "We were *team*. *All* team. I wouldn't trade that experience with those girls for anything."

The Sparkplugs started their 1985 tourney drive in the Decatur Central sectional. "It was a miracle we ever got out of there," Julie recalls. "There were six teams in the sectional and we had to play three games. We won them all by a total of seven points, one in overtime. Then in the regional tourney we had to play Indianapolis Howe, ranked number 4 in state. But we had a great coach Claire Caito, who watched miles of tapes and set up a good plan. It came down to wire and we won. Finally we had to play Warren Central in the Ben Davis semi-state. There were 5,000 people there. Their coach had chains on her boots. They had Linda Godby who was 6'5" and good, and two 6'3"s. We were much smaller. We were scared. Coach gave us a lecture: 'Look,' she said, 'everyone puts there bras on the same way.' We went out there and slowed it down. We were only down 13–12 halftime but then they busted loose and beat us 48–32. We didn't care how big a school was: we figured we could beat anyone and we proved it too: we beat Howe, Southport, Perry Meridian, Ben Davis, Indianapolis Washington. Bring 'em on, that was our feeling."

⋆ ⋆ ⋆

Julie Nash remembers that her daughter Allison's first word was "basketball." "She's my baby. She's very competitive." Allison Nash grew up as tall, athletic and a dominant scorer. Unlike her mom, Allison loved to shoot. But Allison Nash was not obsessed with basketball. She also excelled in volleyball and other sports. She sang in the Sparkleaires choir and acted in the school musical. Only at the end of her sophomore year did she decide to concentrate on basketball. In addition to her play at Speedway High, she joined AAU traveling teams, crisscrossing the Indiana highways once she got her license to play games.

In her junior year, Allison got a chance to study shooting with a very special tutor: the legendary Rick Mount. Mount, who many believe to be the greatest long-distance jump shooter ever, for decades has given private shooting lessons to a very few promising students. Allison was taken to Mount's home in Lebanon, Indiana by Garry Donna, editor of *Hoosier Basketball* magazine. "I just recognized Allison's potential," Donna says. "I thought Rick could really help her."

Allison describes it. "We shot in his driveway, just a net and a ball and some runners who would go after the ball and throw it back. He's an incredible shooter. Mostly he just watched me shoot, and he pointed out things. He told me I needed to lift my shot and follow through all the way. He said I was pushing the ball out so I could still see my hand at eye level instead of shooting it. He wanted me to raise the shot. He was very precise. Before meeting Rick, I had a little fifteen-footer, but there was very little range to my game. I averaged 5 more points per game in junior year, from 12 to 17. Rick Mount transformed me."

Speedway had not won a sectional tourney in three decades, but if it was ever going to happen, it was now, in 2013. Allison had seven seniors with her, players she'd grown up with. They would be gone the following year. Also they had a fine coach in Jordan Dever, then in his third season. And it came together. For the first time since the Julie Nash–led Plugs of 1985, Speedway captured the sectional title with a final-game win over Cascade. Allison scored 31 points. They also won the first game of regional but then fell to Heritage Christian. A year later, they lost the sectional final in Allison's senior year, with Allison turning in a performance that Rick Mount himself would have been proud of— 45 points, 14 rebounds, 6 steals and 4 assists. "It's one of the greatest individual efforts I've ever seen," said Gary Donna. "Total strangers came up to me and said they'd never seen anything like it," says Julie Nash.

★ ★ ★

Julie and Allison Nash have talked a lot about what was gained and lost by dividing the tourney, and about each other's experience of the nearly century-old event. Some things have not changed at Speedway High in the three decades

Speedway's Allison Nash rises high to score. *Courtesy of Mike Wolanin.*

between their tenures at Speedway. The town is basically the same size: Julie had 104 classmates in her graduating class, Allison has 120. It's the same school gym, big enough to hold the student body several times over, though fewer fans attend these days.

"If I had played in Allison's time we'd have been in class 2-A, just like Allison's," says Julie. "With the team and coach we had maybe we would have won a state championship, we'll never know." Asked if she would trade her tourney experience for the chance to put a 2-A state champs trophy into the Speedway High trophy case, the answer comes without hesitation. "Nope," she says. "I liked what we had."

Still, she counts herself a convert. "When they first started talking about dividing the tourney, I wasn't a fan," Julie says. "I was like, we beat Southport, we beat Ben Davis, beat Indianapolis Howe. Why do we need a hand? But when I started coaching, each summer I'd go out and work at a basketball camp at Southwest Missouri. I met coaches from other states who kept saying class basketball gives more people a chance to shine. And it rang true. Our Speedway boys won a state championship in 2002—It's still on the welcome sign when you enter town—that wouldn't have happened without class basketball.

"Still I believe in the movie *Hoosiers*. Hickory High did it. And *we* did it too—the Speedway girls went all the way to the semi-state. It *can* happen. Yeah, it's a movie, but *we did it*. I wish that for everybody, but things change. Progress is progress. It's still hard to win a sectional, no matter what. I guess I feel that even though class basketball gives more kids an opportunity, my heart wishes it hadn't had to happen."

★ ★ ★

Allison Nash can recite chunks of dialogue from the film *Hoosiers*, even though she didn't see it for the first time until her junior year. Like her mom and so many others, her heart responds to the underdogs from tiny Hickory High. Asked if she envies her mom's experience of the tourney that took on all comers, Allison takes a while to answer. It is what Julie calls a "big girl question," and Allison has learned to answer them carefully. "Yes, personally I do," she finally says. "I'd like to see how I would have measured up against other guards from bigger schools. But for the team as a whole, we would have really struggled against a big power like Ben Davis. We lost seven seniors from the year before. Opening the season I had played in 70 varsity games; the next most experienced girl had played in 10. It wouldn't have been fair. So for me yes, for us, no.

"My mom's team took it much more seriously. They didn't go out just for the fun of it. She loved non-class basketball. We both feel that it was good, but that times have changed. My mom had a team that was strong willed and dedicated, willing to put in the work. Now it's more common for kids to go out to be with their friends. Class basketball wasn't so necessary back then because the work ethic was different."

★ ★ ★

One person who has no ambiguity about it is Allison's shooting coach Rick Mount, who played in the wide-open tourney of the 1960s. "Four-class basketball has killed the tournament," he says flatly by phone from his home in Lebanon. "They ruined it. Back when I played Lebanon would have been in class 2-A. My senior year we played sixteen schools that would now be classified 4-A—much bigger than us. That was the *fun* of it. Going to Kokomo in the regional. Going up to Lafayette Jeff in the semi-state. Sure, we might have won two state championships if we were in Class 2-A like it is now, but what a waste. We'd have missed out on all the fun. The competition, that was the fun."

Brad Stevens, coach of the Boston Celtics, who led Butler University to two final game NCAA Men's Division One appearances, knows a thing or two about Davids and Goliaths. Had a long-distance buzzer shot by Gordon Hayward been two inches truer, Butler would have beaten Duke for the national title and Hayward would be the collegiate Bobby Plump. Stevens played for Zionsville High School at the tail end of the one-class tourney days. Two decades later he's still on the fence about splitting up the tourney. "When we won the sectional it was the most memorable basketball game of my life. It still is, actually, because playing's way better than coaching. Winning the sectional was what we shot for the whole year, and we did it.

"That said, we were a small school—a few years later we would have been class 2A or maybe 3A. We likely could have had a chance to go even further. Maybe we could have gotten to play in a big fieldhouse like Hinkle, or maybe all the way to Market Square or Canseco. At first I favored the one-class system but now I'd say I'm more torn because I've seen the benefits it brings to communities of all sizes.'"

★ ★ ★

Six-foot, nine inch Mack Mercer sits down to eat dinner in the Belmont (Tennessee) College cafeteria after basketball practice. He's a 19-year-old freshman there, on a basketball scholarship and still getting his bearings after leaving home and family in Plymouth, Indiana, a couple of months before. Adding to the adjustment is a bout with Wilson's Disease, a rare disorder in which copper accumulates in the tissues. He is still trying to gain back the 25 pounds he lost last winter. The cafeteria cuisine isn't helping. "I guess this is supposed to be chicken pot pie," he says, inspecting the glob on the end of his fork. "And this must be the grilled cheese turkey. I wouldn't really call this food. . . . I'm gonna have to go into Nashville tonight for some good Southern cooking."

Mack has been referred to me by an Indianapolis sportswriter as a young player who has clear and thoughtful opinions about the Indiana high school tourney and who isn't shy about expressing them. As a power forward for the Plymouth Pilgrims, a school in north central Indiana with an enrollment of about 1,100 students, Mack played four years in the tourney, the first three in class 3-A and his senior year class 4-A, with the biggest schools. "The day they set the pairings we were over the 3-A limit by twelve students," Mack recalls. "Actually, by the time the tourney started we were back under the limit. We were the smallest 4-A school in Indiana. We ended up playing against teams four times our size."

The experience of playing in Indiana's modern tourney left Mack with a deep longing for the old days, when sectionals were fueled by passionate county-wide rivalries. "I hate how the system is now," he says. "What made Indiana basketball famous was the one-class tourney that gave a little team a chance to beat a big team. In the old days, we would have played everyone in Marshall County for bragging rights in the sectionals. Everyone would have been there. The rivalries would have been hot. But now teams travel long distances to play against teams from different parts of the state just because of their enrollment. What's the bragging rights to beating a team from South Bend or Mishawaka that you don't even know? It would have meant a lot more to win a sectional back then."

Asked if he ever caught a whiff of what it must have been like in the old days, Mack isn't sure. "I think the real heyday of Indiana basketball was back in the 1980s, the great rivalries between Marion's James Blackmon and Anderson's Troy Lewis, when games were really heated. My dad played for Alexandria, near Anderson and the Wigwam. He graduated in 1982. He played in the tourney when the Wigwam was full, 9,000 fans. He said there were cops on horseback outside the Wigwam to control the crowd. He saw the Maiden and the Brave do their dance at center court. He said it gave him chills, even though he tried to ignore it and focus on what he had to do. He said the sound of that many people cheering was so crazy, so intense.

"But yeah, maybe I caught a little of it. My junior year we played in the regional final against Andrean, a team from the Region. It was the first time in ten years our gym had sold out. For three games, we played before 4,600 people. There is no other feeling like a sold-out gym packed with Indiana basketball fans. It was so cool to see the passion on everyone's faces. So yeah, maybe that one time, I did catch a whiff of the Indiana basketball my dad told me about. I'll never forget it."

Plymouth forward Mack Mercer lofts a free throw in a tournament game. *Courtesy of Hoosier Basketball Magazine and Plymouth High School.*

players, on a per capita basis, was Indiana. Likewise, if you're looking for a talent-rich American city, you can't do better than search the small cities in Indiana. Again on a per capita basis, Muncie took the nation's top spot, with Terre Haute coming in fifth and Anderson eighth. The reason? No one knows for sure, but all those highly organized school programs, all the camps and AAU programs, and all the high-quality coaches it takes to support such infrastructure have to figure in.

MOUNTS

In the second edition of *Hoosiers* we concluded the chapter on the Mount family by wondering if Richie would stay in Lebanon and sire more players to extend the line of Mounts in Lebanon. A generation later, the answer is an emphatic yes. Richie Mount had a fine career at Lebanon high as a high-scoring guard. He made the Indiana All-Star team after being voted the fifth-best senior in the state. After a year at Purdue, he transferred to Virginia Commonwealth and then returned to Lebanon where he joined the police force. He took up weightlifting and developed an impressive physique. And he became the father of four: Jordan, 16; Derrik, 13; Jade, 6; and Ava, 4.

Jordan Mount is first up for the Lebanon Tigers. He led the Lebanon reserve team in scoring last year and figures to play a lot for the varsity this year. He has the Mount body type, tall—6'2"—and lean. He can dunk, which the taller Rick could not do ("small hands"). "He's a gym rat," says Rick proudly. "In the summer he'll come over to my house and we'll put up a thousand shots in my driveway. Shots off the dribble, shots left, shots right. He has quick footwork. I suppose I shouldn't say this, but he has a chance to be a really good player."

16

PASSAGES

What Has Become of Selected People, Places, and Buildings of Hoosier Hysteria

. . . .

MILAN AND BOBBY PLUMP

More than sixty years after lightning struck, Milan High school still stands proudly, educating the youth of Ripley County. The Indians remain scrappy and competitive on a smaller stage, in class 2-A. The Milan '54 Museum, dedicated to remembering the 1954 Indiana state champion team, received visitors from 30 states over the summer of 2014. The famous gray water tower with "State Champs 1954" inscribed in white paint still looms over the little town's railroad track. Still, even though nearby Batesville still has two major employers in Hill-Rom and Batesville Casket, Milan's economy struggles. Some Milan residents grumble that the movie *Hoosiers*, which dramatized their experience, did not do much for the town.

Bobby Plump remains the embodiment of the Hoosier Dream. In January, 2014 donors from across the country honored Plump, the hero of the 1954 "Milan Miracle," by announcing a $50,000 gift in his name to Butler's Campaign

Bobby Plump.

for Hinkle Fieldhouse and naming of a portion of the fieldhouse for him. This honor was part of a $35 million effort to preserve the 86-year-old national landmark.

CRISPUS ATTUCKS SCHOOL

In the years after the school's great championship teams, Attucks changed forms again and again and struggled to survive. A highway bisected the neighborhood, isolating families. When Attucks was racially integrated, neighborhood whites fled for the suburbs. Enrollment plummeted and closure was considered. The school was converted from a high school to a junior high school in 1986, then back to a middle school in 1993, and then back to a high school in 2006. The basketball program was scrapped in 1986.

In 2006, Indianapolis School Superintendent Eugene White announced the formation of "The Medical Magnet at Crispus Attucks," thus changing the school from a middle school to a "medical preparatory high school," designed

Crispus Attucks Tigers: 2014 class 2A sectional 43 champs. *Courtesy of Hoosier Basketball magazine and Crispus Attucks High School.*

for students pursuing careers in the sciences or as medical professionals. The move takes advantage of Attucks's proximity to the campus of Indiana University School of Medicine and associated hospitals. With the school's future more promising, the historic Attucks basketball program was restored in 2008.

And the Tigers roared back! In March 2014, Attucks claimed its first sectional title since 1973 with lopsided wins over Irvington and Indianapolis Manual in class 2A sectional 43 at Triton Central. Winning still felt good. "Nobody on our team has ever tasted anything like [the sectional win], when they were able to hold that big trophy up," Coach Phil Washington told the *Indianapolis Star*. "Hopefully that will drive them to want even more."

STEVE ALFORD

"Hopefully someday I'll be able to write a book about my four years at Indiana," said Steve Alford in our interview. Well, he did it. With the assistance of a pro-

Steve Alford—UCLA men's basketball coach.
Courtesy of Indiana Basketball Hall of Fame.

fessional writer, Alford penned *Playing for Knight: My Six Seasons with Coach Knight*. After a fine career at Indiana University, highlighted by a starring role on an NCAA championship team, Alford played four years for the NBA's Dallas Mavericks and Golden State Warriors. After retiring as a player in 1991, Alford became a collegiate basketball coach taking positions at Manchester University, Southwest Missouri State University, the University of Iowa, University of New Mexico, and, as of this writing, the University of California, Los Angeles.

THE WIGWAM

On March 8, 2011, the Anderson School Board considered a motion to close the 8,996-seat Wigwam to save an estimated $700,000 annually. *Forbes* magazine's Bob Cook wrote a heartfelt Wigwam epitaph: "Even though the stands are rarely half-full anymore, and even though it's almost impossible to justify $350,000 per year just in utility costs for a building that's not even attached to a school, it will be a sad moment if and when the school board decides to put the Wigwam out of its misery. Anderson, the Flint of Indiana, has taken a lot of kicks in the head over the last 30 years, and closing the Wigwam is an acknowledgement that the city can't take any more." Indeed the Board voted 6–1 to give up on the famous basketball temple.

But the Wigwam had one ace card: it was too expensive to demolish. It survived one school board meeting after another. And in August 2014, just a few days before an ominous-looking, final-seeming up-or-down vote on demolition, an angel appeared with a miracle in his pocket: a well-financed plan to save the Wigwam. Indianapolis-based Black and White Investments and Pinebrook proposed to maintain the gymnasium until at least 2030 as part of a multi-use plan for the facility featuring multifamily housing units, offices, and community spaces.

The plan was promptly approved by the Anderson Redevelopment Commission and the Anderson Community School Board. Anderson Community Schools pledged $630,000 to the project and in return secured rights to use the facility rent-free 12 days per year. Renovations are expected to begin early in 2015.

THE WARSAW TIGERS

Title IX, signed into law by President Nixon in 1972 requires gender equity for boys and girls in every educational program that receives federal funding. In 1971, the year before Title IX became law about 310,000 girls nationwide participated in high school sports, about one in 27. Today, the number is 3,373,000, or approximately one in every 2.5.

Major changes came swiftly. In Judi Warren's first year with the Warsaw Tigers, the team wore shorts and tee shirts with numbers ironed on. Shortly after the Tiger's victory in the first girl's tourney, a sporting goods store owner recognized an unclaimed market and started selling customized uniforms for girls' teams, including Warsaw. In its second season in 1977, the girls' tourney exploded, with 96 per cent of Indiana High School Athletic Association member schools entering, according to research published in the *Republic*, of Columbus, Indiana. And in the decade before the start of class basketball—from 1987 to 1997—98% of all schools entered, with the state finals averaging over 27,000 fans and averaging $83,067 in profit. Other innovations, such as a one-inch-diameter-smaller ball and the three-point shot, helped girls.

Of course, not everyone jumped right on board. "That first year after the girls had a tourney, we had 26 coaches of boys high school teams contact us and say we ordered your magazine but we heard you're including girls so cancel our order," recalled Garry Donna, publisher of "*Hoosier Basketball* magazine.

MEADOWOOD PARK

About a decade ago, Meadowood's basketball court was broken up and removed in chunks from the park. Park officials in speedway were concerned that fewer and fewer high school players used the park because rule changes allowed young players to play indoors in the summer. The teens were replaced by older players. Fights broke out and more of a police presence was required. "In the old days you played outdoors at places like Meadowood to impress your coach, who could stand by the court and watch but not speak to the players," recalls Tom Smith, a former Speedway High player and school principal. Now Hoosier gyms are open in the summer, unlocked for AAU team practices and for summer camps that showcase clusters of players for college coaches in a meat market atmosphere. At its peak, the Meadowood court gave players the pleasure of playing outdoors on a shaded court in a lovely park. They learned to shoot into the wind, to get along with unlikely teammates, and to make their own rules in an atmosphere unstructured by adults.

INDIANA UNIVERSITY COACH BOB KNIGHT

The General moved on. On March 14, 2000, just before Indiana was to begin play in the NCAA tournament, the CNN Sports Illustrated network ran a piece in which former player Neil Reed claimed he had been choked by Knight in a 1997 practice. Knight denied the claims in the story. However, less than a month later, the network aired a tape of an Indiana practice from 1997 that appeared to show Knight placing his hand on Reed's neck. The Hall of Fame coach was put

Assistant Butler University Women's Coach Damon Bailey offers
sideline strategy. *Courtesy of Indiana Basketball Hall of Fame.*

on a zero-tolerance leash by Indiana University's then-president Myles Brand.
Knight snapped the leash right away. That September, Knight was fired after a
student accused him of grabbing his arm. Knight took a coaching position at
Texas Tech, remaining for eight seasons. When he retired after the 2007-2008
season, Knight's teams had won 902 Division I Men's games, second most ever at
the time. More than a decade after he last wore the red sweater, Knight still has
a slowly shrinking following—sometimes described as fanatical—in Indiana.

DAMON BAILEY

Indiana legend Damon Bailey was cut from the NBA Indiana Pacers after one
season on the team's injured list and a series of pre-season games the following
year. He was picked up briefly by the Cleveland Cavaliers and released. Bailey

enjoyed several productive seasons playing in the Continental Basketball Association and was named 1997–1998 All-CBA First Team. He retired from professional basketball in 2003. Bailey next turned to coaching. After a stint as boys' coach for his high school alma mater, Bedford North Lawrence (BNL) High School, he became assistant coach of the BNL girls' team, the Lady Stars. The team won the 2012–2013 class 4-A Indiana high school state basketball championship, and then another. BNL's starting point guard was Bailey's daughter, Alexa. Bailey next jumped to the college level, becoming assistant coach of the Butler University women's team. Alexa Bailey has likewise committed to play for Butler.

STEPHANIE WHITE

"This is a moment that I feel like I've been preparing for my whole life. . . . I'm so glad that it is happening in this state. I'm so glad that it is happening with this franchise." That's what Stephanie White told a room full of reporters at a September 14 news conference introducing her as the new head coach of the Women's NBA Indiana Fever. When Stephanie was a girl, in a world that contained or prefigured no professional basketball league for women, she set her sights on becoming an astronaut. Now maybe this was even better.

After becoming Indiana's Miss Basketball in 1995, and being named *USA Today* National High School Player of the Year, White led Purdue to the NCAA women's national basketball championship. She received the Wade Trophy as top college player and was drafted in 1999 by Charlotte Sting and then traded to the Fever in the franchise's first trade. She spent one year with Charlotte, four with the Fever, and retired in 2004

Stephanie White is the rare player who played and coached at all levels in her home state. Speaking of her chance to lead the Fever she said, "I get to share it with all the people who shared my entire career."

Phillip Hoose is the widely acclaimed author of books, essays, stories, songs, and articles, including the National Book Award–winning book, *Claudette Colvin: Twice Toward Justice.* He is also the author of the multi-award-winning title, *The Race to Save the Lord God Bird,* the National Book Award Finalist *We Were There Too!: Young People in U.S. History,* and the Christopher Award-winning manual for youth activism *It's Our World Too!.* The picture book, *Hey, Little Ant* which began as a song by the same title was coauthored with his daughter Hannah. The book is beloved around the world with over one million copies in print in ten different languages. Teaching Tolerance Magazine called it "a masterpiece for teaching values and character education." Phillip's love of the game is reflected in his acclaimed books, *Perfect Once Removed: When Baseball Was All the World to Me,* which was named one of the Top 10 Sports Books of 2007 by Booklist, and *Hoosiers: the Fabulous Basketball Life of Indiana.* A graduate of the Indiana University and Yale School of Forestry and Environmental Sciences, Hoose was for 37 years a staff member of The Nature Conservancy.